Decommissioned Russian Nuclear Submarines
and International Cooperation

D1609910

To Carolyn, the children,
Mom and Dad

Contents

List of Figures

Foreword

(by William J. Perry)

When I signed the 1996 Arctic Military Environmental Cooperation (AMEC) agreement as Secretary of Defense with my counterparts Jorgen Kosmo of Norway and Igor Rodionov of Russia, I was confident that we were making a real contribution to solving a very difficult and dangerous environmental problem. The AMEC agreement initiated a program for military to military cooperation among our three countries to deal with the hazards posed to the Arctic region by decommissioned Russian nuclear submarines and their nuclear spent fuel. The agreement established a commitment to work on six specific projects (since expanded to seven), including the design of a new type spent fuel storage container, to help manage the problem and to move forward toward a solution. The hazards were very real, both from the large amount of radioactivity contained in the nuclear spent fuel on the submarines and in storage and because of the potential danger from misuse and proliferation of weapons usable nuclear material. Even Russian leadership now describes the situation in Northwest Russia where the majority of the submarines are based as "a Chernobyl in slow motion."

Russia built over two hundred nuclear submarines at a frenzied pace during much of the Cold War, but now lacks the facilities and financial resources to care for and dispose of the radioactive material from the submarines properly and within a reasonable period of time. The international community has become involved over the past several years and has helped to focus attention and resources on the issue. Efforts include bilateral agreements like those between Russia and Norway, multilateral initiatives like AMEC, and international organizations like the IAEA Contact Expert Group for International Radwaste Projects. The US Cooperative Threat Reduction program (CTR) has made a significant contribution as well, sending equipment and technology to help dismantle Russia's ballistic missile submarines and paying Russian workers to do the job. Moreover, naval and civilian leaders in Russia are lately more organized and committed to moving forward on this vexing problem.

More could certainly be done. A comprehensive plan for defueling, dismantling, and disposal of Russian submarines and their spent fuel is still lacking — the likely victim of conflicting priorities and minimal resources within Russia and of insufficient commitment among the international actors that will fund and monitor the program. Basic decisions must be made on issues such as reprocessing capability and sites for interim and permanent storage of the spent fuel and roadblocks like taxation and liability must still be overcome. Some of the work in progress, like construction of liquid radioactive waste purification facilities for the Northern and Pacific Fleets, have had misunderstandings and delays along the way and are only now nearing completion — well behind schedule. And Russia as a whole has not done well in the past three years, with political and economic turmoil making it difficult to focus attention on issues that are not immediate crises. Disorganization and corruption in many of the country's affairs make cooperative ventures with foreign actors difficult as international assistance sometimes evaporates before it has a chance to do any good. Nor is the West without fault. Western governments have not been very forthcoming with financial aid, with Norway and perhaps Japan excepted, and the US attitude toward Russia has hardened over the years. Many in the current Congress are unsympathetic to foreign aid in general and to aid for Russia in particular.

And this was before NATO's Kosovo air campaign made political and economic engagement between Russia and the West more difficult. To many Russians, Kosovo seemed a logical escalation of repeated assaults on their interests and national pride. The enlargement of NATO into the former Warsaw Pact was the major complaint, but failed promises of aid and assistance, competition for energy access and profits in the Caspian region, and a disregard for Russia's place and opinion on matters of international importance were concerns as well. The new alienation has not been confined to political elites and the military but also affects the Russian people, something new for the post–Cold War period. After Kosovo, Russian opinion was less inclined to support US and Western European positions on international issues, while the country's deep financial crisis further undermined faith in a Western-style economic system. During the conflict Russia broke off all military to military cooperation with the West, including AMEC.

Several months after the Kosovo crisis US-Russian relations seem to be improving. At the June 1999 G-8 meeting in Cologne, Germany, President Yeltsin of Russia and the heads of state from several Western countries worked on programs for additional financial assistance to Russia. At about the same time, the CTR program was renewed for an additional seven years — an extremely important development that will keep many nuclear cooperative ventures going between Russia and the United States. The Northern Fleet liquid waste purification facility should be completed soon and AMEC seems likely to be reinstated, with a prototype storage container completed on schedule. In Russia itself, the financial and economic crisis that began in August 1998 turned out to be less of a disaster than originally feared and some business confidence is returning. It will still be a long time before a truly representative and efficient Russian government and a hopeful Russian society emerge, but the opportunity exists.

This book provides a valuable guide to the problems associated with decommissioned Russian submarines and their nuclear spent fuel. Professor Krupnick explains the technical and environmental aspects of the issue but also a good deal more, including the economic and political challenges of contemporary Russia, the development of the Russian Navy, and the various international cooperative initiatives in place to help remedy the spent fuel problem. His application of the Russian submarine spent fuel issue to the broader study of international relations is a noteworthy contribution to contemporary scholarship. The book is of particular value for gathering much of the information about the Russian spent fuel problem into one place, well documented, but without the mass of data that can make other reports on the subject difficult to read and analyze.

We have an opportunity today to help achieve a better environment and greater international peace and security. With Russia's destiny still an unknown, US strategic interests would be well served by helping Russia establish a self-respecting place for itself in the world and by promoting a stable political and security order for all of the former Soviet bloc. The military to military cooperation of AMEC and the other collaborative efforts by the international community to help resolve Russia's submarine spent fuel problem are part of a policy to make this happen. Despite the difficulties and uncertainties, it is precisely the right time for the United States and the rest of the West to make a greater commitment to Russia.

William J. Perry • *Summer 2000*

Dr. Perry, Secretary of Defense, 1994–1997 (and Deputy Secretary 1993–1994, and Under Secretary 1977–1981), received degrees from Stanford and a Ph.D. in mathematics from Penn State. He is the Michael and Barbara Berberian Professor at Stanford University, a Fellow at the Hoover Institute, and co-director of the Stanford-Harvard Preventive Defense Project. He is the founder of ESL, Inc., the former executive vice-president of Hambrecht & Quist, and the former chairman of Technology Strategies & Alliances; he serves on the boards of Boeing and United Technologies and as chairman of Global Technology Partners.

Preface

This book looks at the problems associated with Russian nuclear submarine spent fuel and how Russia and the international community are responding to the challenge. With the end of the Cold War, Russia's submarines were no longer needed to deter or fight Western navies and were very expensive to operate and maintain. Older submarines have subsequently been taken out of service in large numbers, but without firm plans and infrastructure in place to remove and adequately to care for their nuclear components. Spent fuel assemblies from submarine nuclear reactors can be a particular hazard to the environment because the enriched uranium they contain is highly radioactive from past high power operations. One fuel assembly of two to three feet in length and a few inches in diameter can contain enough radioactivity to contaminate severely several acres of land, and there are tens of thousands of fuel assemblies requiring attention. Russian spent fuel assemblies also contain enough nuclear weapons usable material to make them a proliferation threat. The problem is particularly acute in Northwest Russia where the majority of the submarines were based. A host of decommissioned submarines are now moored along the shores of Russia's outlets to the Arctic Ocean, enduring a harsh climate with minimum manning and materiel support. The fuel assemblies already removed from submarines are being kept at regional storage sites that are badly out-of-date and that lack the kind of security and environmental control and protective systems found in storage facilities in the West. These sites pose an even more immediate threat to the environment than the fuel assemblies still installed on Russia's submarines.

With Russia in the midst of a difficult transition from a centrally controlled political and economic system to one that might eventually resemble Western models, lines of authority are confused and little money is available for projects not perceived as absolutely essential. On its own, Russia simply cannot afford to finance the defueling and dismantlement of these submarines and the proper storage or reprocessing of their spent

5

fuel assemblies. International participation is needed and has been forth-coming to a modest extent, although helping Russia is no easy task. Taxes of 30 to 40 percent may be levied on foreign aid by various Russian government agencies, money designated for specific projects can be siphoned off for other use or to the pockets of corrupt officials, and donor governments and foreign contractors are fearful of liability claims should a nuclear incident or accident occur with their involvement. Even with substantial international aid and the best of domestic circumstances, the Russian submarine spent fuel problem will be with us for at least another decade and probably two.

The book begins with discussions about Russia's economy, its environment, and the Russian Navy, and then covers in detail Russia's submarine spent fuel and related nuclear problems. The remainder of the book deals with the engagement of the international community on the issue. Involvement began when nongovernmental organizations (NGOs) like Greenpeace and the Bellona Foundation helped to identify the environmental hazards of decommissioned Russian submarines and to publicize them to national authorities and the international public at large. These NGOs provided early expertise and helped to establish an agenda for further action. National governments and intergovernmental organizations (IGOs) soon became involved and began to work directly with Russian governmental and industrial organizations to identify and fund various studies and preliminary projects to help mitigate the dangers. International regime activity helped to improve communications, to build trust and track commitments, and to establish standards of expectation and performance and various mechanisms for further collaboration. A final resolution to the problem will require much greater international commitment and probably the active involvement of multinational corporations. Encouraged by potential profits and in alliance with one another and with Russian enterprises, large Western firms like Kvaerner of Norway, BNFL of the United Kingdom, and Lockheed Martin of the United States can help develop and implement comprehensive programs to remedy the spent fuel hazards.

The pattern of engagement in the Russian spent fuel problem is supportive of a collaboration model developed by Barbara Gray in 1989. Gray observed that international cooperation on both conflictual and consensual issues can develop in three phases: a problem setting phase that identifies the issues of concern and their boundaries; a direction setting phase where key decision-makers become involved and establish formal collaborative processes; and, an implementation phase where relevant actors pursue and complete projects essential to the task. I elaborate on Gray's model by identifying the specific types of international actors most closely associated with each phase of collaboration on the Russian spent fuel problem: NGOs with problem setting; IGOs and national governments with direction setting; and, multinational corporations with implementation. The pattern observed could be a useful model for other efforts at large-scale environmental engagement with the countries of the former-Soviet bloc, and perhaps portions of the developing world as well.

Because of the sensitive nature of the nuclear and defense issues concerned, primary source information was often not available for this research. For the Russian submarine spent fuel problem itself, I used available documents and a large number of interviews but was not privy to technical negotiations or proprietary information; for topics related to the spent fuel issue, such as the radioactive waste problems at Russia's reprocessing and other nuclear weapons facilities, I relied heavily on secondary sources. Useful documents from governmental or intergovernmental agencies included the NATO Committee on the Challenges of Modern Society (CCMS) 1995 and 1998 reports *Cross-Border Environmental Problems Emanating From Defense-Related Installations and Activities*, the US Congressional Office of Technology Assessment (OTA) study *Nuclear Wastes in the Arctic: Analysis of Arctic and other Regional Impacts from Soviet Nuclear Contamination*, and the European Commission's *Inventory of radioactive waste and spent fuel at the Kola Peninsula region of north-west Russia*. From environmental advocacy groups and individuals, Bellona's *The Russian Northern Fleet: Sources of Radioactive Contamination*, "Nuclear Submarine Decommissioning and Related Problems" written by Susanne Kopte of the Bonn International Center for Conversion (BICC), and Joshua Handler's several articles on the Russian submarine fleet were particularly useful. The most comprehensive published coverage of the nuclear waste problem in Russia is certainly Don J. Bradley's 1997 volume *Behind the Nuclear Curtain: Radioactive Waste Management in the Former Soviet Union*, while the American Association for the Advancement of Science (AAAS) book *Reducing Wastes from Decommissioned Nuclear Submarines in the Russian Northwest* provides a great amount of specific information about Russia's submarine spent fuel problem. Both were used extensively in creating this volume. For current political and economic information and analysis, I relied on the *Financial Times* of London; for additional commentary and data I made full use of *Lexis-Nexis* and other Internet resources.

I investigated the Russian submarine spent fuel issue during the period 1997–1999 as part of my research into post–Cold War European security cooperation. Prior to my academic pursuits, I served in the US Navy as a nuclear submarine officer and developed some appreciation for the technical aspects associated with Russian submarine and nuclear spent fuel issues. The research was conducted while I was serving as a professor of military strategic studies at the US Air Force Academy, Colorado Springs, Colorado. I am grateful to my academic department and to the Academy for providing me with the time and resources necessary to conduct this investigation. I am obliged as well to the US Air Force Institute for National Security Studies (INSS) for supporting my research travel, both within the United States and to Western Europe and Russia. I also wish to thank the Secretariat and members of the International Atomic Energy Agency Contact Expert Group for International Radwaste Projects (IAEA CEG) and other attendees at IAEA CEG meetings for their time and willingness to discuss the submarine spent fuel issue.

My contribution will, I hope, be a readable and up-to-date coverage of the Russian submarine spent fuel problem, along with a theoretical analysis of how the international community can help remedy a troubling environmental problem in a difficult country. While indebted to many for the completion of this project, the responsibility for it belongs to me alone. The views expressed in this book are mine and do not reflect the official policy or position of the US Air Force, the US Department of Defense, or the US Government. On matters of responsibility but on a hugely different scale, one is reminded of a comment by Marshall J. C. Joffre who commanded the French Army in the early months of World War I. When asked by a post-war commission about the French and British victory over the German army at the Battle of the Marne in 1914, he replied: "I don't know who won the Battle of the Marne, but if it had been lost, I know who would have lost it."[1]

Chapter 1

Russian Dilemmas

... [The Soviet Union] has passed from the relative simplicity of a bipolar world, in which the only issue was "we" and "they"— who-whom, kto-kogo, as Lenin put it — and has come into an international setting marked by real complications and contradictions. People who have only enemies don't know what complications are; for that, you have to have friends; and these, the Soviet government, thank God, now has.[1]

— George F. Kennan

Kennan's 1960 assertion about the Soviet Union is now true for the Russian successor-state. This book investigates in detail the hazards associated with Russian nuclear submarine spent fuel and the various technical issues that must be solved in order to alleviate them, but also looks at how Russia and its new friends and associates are trying to solve the problem — despite numerous difficulties and setbacks.

Submarine spent fuel and other nuclear dilemmas are part of the enormous challenge Russia faces in transitioning from its Soviet past to some distant and as yet ill-defined future. Churchill's oft-quoted adage about the riddle, mystery, and enigma that identify Russia's motives emerges as we contemplate the country's ultimate destiny. Will it be a prosperous democracy, a resurgent totalitarianism, or a chaotic and economically depressed region of feudal fiefdoms? Most likely it will muddle through today's crises to a circumstance somewhat worse or a little bit better than its current troubles, at least for the next decade or so. To understand better how and why the Russian submarine spent fuel issue evolved as it has and to speculate knowledgeably about what must be done in the future to solve the problem, this chapter reflects on the contemporary Russian economy and environment and on the problems of international cooperation with Russia.

Russia and the End of the Cold War

The Cold War was a period of great tension and manifest danger in the world. The Soviet Union and its satellites faced the United States and its allies across a rigid divide, while citizens on both sides of the Iron Curtain lived with a persistent fear of nuclear destruction. The Cold War later developed a surprising and tolerable stability, due in part to the sublimation of each side's internal rivalries to the needs of the confrontation but also to the same nuclear weapons that had earlier created such anxiety.[2] Fear of surprise attack gave way to a robust mutual deterrent structure and to exceptional caution in foreign and security policy. Stability, however, meant neither freedom nor prosperity for those under communist rule and should not be mourned, but the collapse of the Soviet system in the late 1980s and early 1990s has been followed by severe economic and social dislocation in many countries of Central and Eastern Europe and the former Soviet Union. It also revealed serious environmental hazards throughout the region.

The end of the Cold War has been particularly traumatic for those living in the former Soviet Union. Only a few years ago, their country dominated half the globe with a single ideology and a large and well-armed military; its support of clients in Africa, Asia, and Latin America gave it worldwide influence while regrettably contributing to destructive local conflicts. Today, its main successor state has trouble quelling secessionist movements on its own territory and often seems on the verge of financial collapse. Although led since its founding by a president with apparently good intentions, the new Russian Federation has had great difficulty implementing reforms and establishing productive and consistent political and economic processes. Loyalties are confused as diverse regions and private enterprises compete with Moscow for control of the country's assets and agenda. The decommissioned nuclear submarine spent fuel problem discussed in this book is primarily the result of decisions and mistakes made by past Soviet and Russian leadership, but remediation and resolution of the hazards has everything to do with Russia's current economic and political problems.

Soviet Economy

Communist control over the Soviet Union and the countries of the Warsaw Pact collapsed for many reasons, including the military, political, and economic challenge of the West and the pressure of restive internal minorities. Most profoundly, however, the communist system simply did not work. The Soviet version of centralized control and management of almost all the affairs of a country was inherently inefficient and usually poorly executed. State enterprises and their managers rarely had to compete for business and had preferential arrangements with the government and with suppliers and customers; for Soviet workers, job security and social benefits were available for life without much concern for performance. The centralized decision-making system removed freedom of choice from the lives of Soviet citizens and proved a clumsy way to govern a nation and to run a modern economy. A sad metaphor of the Soviet system was the long lines of citizens waiting to purchase scarce consumer goods; although the goods were usually not expensive, their quality was often poor. Soviet-manufactured televisions were notorious for blowing up during use and Soviet buildings for cracking walls before the first occupants arrived. Although sufficient goods, services, and security were provided for people to survive with a passable lifestyle, the communist system removed the incentive to get ahead through hard work and creative thought. Productivity tended to be low in industrial enterprises and the familiar refrain of workers that "they pretend to pay us and we pretend to work" was compelling commentary on the problems of the Soviet system as a whole.

When the growth rate of the Soviet Union flattened out in the early 1970s, observers both inside and outside the Soviet bloc began to recognize that the country's command economy was in big trouble. The difficulties became ever more apparent during the information and technology revolution that took off in the West shortly thereafter. Entrepreneurial Americans like Bill Gates of *Microsoft* and Steven Jobs and Stephen Wozniak of *Apple*, among many others, revolutionized the way the world did business and communicated, and created enormous new wealth along the way. The "intensive industrial revolution" of the 1970s and 1980s spread to Europe and particularly to Japan and other parts of East Asia.[3] It was one thing for Russia to be eclipsed by the United States or the countries of Western Europe and Japan, but quite another to be non-competitive with industrial upstarts like South Korea and Taiwan.

Full recognition of the Soviet Union's systemic problems led to the policies of President Mikhail Gorbachev and his reform-minded associates in the mid–1980s. They tinkered with the political and economic organization of their country hoping to make it more competitive with the rest of the world, while trying to keep control of their vast and diverse domain. They also wanted to retain what they perceived as "the good" still left in communism: capitalism after all creates different classes within human society, separating people and groups into haves and have-nots — exactly what the founding fathers of Marxism and communism said they wanted to do away with through centralized political and economic control. But the state Gorbachev was trying to reform had rotted for too long from within and could not be salvaged through a Russian version of social democracy. Under pressure of economic necessity and an unexpected rise of nationalism within its ethnic republics, the Soviet Union became part of the rubbish heap of history at the end of 1991.

To the everlasting credit of Gorbachev and his political and military leaders and advisors, the Cold War for the most part ended peacefully.[4] Communist East Germany was allowed to unify with the democratic Federal Republic of Germany to the west, the Central and Eastern European countries of the Warsaw Pact were permitted to go their own way, and the Soviet Union itself fell apart into 15 independent nation-states — splitting off even the ancient Russian heartland of Ukraine from Moscow's control. Some of the former Warsaw Pact countries have since become reasonably stable and prosperous and have joined NATO and are in line for the European Union; other countries that never existed before, such as the southern Islamic republics of the former Soviet Union, are trying to make a go at independence — however difficult. And Russia itself, as the greater part of the former union, has been struggling to make more democratic and capitalistic policies work. Few diplomats, politicians, or political scientists before 1988 had predicted that anything like this new Russian revolution could possibly have occurred.

Despite its collapse and its dismal economic and human rights record, the Soviet Union did not fail in all it did. When truly mobilized for projects of national importance or of particular interest to the leadership, remarkable achievements could be made — albeit at great human and material costs. The industrialization of the 1930s and the enormous military sacrifices of World War II were early examples. Millions died in those efforts but the country survived and to some extent prospered as a result. During the Cold War, the Soviet Union focused its best minds and enormous resources on sending equipment and people into outer space. The country's scientists and brave cosmonauts achieved early wonders that impressed and unnerved Western leaders and citizens. Politically directed industrial efforts targeted military projects as well, such as strategic missiles and the production and operation of nuclear submarines. Substantial advances were made on these projects, stimulating counter-efforts by the United States and the other countries of the West. Untold rubles and dollars were spent on the Cold War arms race. In the "Atomic Audit: The Costs and Consequences of US Nuclear Weapons since 1940" released by the Brookings

Institution in June 1998, analysts estimated that the United States has spent almost $5.5 trillion on its nuclear capabilities since the end of World War II, including development, management, protection, and cleanup.[5]

Even though the per capita wealth of its citizens was relatively low, the Soviet Union could succeed with specific national projects because of its command political and economic system; resources were simply allocated to projects with the highest priority, regardless of efficiency and opportunity costs. The tremendous quantities of radioactive waste (Radwaste) leftover from the Cold War would benefit from such a command effort, but this simply is not possible or desirable in the more democratic and free market-oriented country that Russia has become. Nor is it financially feasible. In the United States, the costs of defueling and dismantlement are estimated at $30 to $40 million per submarine.[6] Russia can perhaps accomplish the task at a significantly lower cost per unit because its wage and environmental overhead costs are likely to be less, but several millions of dollars per submarine will still be required. And the cost of submarine defueling and dismantling can not be separated from other nuclear operations and Radwaste procedures, such as the operation of Radwaste processing and disposal facilities and the complex transportation network necessary to move the waste around. US cleanup cost for its military nuclear establishment is estimated at $365 billion.[7] Russia's total cost for military Radwaste cleanup may well be along the lines of the US estimate, and this from a country with a gross domestic product (GDP) now smaller than Switzerland.[8]

Russian Democracy and Capitalism

Since its founding by Boris Yeltsin, the Russian Federation has generally tried to establish a more pluralistic and citizen-responsive political system that can nonetheless still govern effectively. The Russian constitution of 1993 created a system on the French model, with a strong president who can appoint the country's prime minister and the other senior officials of the state. The president and his bureaucracy have substantial authority and can do much by decree, but must work with the *Duma* (the Russian lower legislative house) to fund themselves and to implement major policy initiatives. With the *Duma* under hostile communist and nationalist control for most of the period since the country's founding, implementing a consistent program of economic and political reform has been practically impossible. The executive branch has not helped, with governmental departments changing their leadership, functions, and relative power with troublesome regularity. The Russian Federation has also become much less centralized than its Soviet predecessor, containing 21 republics and various other political sub-units with different degrees of autonomous authority and competing social priorities and economic imperatives.

Government structure and makeup are only part of the problem. Some Russian leaders had hoped to convert their ponderous state-controlled enterprises quickly into private businesses operated for sales and profit. But how can workers be changed overnight from a patronage system and shadow economy to one where hard work and ambition bring success, particularly when the rewards are neither firmly established nor immediately self-evident? Converting collective farms to private operations has been a failure, for example, and contributed to the 1998/99 food shortage. According to Viktor Remizov, a farm manager both before and after privatization was attempted: "Nobody wanted to leave [the collective farm]." "People seem to be afraid of the uncertainty and financial difficulties."[9] And how can a massive change of ownership of state enterprises be implemented fairly and efficiently; who should the new owners be, the old managers, the workers, or some financial group that makes the highest bid for a company at auction? In fact, the old managers and their friends and associates in government generally took control. Bankers who were well connected and capitalized immediately after Russia's re-founding became part of the controlling interests, taking advantage of bargain-basement prices and amassing huge holdings in the process. As the new state became institutionalized, it resembled more and more the old hierarchy of Soviet *apparatchiks* and company managers. Changing social and bureaucratic arrangements in Russia, some in place from well before the communist era, will be very difficult.[10]

Boris Berezovsky is the most famous of the new elite. He is one of the so-called oligarchs, the 10 or 20 business leaders who have become enormously wealthy since the fall of communism. They control perhaps 50 percent of the Russian economy and exercise power primarily through their banking interests, although they are connected with media and industrial activities as well.[11] Berezovsky made his fortune by buying and selling assets of formerly state-owned oil, automobile, airline, and television companies.[12] In his government position as Executive Secretary of the Commonwealth of Independent States, he vigorously promoted for example the construction of nuclear power plants in Iran.[13] Berezovsky is personally close to former prime minister Viktor Chernomyrdin who himself has made millions, if not billions, through his association with the state energy firm *Gazprom*.[14] The oligarchs focused primarily on immediate profit, with little concern for long-term profitability from the companies they owned. According to Andrew Ipkendanz of Credit Suisse First Boston, the new Russian elite plundered the country's assets and funneled most of the proceeds offshore rather than reinvesting in domestic industries for future profit and the greater good of Russia.[15]

Many of the industries, however, were undoubtedly too outmoded and decrepit to save. At a fertilizer factory in Voskresensk, one worker complained that: "The air was very polluted and it was very hard to breath. Acid was everywhere." Letting the factory fail might be a better plan than any massive upgrading, but doing so without remedial action for workers and their families would create terrible hardships because Russian enterprises provide some of the last remaining social benefits for millions of Russians.[16] Any expectations that industry would become efficient and competitive overnight and that social and bureaucratic processes would flow smoothly from paper reforms were quickly dashed. According to estimates by Radio Free Europe and the Radio Liberty Research Institute, the Russian gross national product (GNP) declined by 40–50 percent between 1990 and 1994 — more than the American collapse during the Great Depression.[17]

The Yeltsin government oscillated between accommodation with the new interest groups and vigorous support for radical reform, and then back to accommodation — provoking and confusing many along the way. A crucial failing has been the government's inability to collect taxes efficiently, leading to problems in paying salaries to the armed forces and civilian government workers and with purchasing services and providing social benefits. According to Russia's former Finance Minister Boris Fyodorov, "New York City collects more in municipal taxes than Russia collects federal taxes."[18] The *Duma* has repeatedly blocked tax reform and any attempt to curb the powers of the state's remaining large enterprises.[19] Summarizing the Russian economy in mid–1998, the *Financial Times* wrote that:

> ... the bulk of the country's Soviet-era enterprises are still subtracting value from inputs rather than adding it. The companies disguise their destruction of value by charging arbitrary prices for their products. Barter is an increasing share of the Russian economy [perhaps 50 percent]. Bankruptcies are rare. The IMF wants tax collection to work, but in the absence of massive bankruptcies, cash starved enterprises will simply be faced with the alternatives of paying taxes or wages.[20]

Corruption has also made reform difficult. According the *New York Times*: "It is probably safe to say a majority of Russians and many foreigners have been shaken down by a local policeman or city official, and it is accepted fact that the shift to capitalism made many Government officials rich overnight."[21] A US CIA report charged Viktor Chernomyrdin of personal corruption while he was prime minister, such as demanding payoffs from foreign business people just for granting an interview.[22] But in contemporary Russia, corruption is also related to organized crime where, according to estimates publicized by the World Bank, such groups control over 40 percent of the Russian economy.[23] In late 1998 Grigory A. Yavlinsky, a reform politician and leader of the liberal Yablokov faction, accused the Primakov government of continuing the corrupt pattern of the past.[24]

Despite all these problems and the overall decline of the economy since the end of the Cold War, from time to time it appeared as if Western-style capitalism was taking hold in Russia and that economic growth was just around the corner. To counter corruption, in 1997 President Yeltsin revamped his cabinet and brought in Boris Nemtsov to spearhead an anti-corruption crusade. He also decreed that all government purchases and services would have to undergo competitive bidding and removed some tax and customs privileges. In the most publicized measure, Yeltsin ordered his government to sell its fleet of foreign-made cars at public auctions and to shift to Russian-made vehicles.[25] Parts of the economy were indeed responding to private initiative and a vigorous middle class was developing in Moscow at least.

Some of this success was due to a policy of monetary stabilization. In the Soviet period, currency value and the price for goods were determined by the state, so there was little concern about the ruble's international exchange rate. Post-Cold War Russia had early bouts with enormous inflation as the artificial Soviet-era fiscal and monetary policies adjusted haphazardly to the realities of the international market economy. This led to a significant "dollarization" of the Russian economy as consumers and merchants sought currency with stable value. By some estimates, more US dollars were in circulation in Russia than rubles.[26] By 1995, the Russian government and financial institutions had settled into a modified-floating exchange rate system that kept the ruble reasonably close to 5000 rubles to the dollar (on 1 January 1998 the Yeltsin government re-denominated the ruble by removing three zeros, converting 5000 rubles to five rubles overnight). The Central Bank of Russia would monitor the relationship and intervene if necessary to maintain the currency's value.[27] This was similar to policies practiced by other emerging and recovering economies of the world and was at least in form consistent with the neo-liberal economic theories that dominated Western thought in the 1980s and 90s.

Monetary stability created a degree of confidence in the Russian government's resolve to combat inflation and to continue its free market reforms. At the same time, however, Russia was being hurt by the decline in oil prices experienced worldwide — one of its few exports and sources of hard currency. With continued problems with tax collection, the growing budget deficit was financed by issuing bonds. As deficits grew, investors began to demand shorter terms for the bonds and increasingly higher rates of return. According to Sylvia Nasar of the *New York Times*, Russia found itself in a classic debt trap: the investors required a high rate of return to invest in the government bonds, raising the cost of servicing the debt and the possibility of default.[28] To keep itself running and to service its growing debt, Russia was forced to borrow repeatedly from the International Monetary Fund (IMF). Its still fragile economy lacked the resiliency to meet unexpected shocks while its new international connections made it susceptible to crises elsewhere in the world.

Crisis of 1998

To understand Russia's economic problems of the late 1990s, one must start in East Asia. City-states and countries such as Singapore, Hong Kong, Malaysia, Indonesia, and Thailand had enjoyed an incredible economic boom throughout the 1980s and into the 1990s, with country after country following the export-led growth model pioneered by Japan, South Korea, and Taiwan. The countries of the region were leaving the have-nots of the developing world and entering the world of prosperity and consumption of the haves. The underlying problems that remained, such as poor bank regulation practices and cozy relationships between government officials and large enterprises, were ignored as exuberance about the region's prospects grew ever larger — setting up the conditions for a shocking collapse. The crisis began with speculative pressure on the currency of Thailand (the baht) in May 1997, followed by a de facto government devaluation in July 1997. This led to further loss of faith in the baht and in the country's overall economic prospects. Like so many dominoes, Indonesia, Malaysia, and even stalwarts like Singapore, Hong Kong and South Korea followed suit or were put under severe economic stress.[29] Japan was immersed in its own systemic economic and political crisis and was not in a position to intervene strongly to help out its neighbors, particularly when encouraged by the United States not to do so.[30] The region went from boom to recession and depression almost overnight; some currencies lost 50 percent of their value in just six months.

By early 1998, the Asian economic crisis had created a flight of capital from other emerging markets to safer havens like the United States and Western Europe. Latin America came under great pressure as did Central Europe. Soon the Russian ruble became a suspect currency as well as speculators began betting against the government's ability to maintain its value. President Yeltsin changed governments to try to discourage negative sentiment, firing stalwart Viktor Chernomyrdin on 23 March 1998 and appointing political novice Sergie Kiriyenko as head of a new reform government, but the tide was probably moving too rapidly against Russia by then. On 17 August 1998, Moscow stunned the international financial community by defaulting on its foreign debt. Foreign investors suffered immediate losses estimated in excess of $33 billion.[31] A few days later, Yeltsin dismissed the Kiriyenko government and attempted to reinstate Chernomyrdin. The change was reportedly precipitated by oligarchs like Berezovsky concerned that the Kiriyenko government would fail to bail out Russian banks that had lost badly on currency and bond market speculation.[32] According to the *Financial Times*, the oligarchs may also have hoped to install a government that could weather what they saw as a coming economic and political storm and perhaps gain a sympathetic successor to Yeltsin. They were worried about a populist strongman like Alexander Lebed coming to power, who might drastically affect their interests.[33]

A major IMF loan to Russia collapsed as a result of the August events and had not been revived by mid–1999. The Russian government soon halted its efforts to support the ruble and allowed it to float, effectively devaluing its currency as Thailand had done to the baht. The ruble's value relative to the dollar plummeted from 6.3 to over 20 within a few days.[34] Interest rates went up to over 100 percent for many of the country's bond offerings; by October 1998, Russian stocks had declined to less than 50 percent of their value before the crisis. Politically, the *Duma* blocked Chernomyrdin's nomination for prime minister and settled on former foreign Soviet minister and apparatchik Yevgeny Primakov, a man likely to be sympathetic with rolling back reforms and with increasing the government's direction of the economy. Russia began to print money again to pay the wages of its employees, raising fears of inflation and further currency troubles.[35] As of mid–1999, conditions were still depressed but relatively stable as the government tried to come up with at viable economic plan; at least it had not begun "printing money like crazy."[36] The greatest casualty of the August financial crisis may well have been hope: virtually no one now believes that Russia will see any degree of prosperity or economic normalcy anytime soon.

The August financial crisis was rooted in the structural problems left over from Russia's Soviet past and in the inertia remaining in Russian society, but other factors contributed. The Russian Central Bank may have misappropriation up to $1 billion around the time of the crisis, aggravating the revenue shortfall.[37] The funds may have ended up off-shore to benefit the few, while the average Russian sank into greater poverty.[38] The international community may also have erred. The United States and the IMF had encouraged Russia's tight money policy and subsequent high-interest rates. This caused domestic investment to remain weak and kept money away from workers and consumers.[39] Others point out that the practice of pegging exchange rates to strong currencies has become "untenable in the conditions of high capital mobility in the 1990s." The pegged currencies of Asian economies collapsed in 1997, Russia's in 1998, and Brazil nearly followed in 1999.[40] Some also believe that Russian reformers, like the Kiriyenko government in 1998, did not really understand the complexity of their monetary management task and erred in believing that their "sado-monetarist" policies could create "credible market institutions."[41] Whatever the cause, Russia's gross domestic product fell 4.6 percent in 1998.[42]

Criticism of past policies is easy but useful suggestions about how Russia can escape from its current situation are scarce. International aid would certainly help and may arrive, but aid-givers are afraid their money will evaporate without achieving its purpose — as much has done in the past. With an adequate social net for its citizens, the Russian government should allow more bankruptcies of mismanaged banks and enterprises, lay-off public employees, and figure out a way to collect more taxes.[43] With soldiers and nuclear workers not being paid, and with other infrastructure and environmental projects on hold, it is not surprising that the potential hazards of decommissioned nuclear submarines in Russia's Northwest have not received greater attention in Moscow.

The Russian People

Even former Soviet President Mikhail Gorbachev was affected by the financial crisis, complaining in late 1998 that his life savings of $80,000 was wiped out when his bank went into bankruptcy.[44] Average Russians have obviously suffered more. Basic needs, like proper food and health care, were increasingly hard to come by even before the current crisis. Russians had waited almost a decade for the benefits of their capitalist revolution, but have instead been subject to an even more difficult life; those who expected to be comfortably retired are working as cleanup personnel or selling flowers in the subway for a few dollars a month. Government institutions like hospitals, prisons, and orphanages have little money for food, medicine, and clothing.[45] Desertion in the military has become common and officers are routinely arrested for selling military supplies to foreign countries.[46] In forgotten Soviet pioneer outposts like the Siberian town of Pevek across the Chukchi Sea from Alaska, there was little food and fuel to make it through the winter of 1998/1999. As the cold set in, Oleg Chetnov of the Russian Red Cross pleaded for help: "It is imperative that we bring help to people who are on the verge of extinction."[47] In a twist to Russia's nuclear submarine problems, three Pacific Fleet submarines were sent to provide electrical power via cables to the remote Kamchatka Peninsula town of Viliuchinsk.[48]

Personal safety has also declined in contemporary Russia, with some describing conditions as an "epidemic of violent crime."[49] Following the November 1998 assassination of St. Petersburg reform politician Galina Starovoitova in St. Petersburg, the Russian newspaper *Izvestia* ran a despairing editorial:

> Evil fears nothing today [in Russia] because it knows that it will not be punished. The proof is in the numerous high-profile crimes that have never been solved, in the widespread embezzlement and bribe-taking by government officials (federal and local), in the unprecedented theft by bankers who have instantly robbed hundreds of thousands of their clients, and finally in the rise of fascism in Russia.[50]

All Russians have suffered hardships and a resulting anomie, but adult males have been particularly hard hit. Their average life-span fell by 7 years to 57.6 between 1987 and 1994; in some parts of the country male life-span has dipped to 49 years or lower — an unprecedented disaster in the contemporary world.[51] According to a report by the UN Development Program, Russia has effectively dropped out of the group of developed states.[52]

Environment

The Russian environment is undoubtedly contributing to reduced life spans. Whole regions that supported the Soviet Cold War economy are in desperate need of cleanup and facilities improvement, or even shutdown. A few examples suffice.

The southern Ural Mountain city of Magnitogorsk was created during the Soviet Union's rapid industrialization program of the 1930s and became one of the world's great steel producing centers. Named for the near-by Magnetic Mountains, its railway, tank, and other war production helped to defeat Nazi Germany. Now its aging factories pollute the skies and degrade the health of its residents, creating a "center of devastation" 120 miles long and 40 miles wide.[53] Some estimate that more than nine out of every ten children born in the city are affected by "pollution-related illnesses: chronic bronchitis, asthma, allergies, even cancers."[54] On the Kola Peninsula in Northwest Russia, Russian industrial enterprises produce twice the toxic emissions as the whole of Finland. The nickel smelters of Nikkel send sulfur dioxide fumes into the Arctic air, blanketing the lands nearby and crossing international borders. Practically no living plants survive in a 400 square mile "industrial desert" near the plant.[55] According to one press report: "The countryside is dead. The pine trees were the first to die and the birch followed. For as far as the eye can see the landscape is of blackened earth and of dead, twisted trees."[56] The Russian people living nearby are of course also affected: respiratory ailments are common and a particular tragedy among the very young. Safe water for Russian families is also a problem. In Murmansk, intestinal disease is common and probably related to contaminated drinking water taken from the Murmansk Fjord.[57] Siberia's Lake Baikal, the world's largest body of fresh water and a natural wonder, is being compromised by industrial pollution, untreated sewage, and a military factory discharging dioxin-laden wastes.[58] Outside Russia in the former Soviet republics of Kazakhstan and Uzbekistan, now sovereign states, the Aral Sea is dying up as a result of irrigation projects to support cotton production — exposing biological warfare testing areas and other new miseries for nearby residents.

Like fixing Russia's economy, no simple solutions exist for these problems. Water and air treatment facilities are expensive and removing sources of industrial or agricultural contamination could even be harmful in the short term. Polluting industries also provide schools, medical care, and other services for their workers — in addition to employment. Modern development may eventually improve Russian industrial processes and reduce pollution, but development has its own environmental costs. The purity of the Moscow River, for example, is now endangered by Western-style subdivisions on the outskirts of Russia's capital and forested regions are being rapidly exploited and perhaps endangered.[59] Proposals by Western firms to develop the mineral wealth of the Kamchatka Peninsula, a spectacular region of volcanoes, ice, deep forests, and exotic wildlife, are being resisted by Russian environmental groups.[60]

Russia's Nuclear Legacy

A serious but also widely misunderstood danger to the environment comes from radioactive material. Life on Earth is exposed to radiation all the time from natural sources. Radiation and radioactive contamination from man-made nuclear sources can add to this exposure and in significant quantities can cause grave harm. Radiation affects living beings by ionizing atoms as the high energy particles or waves pass through cells, triggering potentially damaging changes to cell chemistry. The human body can be exposed directly to radiation or radioactive isotopes (called radionuclides) can be inhaled or ingested if radioactive particles get into the air or food chain. Most radionuclides are a problem for only a very period short time, but some have half-lives of thousands of years.[61]

The nuclear programs of the Soviet Union have created some of the most threatening environmental problems in the world. During the Cold War, the Soviet Union produced upwards of 50,000 nuclear weapons; it conducted nuclear testing from 1949 until 1990 and detonating a total of 715 nuclear devices.[62] The residue from tests conducted on the island of Novaya Zemlya is still the primary source of man-made radionuclides in the Arctic region. Much of the nuclear material used in Soviet nuclear weapons was produced in and around secret cities like Chelyabinsk 65, Krasnoyarsk 26, and Tomsk 7, located in an east-west belt across southern Siberia. In the Soviet Union's plutonium and uranium production process, hundreds of millions of curies of Radwaste were created. Some of the highly radioactive waste was dumped or escaped into the surrounding rivers and lakes, creating substantial contamination and local cleanup problems.[63] Contamination also migrated into waterways that led to the Arctic Ocean. The security imperative caused by the arms race with the West placed an urgency on Russian weapons production, not on safety and the environment. According to the deputy governor for the Chelyabinsk regions, Bennady Podtyosov, even today: "Ecology ranks last on the government's list of priorities."[64]

Civilian nuclear power stations in Russia and other countries of the former Warsaw Pact are a grave concern as well. Twelve Chernobyl-style RBMK reactors are still operational in the countries of the former–Soviet Union, such as those at Sosnovy Bor southwest of St. Petersburg in Russia and at Ignalina in Lithuania. These are very large and relatively efficient electric power producing reactors, but with significant operational safety and waste disposal problems. RBMK reactors use graphite for moderation and have complicated and undesirable operational characteristics; a serious reactor accident could release radioactivity directly into the atmosphere because RBMKs have no containment structure to prevent it. Other Russian reactors also have design problems, like those at the Kola Nuclear Power Plant that have little containment or emergency cooling capability. Since the end of the Cold War spare parts for nuclear power plants have become scarce and nuclear workers disgruntled because of pay arrears, add potential maintenance and operational problems to those of design.[65]

Another part of Russia's nuclear legacy concerns its submarines. During the Cold War they were at the cutting edge of Soviet technology and the very measure of superpower prowess. With the end of East-West competition, decommissioned nuclear submarines have become an expensive and hazardous burden for Russia. Ironically, Russia's nuclear submarine and spent fuel disposal problems now offer an opportunity for increased cooperation and improved relations between Russia and the rest of the world.

Russian Decommissioned Submarines

Over a period of almost half a century, the Soviet Union and Russia built 235 nuclear submarines.[66] Northwest Russia became one of the world's most concentrated repositories of operating nuclear reactors, in part because Russian nuclear submarines usually had two reactors instead of the one normally installed on submarines built by other countries. As the Cold War was ending in 1989–90, approximately 197 Russian submarines were in service and 20 out of service.[67] Approximately 120 or so of the operational units were assigned to Russia's Northern Fleet, a number almost equal to the entire US nuclear submarine force at the time. By late 1998, about 170 Russian nuclear submarines had been decommissioned or put in a lay-up status Navy-wide; of these only 40 had been defueled and dismantled. Of the remaining 130 decommissioned ships, 110 to 115 still have not been defueled.[68] In the Northern Fleet, 95 or so nuclear submarines have been decommissioned but only 26 have been defueled.[69] Additional submarines will be decommissioned in the next few years and operational submarines refueled, adding to the Radwaste dilemma.

Russian Submarine Status		
	1989–1990	**Late-1998**
In Service	197	61
Decommissioned	20	110-115 (fuel still installed)
		~71 in the Northern Fleet

Given unlimited funding and appropriate organization, Russian Northern Fleet headquarters in Severomorsk would have a master PERT chart identifying the defueling and dismantlement timetable and industrial commitments for each submarine of the Northern Fleet.[70] At specified times, the submarines would be defueled at remote or developed sites, the solid and liquid radioactive waste generated would be reduced, processed, or stored, and the rest of the submarine cut-up for scrap; after transport and possible interim storage, the nuclear spent fuel assemblies would be reprocessed or placed in permanent geological storage — all done with safe, secure, and environmentally friendly procedures. Defueling would take one to two months per submarine and total submarine dismantlement perhaps a year. With adequate redundancy of equipment and personnel, Russia's entire decommissioned submarine fleet would disappear within 10–15 years.

The reality is very different. Russian submarines have been taken out of service without any prospect of near-term defueling; the defuelings already accomplished have created an overflow of nuclear spent fuel at sites not designed for proper long-term storage of high level Radwaste. Bottlenecks exist at almost every phase of the defueling process, preventing rapid progress in alleviating the backlog and in pursuing a consolidated plan. Needed equipment like storage containers and railway cars to transport fuel assemblies is in short supply; confused or conflicting organizational interests often impede decision-making because Russian agencies bill each other for nuclear services, but few have the money to pay their debts. Progress is also inhibited by past practices: early Russian reactor components were sometimes poorly designed and perhaps improperly operated, leading to damaged fuel assemblies and radioactive contamination and making routine handling operations impossible.[71] Perhaps one or two decommissioned submarines per year have been defueled in the Northern Fleet since 1988, well below the ten or so per year needed to solve the problem in a reasonably expeditious manner.[72]

Under normal conditions, spent fuel that remains installed in submarine reactors is very safe. It has adequate cooling, rugged protection from mechanical and chemical shock, and substantial security from theft. Unfortunately, conditions are not normal in the contemporary Russian Navy. Sailors are not being paid with regularity and equipment may not be well maintained, compounding problems already created by past manufacturing and repair practices. Out-of-service submarines have already sunk at their moorings; collisions and other serious accidents are possible and could lead to pollution from radioactive material. One report noted that a submarine in the Murmansk Fjord was so dangerous that no one dared move it; in late 1998 an explosion apparently occurred onboard a

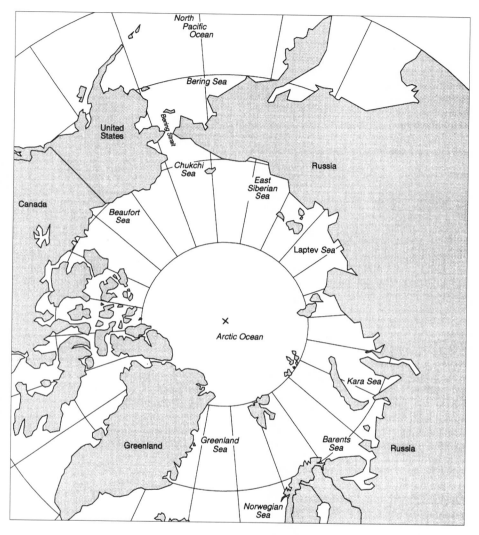

Figure 1. Circumpolar view of the world. From *Nuclear Wastes in the Arctic: An Analysis of Arctic and Other Regional Impacts from Soviet Nuclear Contamination,* OTA-ENV-623 (Washington, D.C.: U.S. Government Printing Office, September 1995), 4.

ballistic missile submarine returning to the fjord, causing near panic in the region.[73]

A greater hazard may be posed by the nuclear spent fuel already removed from Russian submarines. Over 30,000 submarine fuel assemblies are in Northwest Russia alone, most in inadequate storage facilities.

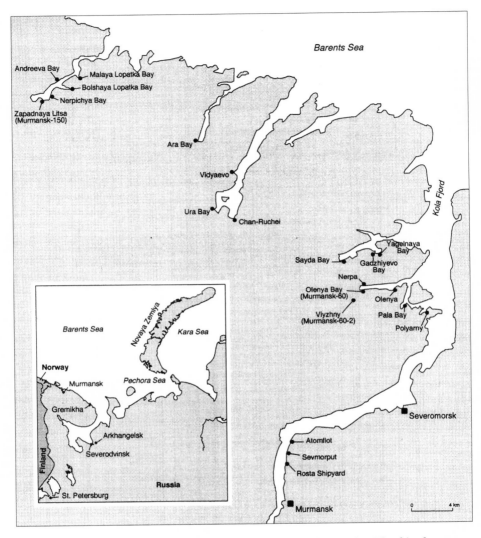

Figure 2. Major Russian naval facilities from the Zapadnaya Litsa Fjord in the west to Murmansk in the east; inset: Northwest Russia, including the Kola Peninsula, the Archangel region, and the island of Novaya Zemlya. From *Nuclear Wastes in the Arctic: An Analysis of Arctic and Other Regional Impacts from Soviet Nuclear Contamination,* OTA-ENV-623 (Washington, D.C.: U.S. Government Printing Office, September 1995), 123. Adapted from Handler, J., "The Northern Fleet's Nuclear Submarine Bases," *Jane's Intelligence Review-Europe,* December 1993. (Reproduced with permission from Jane's Information Group and Joshua Handler.)

They are either stored on moored service vessels or at land bases near waters connected to the Arctic Ocean. At Andreeva Bay in the Zapadnaya Litsa Fjord, 21,000 spent fuel assemblies are stored in tanks originally constructed for liquid waste — less than a quarter mile from the fjord.[74] According to Russian Navy Colonel A. D. Belikov:

> The deceleration of the rate of shipping SNF [spent nuclear fuel] to reprocessing plants, the termination in 1992 of the practice of dumping radioactive wastes at sea, and the lack of productive capacity for reprocessing radioactive wastes and SNF within the Navy have led to the accumulation of these hazardous materials at naval bases and have adversely affected the radio-ecological situation.[75]

Nuclear Hazards in the Arctic

Uranium fuel in both land and marine reactors becomes highly radioactive during power operation and remains so even when the reactor is shut down. Fuel assemblies require special care and handling from then on, whether installed in a reactor or removed after defueling operations. The hazards can be grouped into three categories: spent nuclear fuel assemblies emit high levels of radiation for many years after operation because of the decay of fission products and can create a personnel hazard to those nearby; they are a particular danger if the material inside is released to the environment where it can directly affect people or enter the food chain; and, they contain un-fissioned enriched uranium (U235) and plutonium (Pu239) that can be recovered by chemical reprocessing, creating security concerns if fuel assemblies fall under the control of unauthorized personnel with the will and means to produce nuclear weapons. The greatest hazard with Russian decommissioned submarine spent fuel is probably the second, that radioactive material might escape to the environment. The issue has generated particular concern in Northern Europe because of the large numbers of Russian submarines and great quantities of removed spent fuel that are located on or close to the Arctic Ocean.

The Arctic Ocean contains relatively little man-made radioactivity, considerably lower than the Black and Baltic Seas for example which were more affected by the Chernobyl reactor accident.[76] What exists is primarily left over from Soviet nuclear weapons testing, from the Chernobyl accident, and from nuclear reprocessing plants in the United Kingdom and France. Nonetheless, a large explosion involving Russian submarine spent nuclear fuel, either shipboard or land-based, could spread significant radioactive contamination into the Arctic lands and water, causing local dangers and perhaps trans-border problems as well. Past mishaps and current storage problems have already created some contamination near Russian naval nuclear facilities. According to the Norwegian environmental group Bellona, sediments taken near Andreeva Bay are on average 12 times normal background readings; high levels of radioactive cesium and cobalt have been detected near the naval shipyard at Polyarny on the Murmansk Fjord. Thomas Nilsen of the Bellona Foundation believes that the measurements show a rapid deterioration of Russian nuclear waste storage facilities.[77] Concern is reflected by fish merchant Svein Ruud of Kirkenes, a small city located near Norway's Arctic border with Russia. An early venture capitalist who tried to enter the Russian market, Ruud noted that Russian taxes and corruption were "normal occurrences" but that he was really worried about Radwaste:

> I am not afraid of damage to fish in the short term, but I am concerned about how the market will react. People used to be very aware of the Soviet military threat on the border. But some say they are more scared now than in the Cold War because of the nuclear waste and the submarines.[78]

The Arctic is a very sensitive environmental region. As one of the world's last frontiers it remains formidable and with many unique physical characteristics, but is surprisingly affected by the rest of the globe. In the spring, the far north is now shrouded in smog and exposed to higher ultra-violet radiation because of a thinning ozone layer; in the summer, global warming may soon cause the North Pole itself to melt.[79] The region also has plant and animal species that have become very specialized, making them particularly vulnerable to climate change and to various forms of contamination. Arctic life tends to concentrate substances to a greater extent than life in more temperate regions and then to pass the dangers on to the Arctic peoples that make use of them. The lichen of the region can absorb radioisotopes that are then eaten by reindeer which further concentrate the radioisotopes in their bodies. Arctic people eat the reindeer and can take in up to 300 times more radiation each year as the average resident of the United Kingdom. Despite the low levels of overall radioactive contamination in the region, Arctic native peoples suffer from relatively high rates of cancer — although the exact connection between contaminants and disease has not been established.[80] Even if potential human health hazards are excluded, the cleanup costs and other economic consequences of a significant radiological accident in the Arctic would be enormous.

International Involvement

Russia has a great deal of operational experience in defueling its submarines and in handling their spent fuel. It also has developed preferences and methodologies for conducting defueling operations, but the numbers of submarines decommissioned since the mid–1980s have overwhelmed the country's existing facilities and feeble economy. Recognizing the need, since about 1993 the West has been actively engaged with Russia's submarine Radwaste problem.

There are several motivations for Western involvement. In the Nordic countries in particular, spent fuel from Russian nuclear submarines is viewed as a very credible pollution hazard. Thousands of spent fuel assemblies are stored only a few miles from the Norwegian border, with Finland and Sweden not far beyond. The level of anxiety is probably not as high as fears of severe accidents at the civilian nuclear power plants in Northwest Russia, but remains substantial. A similar concern is felt by Japan because of the Radwaste and reactor safety problems of the Russian Pacific Fleet. Environmental groups and government officials in these countries have publicized the issue and taken actions to attempt to mitigate the dangers to their populations. Western industrial corporations are also interested in Russian nuclear waste disposal problems because of the possibility of profits and new technology. Hence much of the international participation is firmly rooted in self-interest, with the amount of engagement inversely proportional to distance from the problem. But engagement also incorporates a number of liberal notions: that a degraded environment is a world and not just a national or regional problem; that collaborative efforts with Russia on almost any project are a good way to build international trust and to improve the likelihood of peaceful future relations; and, that contributing to the health and welfare of a people in need is basically a good thing to do.

Because of its proximity to Northwest Russian and its relative prosperity, Norway has been in the forefront of Western efforts to help with Russia's Radwaste and nuclear safety problems. The Norwegian Ministry of Foreign Affairs was allocated $50 million for Russian Radwaste projects during 1995–97 and is prepared to spend more.[81] Sweden and Finland are also engaged in a number of projects, while multinational corporations from the United Kingdom and France play a significant role as well. An important part is being played by the European Commission, the supranational bureaucracy of the European Union. Through its TACIS program (Technical Assistance to the Commonwealth of Independent States), substantial European Commission funding is being directed toward nuclear safety and Radwaste initiatives in Russia and elsewhere in the former–Soviet Union; its DG XI unit has contributed directly to the marine spent fuel and Radwaste issues of Russia's Northwest. The United States is a major player in the submarine spent fuel issue as well through its Cooperative Threat Reduction (CTR) program. Formed to help Russia and the other states of the former–Soviet Union dismantle safely and securely the nuclear weapons and weapons systems no longer required after the end of the Cold War, CTR has contributed millions of dollars and made significant progress in dismantling Russian ballistic missile submarines. Elsewhere, however, the United States has proved a relatively minor funding source — given US resources and expertise in the field.

Problems with Assistance

Helping Russia with its submarine spent fuel problem is a difficult and complicated affair. With nuclear power issues in general and nuclear submarines in particular, the relationship between environmental concerns, advanced technology, corporate profit, and national security is complex and without obvious preferential paths or easy solutions. Western collaborators need to be qualified to help and must find common ground with appropriate Russian actors to move forward in a way acceptable to all. Differing priorities between aid-givers and aid-receivers increases the likelihood of brinkmanship beyond the normal hindrances of lack of trust and poor communications in international relations. Bargaining positions can tend to the extreme: Russia, which controls access to the problem, would like unlimited foreign financing and free reign to distribute funds and to prioritize projects as it wishes; the West, which controls the money and to some extent the needed expertise and equipment, would like open access to Russian technical data, control of project priorities, Russian acceptance of international standards on the environment, safety, and security, and good profits for Western corporations.

Security and Politics

Russia is not integrated into the security system of the West and remains a subject of considerable mistrust, despite its membership in many global organizations and participation in a variety of NATO and European arrangements. Russia's leaders differ publicly and vociferously with the

West on a number of important security issues, including NATO expansion (Russia is opposed to it), Balkan politics (Russia tends to be more sympathetic with Serbian positions), and Iraq (Russia opposes the active containment policy pursued by the United States and the United Kingdom). Foot-dragging by Russian *Duma* on approval of the START II strategic weapons treaty has harmed cooperation as well. In addition, the military leaders of all countries tend to base their doctrine and strategy on a potential adversary's capabilities and not on its stated intentions, hence Russia's residual military power is a lingering concern for other defense establishments — despite Russia's assurances of pacific motives and its devastated economic circumstance.

A particular dilemma concerns Russia's continued efforts to build new and improved nuclear submarines. In October 1996, Norwegian Prime Minister Gro Harlem Bruntland threatened to curtail funding for several economic programs in the Barents region, including a project to upgrade the polluting nickel smelter on the Kola Peninsula, because Russia began construction of the *Yuri Dolgorykey* at Severodvinsk — the first of the *Borey* class ballistic missile submarines.[82] United States officials are also concerned that the Russian Navy might divert funds or other aid intended for submarine defueling and Radwaste disposal projects toward construction of new submarines and maintenance of operational submarines, helping to improve the military capability of a too recent adversary. A July 1999 report highlighted the difficulty. "I realize everything that has happened [the Russian submarine Radwaste problems] is the fault of Russia," said Nina Yanovskaya, in charge of the submarine decommissioning project for Russian Ministry of Atomic Energy (MINATOM). "It's our doing. The old Cold War is responsible for [the] situation." Then she stressed the urgency of immediate funding. "Either help us create the infrastructure or we will disrupt international agreements, and then it won't be only our fault." "That is blackmail!" warned David Garman, chief of staff for Senator Frank H. Murkowski of Alaska, chairman of the Senate Energy and Natural Resources Committee, who follows the Russian nuclear submarine problem closely. "If you give money to Russia, you are helping them take care of the back end and freeing up resource to make more nuclear subs. Unless they are willing to forgo a navy, it's going to be tough love."[83]

Technology is also transferable and Western assistance could be used to make the Russian Navy and other defense organizations more efficient in their nuclear activities. Even if Russia itself is not perceived as a current threat, Western technology delivered to Russia could leak to other countries. Recent sales of Russian missile and nuclear equipment to countries labeled as terrorist supporters or as probable proliferators by the United

States, such as Iran and North Korea, are potent detriments to further information sharing. Transferring nuclear and other militarily useful technology to larger powers like India and China is also a concern. Nor is Russia just a receiver of technology. Russian nuclear expertise is considerable and in some areas probably more advanced than the West, particularly in reactor and fuel design. Russian organizations are suspicious of Western requests for access to sensitive facilities and for detailed technical information about their nuclear activities; some Russian officials have expressed concern about US intelligence agencies penetrating their nuclear installations.[84]

Nikitin Affair

The arrest of Alexandr Nikitin is also a factor. Nikitin was a Russian submarine commanding officer who now works for the Bellona environmental group of Norway. He was arrested in early 1996 by the Russian Federal Security Service (the FSB — a successor to the KGB) and charged with giving away state secrets. Nikitin was accused of gaining access to classified information in a Navy library and giving Bellona "data which disclose design faults in naval submarine reactors."[85] Bellona claims the information was freely available and has vigorously rejected the charges.[86] During the same period, the Bellona office in Murmansk was raided by the FSB and its personnel followed.

Nikitin has been called post–Cold War Russia's first "prisoner of conscience." He spent nine months under arrest without a trial and was not released until December 1996. He was reportedly denied medicine for his ulcers and his lawyer beaten up by thugs. Nikitin was released from prison only after intense lobbying at all levels, from Amnesty International to US Vice President Al Gore, but still remains confined to the St. Petersburg region.[87] The initial charges carried a possible penalty of execution, but were later reduced to ten years in prison. Nikitin's case has been lobbied heavily in Washington's corridors of power by his supporters, with Bellona reportedly spending over $1 million in his defense. In October 1998 a Russian judge rejected the case for lack of evidence, but also advised the FSB to continue the investigation. At first, the judgment was taken as a victory for human rights and the environment. According to Thomas Nilsen of Bellona: "Never before in Soviet and Russian history was an indictment of treason through espionage dismissed by the court. Therefore, today's decision is of historic value."[88] His prosecutors, however, have continued the investigation and its ultimate disposition may rest with Russia's supreme court. Nikitin seems resigned to eternal prosecution: "If I'm locked up,

I'll survive. But will anyone ever again want to investigate military environmental issues here?"[89]

Some believe that Nikitin's arrest was precipitated by high ranking officials in the Russia military or civilian establishment; another source claims the FSB commitment to the Nikitin affair was triggered by its failed role in the Chechnya debacle and a desire to impress the Yeltsin government with an intelligence success.[90] Harassment of whistle-blowers seems to be increasing in Russia. An amended states secret list came into effect on 9 October 1997 that environmental advocacy groups fear will create new restrictions on information about Radwaste.[91] Gregory Pasko, a correspondent for the military newspaper *Boyevaya Vakhta* in Vladivostok, faced charges similar to Nikitin for passing documents and videos to the Japanese media that described Russian Navy dumping of nuclear waste.[92] Alexei Yablokov, a former top aide to President Yeltsin on the environment, is suing a spokesman for MINATOM and the newspaper *Nexavisimaya Gazeta* for accusing him of unpatriotic behavior. He wants a retraction and monetary damages for accusations against him that "laws which banned ecological data from being classified as secret had been initiated to benefit foreign intelligence services" and that he had "exploited the legislation to include such things as information about nuclear reactors and navy vessels."[93] The Nikitin affair and other recent anti-dissent activities by the Russian government hamper Western efforts to help with the submarine spent fuel issue by giving opponents of aid to Russia an argument of high principle.

Business Concerns

Russia is transitioning from a command political and economic system to one that might eventually resemble a Western country. This will require a stable and convertible currency, a code of law for social and business encounters, and regularized political and bureaucratic practices that acknowledge the international rules of the game. In the interim, many of Russia's government and private enterprises have become autonomous fiefdoms that vie for survival and profit in a system lacking clear lines of authority. Disappointments range from a General Motor's truck manufacturing plant in the Urals to projects developing oil and gas resources in Russia's northern tier and near Sakhalin Island.[94] Western companies dealing with nuclear operation and waste issues have the same problems as other businesses working in Russia. Along with the expected hassles of doing business in a developing economy, companies must deal with taxation, liability, and corruption concerns.

According to writer Martin Walker, Western businessmen complain about the "... lack of any legal structure to safeguard their investments and their contracts and the combination of anarchy and corruption in the taxation system."[95] A Russian firm of ten people may need two of them working full time to handle the country's complicated tax code. Deputy Technical Director at the Murmansk Shipping Company Vladimir Volkov, whose firm has its own Radwaste problems, complains that, "when other countries are ready to help, the Russian government wants us to pay a tax on the aid, so we are reluctant to take it."[96] Liability is also a major concern for nuclear contractors and Western governments. If Norwegian personnel, equipment, or funding are involved in any way in moving Russian nuclear spent fuel assemblies, Norway wants legal protection. The chemical explosion at Bhopal, India, in 1983 caused many deaths, injuries, and significant environmental degradation and resulted in hundreds of millions of dollars in damage claims against the Union Carbide Corporation. A severe nuclear accident in a populated region of Northwest Russia could also result in personnel casualties and environmental damage, and subsequent enormous financial claims. Russia needs to improve domestic legislation and to more closely conform with international norms on the liability issue.

Corruption in business means making decisions for a company based on factors other than a cost-benefit analysis of what would be required for greater profit. It is an externality that can add significantly to cost and time, either through the requirements of a compromised bureaucracy and financial system or because of an informal system of influence peddling — enforced by financial or physical coercion. According to a "corruption perception index" published by Transparency International and Gottingen University, Russia is exceeded in corruption only by Nigeria, Bolivia, and Colombia. Columnist John Lloyd wrote that "Russian business now succeeds only insofar as it corrupts the state, or protects itself with small private armies, or both."[97] The Russian Minister of Nuclear Energy has complained that criminal structures affect the normal finances of even nuclear enterprises. All of these problems affect the business climate, foreign aid and investment, and Russia's access to capital from international lending institutions.

Radwaste Problems in Other Countries

Russia is not alone with its Radwaste problems. Three Western European reprocessing plants have contributed more to radioactive contamination of the Arctic Ocean than the entire Russian nuclear fleet. The plants are located at Sellafield and Dounreay in the United Kingdom and at Cap de la Hague in France; their discharges to the Atlantic Ocean are transported along the Norwegian coast to the Arctic by the Gulf Stream.[98] In addition, the United Kingdom has dumped more than 74,000 tons of nuclear waste in the Northern Atlantic, making it responsible for more than three quarters of the radioactive material deposited there. A solution to the Radwaste problems of the United Kingdom is probably decades away following the political defeat of proposals to use a deep water repository at the Sellafield reprocessing site.[99] France too has yet to come up with a plan for the permanent disposal of its high level Radwaste and has seen a gradual increase in public concern about its nuclear affairs.

The United States is spending over $2 billion a year to clean up its nuclear defense installations, such as Rocky Flats in Colorado and the Savannah River Plant in South Carolina.[100] Cleaning up the waste left over from nuclear weapons production will cost hundreds of billions of dollars and will take about 75 years.[101] Much of the US problem is concentrated at the Hanford Site in the state of Washington which produced nuclear weapons material during the Cold War and is currently a temporary repository for about 210,000 spent fuel assemblies. These were originally scheduled for reprocessing, but a phase-out of reprocessing activities began during the administration of President Jimmy Carter. Some of the stored fuel assemblies have begun to deteriorate — making their acceptability for permanent storage problematic and more expensive. The Hanford Site is of particular concern because of its proximity to the powerful and fast-flowing Columbia River.[102]

Elsewhere in the United States, after many years of wrangling the Waste Inspection Pilot Plant (WIPP) in southeastern New Mexico is finally coming on line. It will store intermediate level Radwaste in the deep caverns of old salt mines. Storage of commercial nuclear waste remains a major issue, with many delays and political skirmishes ahead before the centralized storage at Yucca Mountain in Nevada will see its first fuel assemblies — if ever. Meanwhile, US nuclear activities are closely scrutinized by environmental action groups. The return of "Atoms for Peace" spent fuel from Asian reactors to Idaho in 1998 caused considerable controversy, particularly as the material passed through San Francisco Bay.[103]

The United States must properly dispose of the spent fuel from its own decommissioned submarines. Approximately 100 US submarines will be decommissioned by the year 2000, about the same number as the Russian Northern Fleet. The United States, however, is not in the midst of an economic or political crisis (although some might argue the points) so its spent fuel management strategy has been moving forward steadily. US submarines can be defueled at a number of different naval or commercial shipyards. The spent fuel is transported by rail to the Idaho Reactor Test Site and ultimately the Idaho Chemical Processing Plant.[104] Prior to 1992, spent fuel from US submarines was reprocessed at the Idaho National Engineering Laboratory but is now stored in stainless steel-lined wet storage basins. A goal is to have all of the submarine spent fuel placed in dry storage by 2023, perhaps in dual use storage/transport containers, with eventual delivery to a permanent geological storage location when environmental concerns and political obstacles are overcome.[105] In 1995, the US Navy reached an agreement with the state of Idaho that allowed it to continue to ship spent fuel to the state for the next 40 years, but with removal required by 2035.[106]

After defueling, the submarines themselves are sent to Puget Sound Naval Shipyard in Bremerton, Washington, for reactor compartment removal and scrapping. Even without nuclear fuel installed, reactor compartments remain highly radioactive for many years and also contain substantial radioactive contamination. The compartments are then barged by sea around the state of Washington and up the Columbia River for storage in shallow trenches dug in the desert of the Hanford Site. By 1998, 71 reactor compartments were stored there.[107] According to Susan Kopte of BICC, by mid–1996, 71 US submarines had been decommissioned with 32 completely dismantled.[108] Defueling is expected to be completed by 2010. While environmental advocacy groups sometimes criticize American procedures, no significant problems seem to have emerged. One knowledgeable observer commented that US nuclear submarines undergoing dismantlement look more seaworthy than Russian submarines still in operation.

Russian Decommissioned Submarines: Problem or Crisis?

An unintended consequence of the end of the Cold War is that the controls and planning characteristic of the Soviet structure have been replaced by the uncertainties and obstructions of freedom of choice, often hindering progress toward problem solution. Russia has greater Radwaste problems than the West in both quantity and difficulty, but with a troubled economy and volatile political and administrative system it is much less able to deal with them.[109] Russian citizens certainly want to move forward to resolve the country's nuclear safety and Radwaste problems and there is some strength in contemporary Russian environmental organizations and regional political leadership. Action by local groups contributed to a shutdown of refueling activity at the Sevmorput shipyard in Murmansk; at Severodvinsk near Archangel, the town administration set limits on the total amount of Radwaste that could be stored in the city.[110] *Duma* official Alexander Pikayev noted how the "unsettled problem of decommissioned but not fully dismantled nuclear submarines became a significant source of social tension" at Russia's major nuclear industrial sites in recent years.[111] At the same time, the historic and remarkable stoicism among the Russian people has allowed them to tolerate what seems intolerable and to deal with the situation at hand as best they can.

The difficulties of submarine defueling, dismantlement, and Radwaste processing could be overcome given sufficient priority and funding by both Russia and the West. But decommissioned submarines are only one of Russia's many dilemmas, so the real question is the appropriate priority to give the problem. And here the Russian spent fuel issue should be kept in perspective. In the hierarchy of concerns, a "situation" is something out of the ordinary that would be changed in a perfect world, but that is not particularly disruptive as is; a "problem" is a condition that really should be changed because, under certain circumstances, it would become hazardous or disruptive to the lives and routine of a population; and, a "crisis" is a dangerous circumstance requiring immediate action. To date, little radioactive contamination of the Arctic can be attributed to Russia's Northern Fleet. Nuclear submarines are designed with shielding to protect personnel from radiation and with equipment to remove heat generated by the decay of fission products in the reactor fuel assemblies. If cooling (or heating in the cold Russian winter) and proper chemistry are maintained, fuel assemblies might safely remain aboard submarines for many more years, depending on the composition of the fuel and clad material and barring physical accidents like collisions and explosions. There is some fear, however, that fuel assemblies on some earlier classes of Russian submarines may have been designed to remain inside reactors for only a specified period of time after which the fuel cladding and other reactor parts that must be intact for defueling may corrode or mechanically fail, preventing normal processing and perhaps releasing radioactivity.

Even after external shocks spent fuel onboard a submarine may stay intact or at least contained within the ship's reactor complex, a very strong welded structure designed for operation at high temperature and pressure. Nuclear submarines lost at sea, for example, have not resulted in significant known contamination to the environment. Theft of an installed fuel assembly for its weapons usable material would require hijacking an entire non-functional submarine displacing several thousand tons, a very unlikely scenario. Spent fuel already removed from submarines is a more immediate problem, but again an unlikely scenario must be postulated for an accident to have more than local effects. NATO's *Phase I CCMS Report* notes that, although the risks associated with nuclear vessels in Russia's Northwest are hard to estimate, accidents leading to large releases of radioactivity can clearly have very significant local consequences but would have only modest cross-border impact.[112] Russia is also a very big country, so places to handle and store radioactive waste that are acceptable to the local population and to the international community at large can almost certainly be found. And while difficulties have mounted in recent years, Russian naval personnel, civilian engineers, and government officials have been dealing with nuclear issues for half a century.

At the very least, caring for Russian decommissioned submarines is a continuing expenditure of manpower and materiel that will only increase as the submarines age. It takes about 40 percent of a regular submarine crew to man the decommissioned ships, a significant commitment for obsolete equipment with no military purpose. According to Russian estimates, the annual expenditure of keeping one submarine in port is about $400 thousand.[113] In addition, with so many locations containing Radwaste, individual problems are difficult to track and to deal with — such as water run-off from contaminated containers and storage sites. Submarine defueling, submarine dismantlement, and Radwaste processing are difficult and expensive procedures to accomplish, but at least they have terminal points of effort and expenditure.

Russian decommissioned submarines and their spent fuel are complex and serious problems that should not, however, be over-sensationalized. Retaining spent-fuel on board decommissioned submarines and at temporary storage facilities is a regrettable expedient that should be corrected as soon as possible. The sheer magnitude of the radioactive material involved commands attention: millions of curies are stored at Andreeva Bay alone, approaching the amount released during the Chernobyl disaster.[114] According to Chief of Naval Operations, Admiral Igor Khmelnov: "Decommissioned but not fully dismantled SSNs [nuclear submarines] represent higher radiation and ecological danger," "… their existence together with possible negative consequences attract growing attention from Russian and international public, which wants ecological safety of the planet."[115] Fundamental Russian and Western interests converge on nuclear issues: reducing weapons usable material stocks and Radwaste and lowering the risk of significant radiological accidents and nuclear proliferation are continuing and mutual concerns.

Chapter 2

Rise and Fall of the Russian Navy

The Russian Navy is capable of fulfilling the main goals it has been set despite the "acute problem of maintaining the fleet's technical readiness owing to lack of due financing."[1]

— Rear Admiral Viktor Batrushev
Chief of the Operational Department, Russian Navy

The Russian Navy has struggled for resources and missions for much of its existence, not just in the post–Cold War period. Conventional wisdom would certainly classify Russia as a land power, not a sea power. England needed a victory over the Spanish Armada in 1588 to survive and the United States a French victory at the Virginia Capes for its independence, but Russia's fate has never depended on a single great sea battle.[2] Vast and with few topographical barriers, early Russia's threats came from the land where men and horses could move quickly across its open spaces. The state was created by the frequent combat of enemy armies and by the forced unification of dispersed groups and their territories. Access to the world ocean was in fact always restricted, even after Russia and the Soviet Union had reached their greatest sizes in the 19th and 20th centuries: to the west by the narrow Baltic Sea; to the south by the Black Sea and Turkish Straits; and, to the east by passages from the Sea of Japan. Any ship using these waterways had to pass near strong and often antagonistic foreign powers before gaining the relative safety of the open sea. And to the north was the forbidding Arctic. Months of cold, ice, and darkness made Russia's northern frontier one of the most hostile places on earth, and much of the coastline had no practical access to the ocean at all. Off the Kola Peninsula to the west, however, a finger of the Gulf Stream kept a strip of coastline relatively ice-free throughout the year; on the Pacific coast off the Kamchatka Peninsula, the waters were not ice-free but ships could at least leave ports relatively unopposed for the open ocean.[3]

Difficulties and rival imperatives notwithstanding, a naval tradition of sorts developed in Russia's Black and Baltic Sea regions and along the country's extensive navigable river system.[4] The Kievan Rus state of 1000 AD had a naval capability stimulated in part by Norse settlement and influence, but this was almost certainly destroyed along with the Kievan state itself by the Mongol invasions of the 13th century.[5] Centuries later, emerging Russia — now centered in Moscow — developed a fleet to confront rivals to the west and south. In 1583, however, it lost access to the Baltic Sea to Sweden. Fortunately for the Russians, in 1553 English merchants had discovered a new sea route to Russia via the Barents and White Seas. The Arctic port of Archangel was founded in 1584.[6]

Peter the Great's Navy

The Russian Navy and Russia's world power status owe much to Peter the Great. Like American naval theorist Albert Thayer Mahan two centuries later, Peter believed that great powers profited from large and powerful navies and declared that "any potentate with a land army has one hand but he who also has a fleet has two hands."[7] With Italian help, the Russian Navy had its first noteworthy naval victory when it captured Azov from the Turks in 1696.[8] In 1703 during the Great Northern War, Peter founded St. Petersburg to reestablish a Russian presence in the eastern–Baltic region. He built a substantial fleet and in 1714 defeated the Swedes at the Battle of Gangut (Hangö), where over 100 Russian galley's overwhelmed the outnumbered enemy squadron.[9] By 1720, the Russian army occupied the south Baltic coast and the Russian fleet controlled much of the Baltic Sea itself.[10] Peter's navy had helped Russia become a European great power.

After Peter's death, Russian naval developments were less focused and generally lagged behind the technological and doctrinal improvements of other great powers. The reign of Catherine the Great was an exception, stimulated in part by recruitment of English and Scottish mariners to man Russian ships. In 1770 the Russian Navy won a decisive victory over the Turks at Chesma, often called Russia's greatest victory at sea.[11] In later 18th century battles against the Turks and the French, Russian Admiral Feodr Feodorovich Ushakov emerged as a naval leader of international stature — by Russian accounts comparable to his English contemporary Admiral Horatio Nelson. Cooperation with England continued during the Napoleonic wars, with Russian naval officers actually serving with Nelson at the Battle of Trafalgar in 1805.[12]

The Russian Navy was sorely tested in the mid–19th century. The Crimean War began well, with Russian battleships using their new exploding shell guns to good effect in destroying a Turkish flotilla at Sinope. Against the British and French, however, Russia was a victim of sea power. Its Black Sea ships were trapped by superior allied forces and its guns and men used instead for shore defense; iron-clad vessels were put in action for the first time when three French "floating batteries" helped demolish Russian fortifications.[13] The British and French control of the seas gave their forces strategic mobility and the means to carry out amphibious operations, helping to secure the eventual Russian defeat.[14] Later in the century Russia was challenged by the rising power of Japan to the east. In the Russo-Japanese war of 1904/5, the Russian Pacific Fleet was quickly taken out of action by Japanese forces. The Baltic Fleet of Admiral Z. P. Rozhdestvensky, after a fabled journey around Europe, Africa, and Asia, was annihilated by Japanese Admiral Heihachiro Togo at the Battle of Tsushima in one of the most decisive naval battles of all time.

More threatening to Russia than Japan was the newly-united Germany to the west and its growing land and sea power. During World War I, the Russian Navy had some success on the Black Sea containing the German and Turkish forces. The Navy also helped to protect Russia's northern flank on the Baltic Sea, although it was generally restrained by German countermeasures and confined to small-scale ship skirmishes and mine laying operations.[15] As the war turned increasingly bleak for Russia, crews of ships like the cruiser *Aurora* began supporting Lenin's Bolshevik revolutionaries. During the 1917 Revolution and subsequent civil war, much of the fleet and shore-based naval infrastructure were destroyed; in a reversal of loyalties, the 1921 rebellion of sailors at Kronshtadt against the Bolsheviks helped to break the bonds remaining between the new political class and the historically conservative naval leadership.

Not until the 1930s, did the Soviet government pay much attention to its navy and again emphasize shipbuilding. The Navy became a high priority after Germany reemerged as a threat during the latter-half of the decade. Soviet dictator Joseph Stalin emphasized submarines early-on, but shifted to a more balanced fleet when Soviet intervention in the Spanish Civil War failed in part because of the lack of surface warships.[16] Despite its high priority and new equipment, the Soviet Navy entered World War II crippled from Stalin's purge of senior military leadership in the late 1930s. Admiral N. G. Kuznetsov was put in command of the Navy, having been a captain only the year before, and lack of good leadership and effective training were to hamper Soviet naval activity throughout the war. Germany soon controlled Denmark, Norway, and Russia's Baltic coastline while Germany's ally Finland and neutral Sweden controlled the rest of the Baltic region — adding further geographic constraints to Soviet fleet action. Soviet naval guns and crews were used for land warfare in the historic defense of Leningrad, just as they were a century before in the Crimea.[17] In the Arctic North, historian Eric Morris points out that all Western commentaries on the subject criticize the paucity of Russian naval support for the Anglo-American convoy operations to Murmansk and Archangel — a source of bitterness in the wartime alliance.[18]

On the Black Sea, the Soviet Navy again had considerable action and some success. This helped shape the Navy's future leader, Sergey G. Gorshkov. He commanded, for example, an amphibious operation that disrupted the Romanian Army besieging Odessa.[19] Despite this and a few other successful ventures, most historians find significantly fault in the Soviet Navy's performance in World War II. Peter Tsouras noted that the failure to develop a British-like tradition of "offensive superiority and victory" was a persistent characteristic of the Soviet Navy and contributed to its generally poor performance.[20] The Red Army, with valuable help from its air forces and in alliance with the forces of Great Britain and the United States, was largely responsible for defeating Nazi Germany — not the Soviet Navy.

Admiral Gorshkov's Navy

After World War II, the Soviet Union again began an aggressive naval construction program. Stalin's goal was to build four aircraft carriers, 40 cruisers, 200 destroyers, and an incredible 1,200 submarines.[21] Although this grandiose program faded after Stalin's death in 1953, the country's political leadership from Khrushchev to Gorbachev generally supported the construction and operation of a large and capable Soviet Navy. The fleet that emerged was shaped by the vision and drive of Admiral of the Fleet Gorshkov, commander in chief of the Soviet Navy from 1956 until 1985.[22]

Gorshkov would be comfortable in the company of Peter the Great and Albert Thayer Mahan. In his book *The Sea Power of the State*, Gorshkov advocated the development of sea-going enterprises of all kinds, from a strong blue water navy to merchant and fishing fleets. He believed that great powers required great fleets to extend their influence during peace and to defend their interests in time of war. In the immediate Cold War contest against the United States and its allies, the Soviet Union could not afford to give up control of the seas to such powerful and hostile foes. Gorshkov's challenge was immense, however, because the West's lead was

2. Rise and Fall of the Russian Navy

too great to compete on a ship for ship basis and the Soviet Union's geographical disadvantage was still severe. Defense against invasion and enemy coastal submarine operations were reasonable and achievable missions for the Soviet Navy, but offensive operations on the high seas required new thinking.[23] Gorshkov looked for vulnerabilities in the opposition and for efficient ways to level the playing field. United States naval strength was concentrated in its attack aircraft carriers, the ships that had helped defeat Japan and that could project American power to almost anywhere on the globe. Aircraft carriers were also very difficult and expensive technologies to master and, for all their offensive might, were large and potentially vulnerable targets requiring extensive airborne and multi-ship systems for defense. A cost-effective weapon to threaten them was the cruise missile.

Soviet Innovation

Cruise missiles are air-breathing winged and generally sub-sonic weapons that can be difficult to detect and counter. The virtually unguided V-1 was used by Germany with some success against allied forces and cities in World War II. With modern navigation and propulsion systems, cruise missiles can transport large warheads hundreds of miles for precision attack against enemy targets. Under Gorshkov's direction, the Soviet Navy began to deploy anti-ship cruise missiles on a variety of naval platforms in the 1950s and 60s. The world awoke to this new threat during the 1967 Six Day War between Israel and several Arab countries. An Egyptian patrol boat sank the Israeli destroyer *Elath* with a Soviet-built *Styx* cruise missile. A similar demonstration occurred in South Asia in December 1971 when India used its Soviet-built missile patrol boats to good effect against Pakistan's navy. NATO forces had much catching up to do to match and counter this new threat.

The Soviet Navy was innovative in other ways. The *Kashin* class destroyer was the first large warship powered by gas turbine engines. Gas turbines can deliver high performance with relatively low maintenance and manning requirements compared to the high pressure steam systems then in use. Several follow-on classes of Soviet warships used them as well and other navies have subsequently adopted them; gas turbines are the propulsion of choice for current large US surface warships except for aircraft carriers. The *Kashin* class had a very elegant exterior as well that helped to establish a "Soviet look" in warship design, with a relatively uncluttered deck, high-rise bow, full-length hull-knuckle, and a pyramidal superstructure and antenna arrangement.

The Soviet Navy also deployed the unique *Moscow* and *Kiev* classes of mixed-mission air-capable cruisers, operational in 1967 and 1975 respectively. They carried helicopters and (on *Kiev*) vertical/short takeoff and landing jet attack aircraft, in addition to ample guns and missiles. They could be used for anti-submarine and anti-surface ship missions, and perhaps amphibious operations as well. Both classes were stepping stones to more sophisticated true aircraft carriers, finally realized with the *Kuznetzov* class in 1989. These were a thousand feet long and displaced 60,000 tons, approaching the size of their US rivals. With the *Kirov* in 1980, the Soviets re-invented the offensive battle cruiser. Powered by two nuclear reactors and with an incredible array of weapon systems, the *Kirov* class ships were the largest non-aircraft carrying warships built anywhere in the world since the end of World War II. These were supplemented by other heavily armed but conventionally powered frigates, destroyers and cruisers, like the *Krivak, Slava, Sovremennyy,* and *Udaloy* classes.[24] According to naval intelligence analyst Paul L. Pierce:

> The weapons found on virtually all large Soviet surface combatants build or modified since 1970 reflect an excellent application of both technology and design concepts. When compared with the ships of Western navies, these combatants, in some respects, are more capable of accomplishing their wartime missions.[25]

Soviet maritime development was not limited to warships. Coastal defense and high seas missions were supplemented by modified Soviet Air Force bombers, particularly the *Badger* but including the supersonic *Blackjack* and *Backfire*. *Bear D* reconnaissance aircraft were a familiar sight to US fleets while the *Bear F* ASW variant gave American and allied submariners something more to think about. Gorshkov's navy was supported by a wide variety of ancillary craft, including the infamous AGI surveillance and intelligence platforms, enormous communications and missile/space tracking ships, and numerous oceanographic and atmospheric research vessels. The Soviet commercial and fishing fleets also grew in size and quality during Gorshkov's tenure. In the North, the frozen waters of the Arctic were kept open by a fleet of icebreakers; beginning with the *Lenin* in 1959, several were nuclear powered.

Soviet Fleets

Because of its geography, the Soviet Union required four nearly independent fleets. The Baltic and Black Seas fleets were regional forces-in-being and helped support Soviet Mediterranean and Indian Ocean deployments. They also handled much of the training and sea-trial requirements of the construction activity of shipyards on the Soviet Baltic coast and along the Black Sea. The real battle navy was represented by the Soviet Pacific and Northern Fleets where most of the major warships and nuclear powered vessels were assigned. The Pacific Fleet developed into the largest fleet in quantity, operating from Vladivostok and other ports along the Sea of Japan coast and the Kamchatka Peninsula, but the Northern Fleet was probably more important. It stood between the Soviet Union's populous Russian region and the potentially hostile NATO powers. It also had access to the open Arctic and Atlantic Oceans without required passage through narrow straits. During the Cold War the Kola Peninsula was host to one of the most formidable assemblies of military hardware anywhere in the world, with nuclear powered battle cruisers, aircraft carriers, submarines, land-based aircraft, and a host of supporting naval craft. In the mid–1980s, it numbered well over 200 major warships.

Soviet warships were a common sight in the Mediterranean Sea, the Indian Ocean, and even the Caribbean Sea during the 1970s and 1980s. Client states like Angola, Yemen, Vietnam, and Cuba provided refit facilities for Soviet ships and recreation for the crews. United States submarines sometimes had to dodge AGI intelligence ships as they deployed for patrol while US and allied at-sea training exercises often had Soviet escorts. The Soviets themselves conducted frequent theater and occasional world-wide training activities, such as the 1975 *Okean* exercise. Just how Gorshkov's naval fleets, auxiliaries, and the Soviet civilian sea-going activities integrated into a grand maritime strategy is a story yet to be told, but the sea-going capabilities of the Soviet Union were undeniably important and potentially threatening to the West. According to 1987 Congressional testimony by Secretary of the Navy John Lehman:

> Whatever the initial rationale for the massive expansion in the capabilities and sphere of operations of the post–World War II Soviet fleet, the USSR has created an offense-capable, blue-water force, providing a major element in the Soviet Union's global military reach that supports the expansion of Soviet influence from Nicaragua to the South Pacific, and from Vietnam to Africa. Daily, no matter where our fleet operates, our ships and men may pass within yards of Soviet naval forces. Familiarity is breeding a well-deserved respect on both sides: we see that the Soviets are good and are getting better — and *they* recognize that we are doing the same.[26]

Second Navy Dilemma

Despite the concern it generated in the West, the Soviet surface navy was an imperfect tool of warfare. Adequate protection against air attack was a significant problem for Soviet ships, particularly earlier classes, and the vaunted cruise missiles often required forward air controllers (aircraft or other ships) to locate and select important targets — reducing the stealth and flexibility of the weapon platforms and their potential effectiveness. Some ships were reported to have sea-keeping problems while others were mechanical nightmares. In 1998, the Russian Pacific Fleet commander lamented that some of Russia's large anti-submarine surface vessels have "never in their lifetime spotted a single submarine."[27] The carrier *Kuznetzov* was the result of decades of evolutionary development, but was still greatly outclassed by America's several *Nimitz* class and similar supercarriers. The Soviet Navy also seemed to be playing catch-up most of the time. United States aircraft carriers were vulnerable to Soviet cruise missiles in restricted or coastal waters, but the need to do so was reduced by longer ranged aircraft and by the shift of US strategic deterrence and attack missions to nuclear submarines.[28]

The Soviet Union also had relatively few deployed bases, a still embryonic at-sea logistics system, and the enduring disadvantage of its geography. In a shooting war, Soviet ships deployed to the Mediterranean Sea and other enclosed bodies of water would be short work for the land and sea-based air power of NATO and other Western powers.[29] Soviet surface craft were also increasingly vulnerable to cruise missile attack as the West began to gain significant capabilities with this technology. The Soviet Navy suffered from personnel problems as well, ranging from the lack of a winning tradition to poor morale and an "overpowering command and control system."[30] Although the comparison should not be overdrawn, the Soviet surface fleet was somewhat analogous to the "risk" fleets of Germany in World Wars I and II.[31] They were useful for showing the flag in peacetime and for smaller encounters in time of war. The fleets certainly posed interesting and tricky challenges for their Western opponents, but would likely be destroyed before they could make a significant difference in an all-out conflict.[32]

That Gorshkov failed to eclipse the Americans and their allies with his surface navy is not surprising; that he made so much progress in so many areas is a tribute to his maritime and political skills and to his commitment. And, as with the German U-boats in the century's earlier conflicts, quick defeat was not such an obvious fate for Soviet submarines.

Diesel Submarines

Early submarines were designed to attack warships and merchantmen without warning. The stealth of German submarines and the skill of their crews made U-boats almost decisive in World Wars I and II. American submarines had a similar impact on the war with Japan. Russia was an early innovator in undersea warfare and, according to Soviet sources, in 1724–1727 developed the world's first underwater vessel designed for military purposes. In the second half of the 19th century, Russia experimented with a German-built submarine and made additional attempts to build a workable model of its own.[33] Prior to World War I, Russia acquired several submarines from the American designer Simon Lake, called the *Kaiman* class, and also built the *Delfin* class beginning in 1902.[34] As the war began Russia had 37 submarines that were about equally distributed among the Baltic, Black, and Pacific Fleets, and built several more as the war went on. These had some success against merchant ships in the Black Sea, but were not used very effectively during the war. Because of war-time losses and the revolution and civil war that followed inside the Soviet Union, the submarine fleet all but disappeared by the early 1920s.[35] New classes began to appear in the late 1920s and, as a result of Stalin's aggressive construction program in the 1930s, the Soviet Union had one of the largest submarine fleets in the world at the start of World War II — with over 200 vessels.[36] Lack of leadership, training, and aggressiveness took their toll, as it did with the Soviet surface fleet, and Soviet submarines had little impact on the outcome despite their numbers. By the end of the war, Soviet submarines had sunk about 128 ships while losing 110 submarines.[37]

After World War II, Gorshkov pushed the Soviet Navy toward a large and capable undersea fleet to help challenge NATO's command of the sea. In *The Sea Power of the State*, he observed that:

> The priority given to the development of the submarine forces made it possible in a very short time to increase sharply the strike possibilities of our fleet, to form a considerable counter-balance to the main forces of the fleet of the enemy in the oceanic theaters, and, at the cost of fewer resources and less time, to multiply the growth of seapower of our country, thereby depriving an enemy of the advantages which could accrue to him in the event of war against the Soviet Union and the countries of the socialist community.[38]

Like the Western allies, the Soviet Union claimed significant quantities of German technology after World War II was over, including submarine

design. The first post-war Soviet submarines, the *Whiskey* class, incorporated a number of German features.[39] Over 200 were put in service with
the Soviet Navy and exported to friendly countries. Several were also used
for research and development of advanced systems, like the Twin Cylinder and Long Bin variants that pioneered Soviet use of cruise missiles on
submarines. A modified *Zulu* class of the same period conducted the first
submarine launch of a ballistic missile. The *Foxtrot* class followed. A much
better ship than the *Whiskey* or *Zulu*, the *Foxtrot* is still in service with several countries as of the late 1990s. But even as these advanced Soviet diesel
submarines were being built, a new means of propulsion was under development in the United States. In 1954 the *USS Nautilus* (SSN 570) was
launched by the Electric Boat Company of Groton, Connecticut, the
world's first nuclear powered submarine.

Diesel engines are used extensively to power submarines because of
their reliability, good fuel economy, and the low volatility and flammabil-
ity of diesel fuel.[40] Diesel powered submarines, however, must spend much
of their time at or near the surface because diesel engines require large
amounts of air to operate. Submerged operation depends on electric
motors powered by banks of batteries that take up a significant proportion of the space on the ship. The best diesel submarines can remained fully
submerged for a week or two on their batteries, but must then run their
diesel engines for several hours to recharge.[41] This makes them vulnerable to radar, sonar, visual, and other means of detection. Formidable when
undetected, submarines are relatively easy prey to a capable enemy that
knows their location. Nuclear power allows submarines to remain fully
submerged almost indefinitely and to move freely and rapidly under the
world ocean, substantially reducing the risk of detection and destruction
and greatly increasing submarine offensive striking power.

Nuclear Powered Submarines

Nuclear reactors have been around since 1942 when Enrico Fermi and
his colleagues brought a pile of uranium ore, graphite, and wood to self-
sustaining criticality in the famous squash court experiment at the University of Chicago.[42] During World War II the United States used nuclear
reactors as part of the Manhattan Project to produce plutonium for its
nuclear bombs but after the war gave some emphasis to more benign uses
of nuclear energy. Because reactors produced heat, they can be harnessed
to electrical generators or other rotating equipment in a conventional

steam cycle. In 1957, the world's first large-scale civilian electrical generating plant powered by a nuclear reactor went into service at Shippingsport, Pennsylvania, although Russia also claims the title for a plant at the Institute of Physics and Power Engineering, Obninsk, Russia, placed in operation in 1954. The reactor was an early pressurized water design, related to those now powering many nuclear power plants in the United States and throughout the world. Perhaps surprisingly, much of the design, engineering, and procedures for Shippingsport were developed by Hyman Rickover and his naval and civilian team — a spin-off of their work to harness nuclear energy for submarine propulsion.[43]

Rickover was born in Russian-occupied Poland in 1900 and brought to the United States when he was six years old. He became a career naval officer, skilled engineer, program manager, and dogged political in-fighter who was able to shepherd the submarine nuclear propulsion project through a host of technical and bureaucratic difficulties. Along the way Rickover developed a deserved reputation for intense and idiosyncratic personnel management; many like myself having endured his attention.[44] But the ends probably justified the means, the creation of an entirely new American ship category with exceptional capabilities and an enviable record of safety.

Submarines and nuclear reactors were technologies made for each other. Reactors gave submarines a revolutionary increase in military capability, much as breech loading did for rifles and artillery and jet engines for aircraft. The extraordinary energy contained in a nuclear reactor per unit size gives nuclear submarines not only great propulsion capability, but also generates ample electrical power for the extensive weapons, sensors, and communications electronics required of modern warfare. Reactors also power atmosphere control equipment that allows submarines to remain submerged for long periods and the pure water production systems used for the propulsion plant and for drinking, food preparation, and sanitation. On nuclear submarines, the crew members actually get to take showers! Nuclear submarines can cruise for weeks without surfacing, for months without re-supply, and for years without refueling. When properly designed and operated, they are virtually undetectable and can effectively limit the use of the open ocean to an adversary. In the 1982 Falklands War, the British nuclear submarine HMS *Conqueror* sank the Argentine cruiser *General Belgrano* with two torpedoes. For the rest of the war, Argentine naval units rarely ventured to sea for fear of British nuclear submarines — whether or not any were actually in the South Atlantic Ocean. When mated to nuclear tipped ballistic missiles, submarines are without question the world's best strategic deterrent weapon. On patrol they remain submerged and maintain quiet conditions, avoiding any evolution that might draw attention to their presence; if called upon for a strategic nuclear strike, they can launch their multi-warhead missiles within minutes. The assured second-strike capability of strategic missile nuclear submarines helped to ensure a stable nuclear balance during the Cold War. In the really frigid Cold War of the 1950s and early 1960s, the success of the US nuclear submarine program gave Americans something to cheer about while the Soviets — after the 1957 launch of *Sputnik* in 1957 — were singularly triumphant in space.

The submarine in turn is an excellent platform on which to operate a nuclear reactor. A submarine pressure hull is essentially a high strength steel cylinder closed at both ends. The submarine crew lives and works within the cylinder, which also contains most of the operating equipment and weapons. A portion of the exterior of the hull is surrounded by ballast tanks that can be flooded to submerge and blown dry with air to surface. The hull and the ballast tanks are all faired together or housed within a streamlined metal exterior — what is actually seen from outside an operational submarine. The nuclear reactor and immediate supporting components form a robust structure in a separate compartment near the mid-section of the cylinder, somewhat further aft on ballistic missile carrying submarines. A submarine hull, made strong to withstand the great pressures of deep water operation, is also a ready-made containment structure should a release of radioactive material somehow occur from the reactor system.

Water is a key to effective power generation in most reactors: it acts as a coolant to control the temperature of the nuclear reaction; as a moderator to slow down the neutrons given off by fission, making them available for further reactions; and, as a heat-transfer agent to carry the heat from the reactor core to a heat exchanger where it can be transformed into useful energy.[45] In addition to the pure water used in the reactor and steam systems of the propulsion plant, sea water is essential to cool various components of the steam cycle and, ultimately, the reactor itself. Submarines are in their ideal operating environment when surrounded by the cool clean waters of the deep ocean.

Soviet Nuclear Submarine Development

The Soviet Union worked hard to match the nuclear submarine achievements of the United States. Soviet nuclear submarines were conceived by several organizations but were especially the product of the Malachite design bureau (St. Petersburg Marine Engineering Bureau). According to Anatoly V. Kuteinikov, in March 1948 Malachite was tasked to develop high-speed submarines with new types of propulsion systems.[46] Rickover's progress was not unknown to the Soviets, so work to develop nuclear propulsion for submarines began in 1952.

In 1958 the first Soviet nuclear submarine, the *Leninsky Komsomol* of the *November* class entered service, having been built at the "Northern Machine-Building Enterprise" in Severodvinsk — not far from Archangel.[47] The *Leninsky Komsomol* was an attack submarine (SSN) of otherwise conventional design, essentially a diesel submarine type hull and weapons platform with a new propulsion system as was the *Nautilus*. The basic engineering of the *November*, called a Type I nuclear design, used two reactors and was also used on the *Hotel* and *Golf* class submarines that appeared almost simultaneous with the *November*. *Hotel* was a nuclear version of the diesel powered *Golf* class and carried 3 ballistic missiles to be launched from its sail or conning tower. The *Echo* class had a revolutionary mission, taking Gorshkov's anti-carrier strategy to the undersea dimension. The *Echos* carried 6 or 8 250 mile range cruise missiles mounted in exterior launch tubes. Although required to surface to fire their missiles, the *Echos* nonetheless posed a substantial threat to US surface forces.

Patrick Tyler, the author of *Running Critical*, detailed an alleged encounter between a *November* and the US aircraft carrier USS *Enterprise* (CVN65) in January 1968. The *November* was tracked at a speed of 31 knots, much faster than US naval leaders and analysts had expected.[48] Type I submarines were probably durable as well, but reportedly also very noisy. They succeeded, however, in taking the Soviet Navy to sea in nuclear powered submarines and in giving their operators and builders much needed experience. Reports of health problems to the crews (such as hair loss and sterility) caused by excessive radiation on these early ships may have had some basis in fact, but have been denied by Russian officials.[49]

A significant leap forward in Soviet design was made with the Type II submarines. These were built from the ground up to optimize the benefits of their nuclear capabilities, including a more streamlined hull design for efficient operation submerged, more powerful nuclear propulsion plants, and better sensor and weapon systems. *Victor* class SSNs began appearing in the late 1960s, with two reactors driving a single large propeller. The *Victor III* variant is considered by many to be a world-class submarine: reasonably fast, quiet, and with considerable offensive capabilities. The *Charlie* class cruise missile submarine used one reactor instead of two and, like the *Echo*, had an anti-surface ship role. Although its missiles were shorter ranged than the *Echo*, the *Charlie* was ground-breaking because it could fire them while operating submerged.

Soviet SSBN design advanced well beyond the *Hotel* with the *Yankee* class, the first Soviet SSBN design roughly comparable to those of the US Navy. It used a more powerful version of the Type II propulsion system and was both fast for an SSBN and reasonably quiet for its time. The *Yankees* carried 16 missiles and looked remarkably like the USS *Ethan Allen* (SSBN 608) class, raising the specter of intelligence leaks from the American submarine program. Suspicions were confirmed when revelations about the Walker spy family became public in the mid–1980s. John Walker was a senior enlisted radioman assigned to various US submarines and had access to large amounts of sensitive information. His espionage may have resulted in the transfer of considerable classified information to the Soviet Union, particularly with regard to acoustics and production methods, and to the expenditure of millions if not billions of dollars by the United States to recover from the damage.[50] The *Yankees* were followed by the more advanced *Delta*, apparently a very successful design. Several versions of the *Delta* class were built to conform with Soviet ballistic missile developments and a significant number are still in active service.

The Type I and II submarines were fairly mainstream projects, but Soviet submarine designers also pursued some radical departures in undersea warfare. One of the most remarkable classes of ship ever built was the *Alfa* attack submarine. Begun in the late 1950s, the *Alfa* combined several cutting-edge technologies: it had a liquid metal reactor plant instead of pressurized water, allowing a smaller propulsion system for a given power output; it was exceptionally streamlined with an almost pure teardrop-shaped hull to maximize underwater speed; and, its hull was fabricated out of titanium for lightness, strength, and low magnetic signature. The seven ships of the *Alfa* class may also have made significant use of automation to permit reduced crew sizes and effective operation at the high speeds and great depths for which they were designed. The *Alfas* were certainly among the fastest and deepest diving submarines ever built.

But the class failed to live up to its promise. Titanium was a difficult metal to fabricate and construction was filled with delays and setbacks. The use of liquid metal (reportedly a eutectic lead-bismuth alloy of 55 percent lead and 45 percent bismuth) instead of water as the reactor coolant required keeping the reactor system above 145° Celsius (about 300° F) at all times or the alloy would solidify, creating obvious operational and maintenance problem. [51] Radiated noise abatement was apparently not given much of a priority in the design because *Alfa* submarines were reported very noisy. Even if detected by allied navies, however, there was reportedly concern among Western analysts and operators that the *Alfas* could just out-run and out-dive the torpedoes fired at them![52] Liquid metal technology was not pursued much further by the Soviet Union, perhaps because of its inherent maintenance disadvantages, but titanium was used on a number of later ships, including the *Papa* and *Mike* (one hull each) and the *Sierra* class discussed below. The *Mike* may have had the deepest operating depth of any front-line submarine, reported to be greater than 3000 feet; according to Russian sources, the *Papa* established the under-water speed record of 44.7 knots.[53]

The first of the Type III submarines began to appear in the early 1980s, signaling another qualitative advance in Soviet undersea technology and capability. Two classes of attack submarine were introduced, the *Sierra* and the *Akula*, both quieter than previous Soviet classes and, according to various sources, approaching American standards.[54] The *Akula* ended up the preferred class and continues in production at Severodvinsk. With powerful and graceful lines, *Akulas* displace approximately 8,000 tons and are armed with torpedoes and the submerge-launched anti-ship missiles. The *Oscar* is the dedicated Type III cruise missile submarine. An incredibly beamy vessel, it carries 24 externally mounted cruise missiles of 300 mile range. It is fast and quiet and could present a significant threat to US aircraft carriers. Even the big *Oscar* is dwarfed by the Soviet Type III SSBN, the gigantic *Typhoon* class. These ships are actually two submarine hulls straddling a missile launch system, all contained within a hydrodynamic outer metal skin. They displace 25,000 tons, about 50 percent more than the USS *Ohio* class SSBN 726 — America's largest submarines.

Soviet submarine construction capability averaged about 10 submarines per year.[55] Norman Polmar, who has researched the Soviet Navy, reported that from 1945 through 1991 the Soviet Union produced 727 submarines — 492 with diesel-electric or closed-cycle propulsion and 235 with nuclear propulsion. This compares with the US total of 212 submarines — 43 diesels and 169 nuclear.[56] By the mid–1980s if not before, American leadership was beginning to get concerned. According to Admiral Carlisle A. H. Trost, a US Chief of Naval Operations during the period: "If we are going to make sea power work in the 21st century, we are going to have to maintain our advantage. When you consider what the Germans were able to achieve in the two world wars... you have to respect the potential of the Soviet Navy." Germany severely damaged allied sea-going forces and activities with a submarine force only 20 percent the size of the Soviet fleet in 1987.[57] Particularly worrisome to many US submariners was that the Type IIIs and possible follow-on classes would reduce or reverse the US advantage in detection capabilities and radiated noise levels.

Figure 3. A *November,* from Russia's first class of nuclear powered submarines (courtesy N. Polmar, *Guide to the Soviet Navy*).

Other Soviet Nuclear Ships

In 1959 the Soviet Union completed the world's first nuclear powered surface ship, the icebreaker *Lenin;* the first US nuclear powered surface ship, the cruiser *Long Beach,* was commissioned in 1961. Eight improved nuclear powered icebreakers of the *Arktika* and *Taimyr* classes were built between 1975 and 1993 and remain in service.

The *Kirov* battle cruisers mentioned earlier are about 800 ft long and displace 25,000 tons. Each has two reactor plants, probably derived from Soviet ice-breaker design. *Kirov* was launched in 1980, followed by the *Frunze* in 1981, the *Kalinin* in 1988, and the *Yuri Andropov* in 1989. The *Kapusta* is a nuclear powered communications ship, very heavily armed and with obvious potential as a command ship. Its nuclear components and hull design may be similar to *Kirov*.[58] The *Sevmorput* is a nuclear powered container ship (a barge carrier) based alongside Russian nuclear icebreakers in Murmansk, with reactor design similar to those of the icebreakers. The third ship of the *Kuznetzov* class of aircraft carrier, the *Ul'yanovsk,* was to be nuclear powered but was never completed.

But Now the Fleet "...Will Rot"

The post–Cold War period has been a disaster for the Soviet Navy and for most of the rest of the Russian military as well. According to Defense Minister Igor Sergeyev, only one third of Russia's aircraft can take to the air; in the Russian Navy, over 70 percent of the ships need repairs.[59] The Russian Navy used to get 23 percent of the Defense Ministry's funds, but now gets only 13 percent of a much smaller budget. Since 1992, the personnel strength of the Navy has been cut in half to about 200,000, the number of ships reduced by 60 percent to about 100 large and medium surface ships, and naval aviation cut by 30 percent.[60] According to Russian Navy Commander-in-Chief Admiral Vladimir Ivanovich Kuroyedov, the Navy has eliminated 190 units and institutions, reduced staffs in 196 units and institutions, and cut 36,000 staff and command positions since the end of the Cold War.[61]

A tour of the waterfront at any major Russian naval base would find few signs of activity, only rows and rows of corroded ships in various stages of neglect. Ships are expensive to maintain and require political support to warrant appropriations; without a clear threat to justify their existence and with enormous needs elsewhere, politicians and constituents tend to view naval forces as added extras for a country's defense — nice to have but not essential for day-to-day existence. The fledgling capitalist economy of Russia can not support the operation of the large and complex fleets Gorshkov created.

The down-sizing has been rapid and haphazard, with ships sometimes retired more by chance and circumstance than from any comprehensive plan.[62] The two Northern Fleet *Kirov*s have been inactive because of propulsion plant accidents, although one was recently brought back into service after an extended overhaul; the Pacific Fleet *Kirov* is non-operational and will probably be scrapped.[63] The newest *Kirov*, now called *Peter the Great*, had an accident-delayed construction period, but in May 1998 conducted sea-trials with President Yeltsin aboard. Russia is reportedly looking for a buyer for the incomplete second *Kuznetzov* aircraft carrier. As the final indignities to the fleet that Gorshkov built, the rusted hulk of the *Kiev* class air-capable cruiser *Minsk* is tied up to a quay in China and will be converted into a hotel/karaoke bar; the remaining operational *Kiev* class ship — named the *Admiral Gorshkov* — will probably be sold to India.[64]

According to the International Institute for Strategic Studies, for three months during the summer of 1998, no Russian SSBNs were at sea.[65] New construction has been shifted to the future; available funding goes to wages, then to strategic units, and last to general purpose forces. Out of the Russian Navy's budget for 1998, 85–90 percent was allocated to personnel and only 10–15 percent to maintain equipment. Admiral Kuroyedov stated that fleet maintenance must have a ratio closer to 60–40 percent or "it will rot."[66] Yet the Russian leadership still hopes to keep the country's maritime tradition alive. Fleet Admiral Feliks Gromov has proposed a vigorous campaign against "negligence, wastefulness, embezzlement and the use of resources for nondesignated purposes" to get the most out of the funding the Navy does receive.[67] In 1997 Minister of Defense Igor Rodionov declared that: "Russia has always been a great sea power and always will be. This is an objective and historical necessity. The geostrategic position of Russia obliges us to have a modern and well-equipped fleet."[68]

Submarine Downsizing

The most cost-effective way for Russia to keep a strong maritime presence may well be to concentrate on state-of-the-art submarines, as it did in the 1930s and for much of the Cold War. According to the US Office of Naval Intelligence (ONI), in the post–Cold War period Russian submarines are intended to fulfill the following missions:

1. Strategic deterrence: Russia depends more heavily today than before on its strategic nuclear force to provide for its security. At the same time, arms control agreements are putting an increased percentage of nuclear warheads on ballistic missile submarines (SSBNs).

2. Pro-SSBN Operations: With an ever-increasing share of their nuclear deterrent force at sea, protection of SSBNs takes on increased importance and requires sophisticated nuclear and diesel-powered general purpose submarines to do the job.

3. Aerospace Defense: The Russians view SSNs and SSGNs as their front line in "aerospace defense." Beyond their potential mission to prosecute enemy SSBNs, these general purpose submarines contribute to aerospace defense by countering enemy aircraft carriers and other warships capable of launching land attack cruise missiles.

4. Anti-assault Defense: Russia continues to place emphasis on defeating invasion from the sea. Submarines, particularly SSGNs [nuclear cruise missile submarines]and SSs [diesel powered attack submarines], have a central role in Russia's anti-invasion plans.[69]

To perform these roles, Russia will need to keep its more modern submarines operational and their crews well trained. Russian officials stated that they would like to retain 20–26 strategic missile submarines, 12 *Oscar* class anti-ship missile submarines, 40 *Akula, Sierra,* and *Victor III* attack submarines, 40 diesel submarines, and perhaps several *Yankee*-class SSBNs converted to fire land-attack cruise missiles.[70] Russia is continuing to build *Akula* SSNs and *Delta V* SSBNs, albeit at a very low rate. It has also begun construction of two new classes of submarine, the *Yasen* class SSN (*Severodvinsk*), laid down on 21 December 1993, and the *Borey* class SSBN (*Yuri Dolgorykey*), begun on 2 November 1996. Yet because construction and overhaul infrastructure is not being maintained and shipyard workers are not regularly paid, it will be difficult to maintain the Russian submarine force where it is today — much less to improve it. *Jane's Fighting Ships 1998–1999* listed 24 SSBNs, 11 SSGNs, and 26 SSNs operational with the Russian Navy.[71] Some expect as few as 50 to remain in service. Daniel Goure, a former Pentagon official now with the Center for Strategic and International Studies, said that the Russian Navy was "dead in the water," including the new *Borey* class SSBN. Construction stalled after the keel was laid while its companion SS-N-28 ballistic missile was suffering five consecutive test failures.[72]

Contemporary problems create an image of inferior Soviet and Russian submarine capability and overall military prowess. With the collapse of the Soviet Union itself, the faults of its communist economy and technology have become all too clear. The focus on military production without due concern for the country's economy and the environment has also created enormous difficulties, a topic further discussed in this report. But to those who went to sea in Western navies during the 1970s and 1980s, the progress of the fleet that Gorshkov built and particularly the Soviet submarine force commanded respect and considerable anxiety. Peter Tsouras wrote that the modern Soviet Navy represented a "remarkable organizational and industrial achievement, and that the Soviets had every reason to be proud."[73] The United States undoubtedly maintained advantages both in surface and submarine naval warfare, but the shear numbers and sustained improvement of the Soviet Navy were impressive indeed and should not be lightly dismissed or quickly forgotten.

Chapter 3

Submarine Reactors and the Russian Spent Fuel Problem

> [In the Soviet era] when they produced nuclear submarines, it's ridiculous, but nobody thought about how to decommission them… How is it possible, even in such a centralized economy, that no one thought about the fate of these submarines? [1]
>
> — Alexei Yablokov
> Co-chairman, Russia's Social-Ecological Union

Russia's reactor spent fuel problem stems in part from the Soviet Union's exuberance for the military potential of nuclear powered submarines. They were the great equalizers in the contest with the otherwise superior naval capability of the West. As Yablokov notes, however, Soviet leaders and military planners did not fully consider how to get rid of so many submarines and their spent fuel. When combined with contemporary Russia's economic and political difficulties, the requirements become overwhelming. This chapter provides detailed information about Russian submarine reactors and discusses the technical reasons why decommissioned Russian submarines have become such a big issue. Chapter 5 discusses Russian actors and the organizational and political issues that contributed to the current problem.

Russian Submarine Reactors

Technical data on Russian submarine reactors is not readily available, particularly for the later classes, but estimates on their design and capabilities have been made in recent years that are probably reasonably accurate.[2] Except for the *Alfa* class and one or two other ships, Russian submarines have all had pressurized water reactors — meaning that common pure water was used as the cooling, moderating, and heat transfer agent. The water in a pressurized water reactor must be kept under substantial pressure or it will change to steam during normal operations and possibly harm reactor performance and components. High pressure in turn requires construction material of substantial strength and quality, so that the reactor complex ends up a very robust system of considerable size and mass. Reactors with liquid metal as the cooling medium can use lighter components for construction because the coolant will not change to a vapor until a much higher temperature than water, hence operating pressures can be lower.

Russian reactor design and composition have progressed along with the overall advance of Russian submarines, to increase power output, lengthen the time between refueling, and improve reactor safety. Most Russian submarines have two nuclear reactors instead of the one chosen by other countries.[3] Their designers and operators no doubt desired redundancy in the propulsion system for reliability reasons and perhaps also to enhance the overall power output for greater speed and endurance. The downside of a two reactor system is greater weight plus increased space and maintenance requirements. Two reactors can also increase the submarine's production of spent fuel and other Radwaste.

A submarine reactor is powered by uranium that is enriched to increase the percentage of U 235 vs U 238, the predominant natural isotope. Natural uranium is only 0.7 percent U 235 and would be an impractical fuel for submarine reactors, although land-based reactors sometimes use natural uranium for fuel — particularly for plutonium production. U 235 will frequently fission, meaning divide into several particles, after it absorbs a neutron. Usually there are two fairly large elements remaining after fission, with each containing about half the mass of uranium, plus various packets of energy and smaller particles — including two or three neutrons. If enough neutrons are created from U 235 fission and subsequently absorbed by other U 235 atoms to cause further fissions, the reaction can become self-sustaining. This process is enhanced by slowing down the neutrons from fission so they are more likely absorbed by other U 235 atoms. This is done by use of a moderator, usually water or graphite (a form of carbon). If the neutron production stays constant from U 235 fissions alone, the reactor is said to be critical. Reactors are usually brought critical by withdrawing control rods that are composed of plates or pins containing neutron absorbing material like boron or hafnium.[4] Inserting the control rods removes neutrons from the reactor fuel that might otherwise cause further U 235 atoms to fission — forcing the reactor to go below criticality and to move to a shutdown status.

If a large number of fissions occur within a critical reactor, enough energy may be produced to raise the temperature of the uranium fuel and surrounding material. The water in the reactor complex (liquid metal in *Alfa* class submarines) will also rise in temperature. Circulation pumps can move the heated water from the reactor to a heat exchanger, often called a steam generator, where heat is transferred across metal tube boundaries to another water system. In this "secondary system" (the reactor side is often called the "primary system") water is turned into steam and used to drive propulsion or electric turbines. The secondary system can be very similar to steam systems used on fossil-fueled power plants. Use of primary and secondary water systems keeps potentially radioactive reactor material out of propulsion equipment and away from the compartments commonly occupied by crew members. The power output of Russian submarine reactors may vary from 55 megawatts on earlier classes to an impressive 370 megawatts on the giant *Typhoon* SSBN.[5] By comparison, a large US or Russian civilian nuclear power plant will produce about 3,000 megawatts (thermal) per reactor.

One of the advantages of reactor systems is that they have few moving parts, despite the enormous power potential they contain. Even the circulation pumps can be augmented or replaced by a natural circulation system. With proper design, coolant will flow through the reactor and into the steam generators because of convection; the hot water rises to the steam generators, transfers its heat, and sinks back to the reactor as colder water to begin the cycle again. Natural circulation has a number of advantages over forced circulation: the heat removal process is virtually automatic and requires little electric power, making reactor operation potentially simpler and more reliable; and, operation without circulation pumps should be quieter as well.[6]

Fuel Assemblies

The uranium fuel in a Russian reactor is contained within a large number of structural units called fuel assemblies. The uranium is alloyed with other metals or mixed as an oxide (UO_2) to form a high strength matrix inside the fuel assemblies. Early Russian submarine reactors may have used a uranium/aluminum mixture similar to the country's plutonium production reactors. Aluminum, however, is a fairly active metal and a poor choice for reactors designed for extended lifetimes. Later Russian submarine reactors probably contained uranium dioxide (UO_2)/ stainless steel or zirconium mixtures, although uranium-zinc compositions have been mentioned as well.[7] Zirconium is a rather exotic metal with good strength and corrosion resistance characteristics and a low affinity for neutrons, making it nearly ideal as a fuel assembly material. A downside is that zirconium could aggravate a reactor accident. If zirconium in the cladding or fuel mixture reaches 900° C, it reacts chemically with the surrounding water/steam mixture to generate heat and potentially explosive hydrogen; at 1200° C the reaction becomes self-sustaining.[8]

The uranium fuel mixture may be formed into cylindrical pins or narrow flat plates (like Venetian blinds), with perhaps two or three dozen pins or plates welded or otherwise bundled together with structural material to form a complete fuel assembly. The pins and plates are also coated with a thin protective coating of corrosion and wear resistant material. This cladding is an extremely important boundary, protecting the uranium fuel from chemical and mechanical damage and also preventing fission products and other radioactive material from escaping from the fuel and contaminating the rest of the reactor system. Russian submarine fuel assemblies have cladding that is probably made of stainless steel or zirconium alloy.

Although specific Russian submarine reactor data is not generally available, the details of Russian icebreaker reactor construction is fairly well understood and believed to be similar to some classes of submarine reactors. A fuel assembly on an OK-150 reactor, such as those previously installed on the icebreaker *Lenin*, has a diameter of 54 millimeters (mm), a length of 2.5 meters (m) of which 1.6 m is active fuel, and weighs 20 kg. It is essentially a zirconium alloy tube containing 36 fuel pins of 6.1 mm diameter which in turn contain 4.5 mm diameter UO_2 pellets of 5 percent enrichment.[9] There are 260 fuel assemblies in each OK-150 reactor. The reactors on Type I Soviet submarines (*November*, *Hotel*, and *Echo* classes) may be similar to this design.

More modern Russian submarine reactors probably resemble the newer generation of icebreaker nuclear reactors, like those on the *Arktika* and *Taimyr* classes. Some information on these is available through a safety report made available on the nuclear icebreaker/cargo ship *Sevmorput* which has a propulsion system thought to be nearly identical to the *Taimyr* class. The thermal output of the reactor may vary between 135 and 180 megawatts; the fuel is 90 percent enriched uranium metal alloyed and clad with zirconium.[10] According to the *Phase II CCMS Report*, present-day submarine reactors are likely to use fuel with enrichments greater than 30–35 percent to ensure sufficient operational capability between refuelings.[11] Like the *Sevmorput*, some may have exceptionally high enrichments — estimated at over 90 percent on the *Alfas* for example. Enrichment may also vary within a particular reactor as part of a scheme to increase power and lifetime without exceeding size and metallurgical limitations. Note that uranium enriched above about 90 percent is considered pure enough for use as nuclear bomb-making material.[12] It is believed that most Russian submarine reactors have about 210–215 fuel assemblies, with each containing 20–40 pins or plates of fuel, for a total of about 200 kg of uranium.

Great care goes into the design and fabrication of fuel assemblies and other reactor components to ensure that power and lifetime objectives are achieved and that physical limits such as heat and stress are not exceeded in any area of the reactor for its entire period of operation. Very little maintenance can be done on reactors after they are installed and operated, so the fabrication and procedures followed must be nearly flawless. Modern submarine reactors can typically go five to ten years before requiring replacement of their nuclear fuel while still being able to perform all of their mission requirements.[13] The original two reactors on the nuclear powered aircraft carrier USS *Nimitz* (CVN 68) are only now being replaced, after almost a quarter century of high-tempo operation.

Reactor Operation

Prior to their initial operation, nuclear reactors are just chunks of carefully formed and precisely machined metal parts fitted or welded together with a number of operating mechanisms and monitoring devices. A crucial evolution in the life of a pressurized water reactor is the addition of coolant to the fuel complex for the first time. The water will begin to moderate neutrons and to bring the reactor much closer to criticality than it was when dry. If coolant is added improperly, power in the reactor might rise uncontrollably and lead to a severe accident. Once installed and fully immersed in coolant, the new fuel assemblies pose little radiation danger until operated at power.

After withdrawing control rods to criticality and raising power to a level where they are producing heat, pressurized water reactors can have very stable operational characteristics because of the nature of water moderation. As temperature increases because of higher power level operation, the coolant expands and moderates neutrons less efficiently — tending to level or reduce power; as temperature decreases, the coolant becomes more dense and increases its moderating capability — tending to raise power. If reactor power were to rise uncontrollably for whatever reason, the characteristics of water moderation would tend to dampen the power rise and to reduce the severity of the accident.

During powered operation, reactors emit intense levels of radiation from uranium fission and related processes, making the immediate vicinity of the reactor (the reactor compartment) uninhabitable. The shielding and distance designed into nuclear powered ships protects the crew from this hazard. For American submarines at least, radiation doses received during reactor operations are very low. Soviet designs seem to emphasize power and speed over radiation protection and may have skimped on shielding, which can add hundreds of tons to a ship's displacement, so the radiation levels in spaces near the reactor compartment on Russian submarines could be higher than their American counterparts. The exposure of the crew can still be minimized, however, by restricting access to compartments adjacent to the reactor during power operations. As the submarine operates, the fuel assemblies within the reactor begin to accumulate significant quantities of fission products and to become highly radioactive, even when the reactor is not operating. From then on fuel assemblies require even greater care in handling, whether installed in the reactor or removed after defueling operations.

Defueling Procedures

Defueling nuclear submarines is a difficult technical operation requiring specialized equipment and highly trained personnel. Moving and storing nuclear fuel must be carefully planned and executed to keep the radiation dosage of personnel as low as possible, to minimize the possibility of radioactive contamination to the work place, and to ensure security and accountability of the reactor nuclear material. Even commonplace procedures, like lifting crane maintenance and operation, require special operator training and quality control procedures. To accidentally drop a spent fuel assembly could spread radioactive contamination in the immediate area; just suspending spent fuel assemblies for a prolonged period of time because of equipment malfunction could cause unnecessary radiation exposure to operating personnel and perhaps damage to the fuel assembly due to lack of cooling. All of that said, reactor fueling and defueling procedures are well understood and accomplished routinely in many countries of the world today.

Before defueling begins, submarines are usually berthed at a naval or civilian facility for several months after their last at-sea operations so that radiation and heat generation can decrease to levels more easily managed by industrial personnel. Temporary facilities are constructed above the reactor compartment to prevent unauthorized access, to restrict the potential spread of radioactive contamination, and perhaps to provide additional shielding against radiation during the defueling process. The reactor system is depressurized and the welded integrity of the reactor complex subsequently breached. Specialized equipment is then used to remove the spent fuel assemblies, involving devices and procedures to latch-on to a particular fuel assembly and then to raise it into a shielded container for transfer off the submarine by crane for further storage and processing. It is believed that Russian fuel assemblies are removed one at a time.

During refueling or defueling operations, an uncontrolled criticality is also conceivable if the configuration of fuel assemblies, control rods, or moderator are changed to increase the power production potential of a reactor or group of fuel assemblies. In 1985 at a shipyard in Shkotovo-22 near Chazhma Bay (on the Russian Pacific coast near Vladivostok), the reactor on a Soviet *Echo II* class submarine had an uncontrolled criticality during refueling operations — causing an explosion, a number of deaths and injuries, and releasing radioactive contamination to the atmosphere, sea, and surrounding land area.[14] The personnel performing the evolution had mistakenly lifted the control rods that were keeping the reactor shutdown.[15] The radioactivity of the sea water returned to background levels after a few months, but sea sediment radioactive contamination remains above normal levels and the area of contamination has been expanding in size ever since.[16]

After removal from recently operated submarines, fuel assemblies are usually placed in water pool storage for about three years to allow radiation and heat generation levels to reduce further. This would not be necessary for reactors from submarines that had been out of service for several years already, like many of the currently decommissioned submarines of the Russian Northern Fleet. The fuel assemblies will have one of two final destinations: they can be cut apart and chemically dissolved, with the fissile material reprocessed into nuclear products for other use and the remainder stored as high level Radwaste; or, they can be stored indefinitely as intact fuel assemblies.

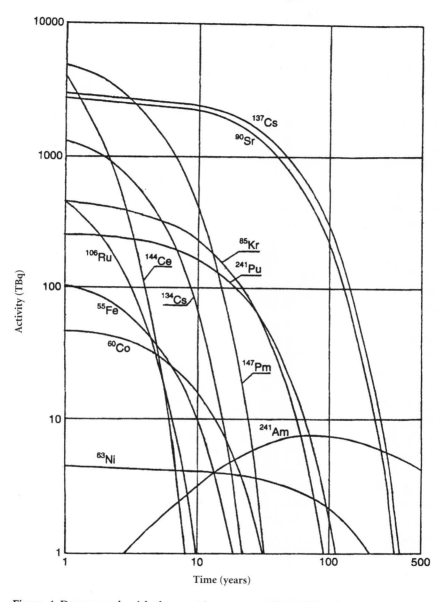

Figure 4. Decay graph with the most important radionuclides from the reactor of the sunken submarine *Komsomolets.* The fission products cesium 137 and strontium 90 are dominant from about five years to several hundred years after operation; from then on the actinide americium 241 becomes the main source of spent fuel assembly radioactivity (NATO/CCMS pilot study, *Cross-border Environmental Problems Emanating from Defence-Related Installations and Activities, Phase I: 1993–1995, Volume 1*).

Spent Fuel Hazards

Spent fuel assemblies must be treated with great care at all times. The hazards they present form the crux of the Russian decommissioned submarine problem. There are three fundamental concerns: radiation exposure, radioactive contamination, and weapons usable material proliferation.

Radiation Exposure

Spent fuel assemblies can emit very high levels of radiation for many decades after operation because of the decay of fission products. The new elements created from fission (the fission products) are almost always unstable isotopes that move toward stability through beta and gamma radioactive decay, i.e., they emit particles and energy that can be dangerous to living organisms. The amount of radioactivity contained within a Russian submarine fuel assembly will vary depending on its composition and operating history, but 1000 curies may be a reasonable estimate — enough to cause a fatal radiation dose in a short period of time to anyone in the immediate vicinity of the fuel assembly.[17] In September 1993, eight Russian servicemen were exposed to excessive radiation when a container with spent fuel was mistakenly handled as though it was empty.[18]

To protect personnel, spent fuel assemblies removed from reactors are stored so that radiation exposure is reduced by distance or by shielding with water, steel, or other appropriate substance. Water pool storage of spent fuel assemblies, with sometimes hundreds or thousands of fuel assemblies suspended from racks at specific distances apart, removes the heat generated by fission product decay and also provides shielding from the high radiation of the fuel assemblies. For fuel assemblies removed from recently operated reactors, the blue glow of *Cerenkov* radiation in the water pool is convincing evidence of the extremely high radiation levels present.[19]

Radioactive Contamination

If a fuel assembly's thin protective cladding is damaged, the radioactive material within it can escape and become air or waterborne, putting people and the environment at risk. In a stroke of bad luck from nuclear physics and human physiology, some of the elements produced by nuclear fission (the fission products) are particularly hazardous to our health. Strontium 90 (Sr 90) is a common product of fission and is chemically similar to the calcium used by the body to build bones. It can readily take calcium's place, putting radioactive material next to the blood manufacturing organs of the bone marrow. Radioactive isotopes of iodine are also produced in significant quantities by fission and can concentrate in the human thyroid gland to levels 100 times higher than in other tissue. Radioactive iodine (chiefly I 131) released by the Chernobyl accident was responsible for the most direct and demonstrable impact of the accident on public health, thyroid cancer in children. Most of the iodine dose to these children was received by drinking milk from cattle that had grazed in contaminated pastures.[20] In the early 1960s, concern about radioactive contamination from the "fallout" of Sr 90 and the various iodine isotopes was among the reasons the United States and Soviet Union signed the Limited Test Ban Treaty and agreed to stop testing nuclear weapons in the atmosphere. The ban has subsequently been observed by other emerging nuclear powers.

Spent fuel assemblies also contain actinides, a series of mostly artificial elements created primarily by neutron bombardment of uranium and subsequent decay. Their atomic numbers range from actinium (89) to lawrencium (103) (uranium is 92). Among these, isotopes of plutonium (94) and americium (95) predominate in spent fuel. Several hundred years after reactor operation, the fission products have essentially decayed away, leaving the actinides as the primary form of radioactivity remaining in the fuel assemblies. Fuel assemblies can remain highly radioactive for hundreds of thousands of years because of the actinides.

Both high radiation and radioactive contamination could result from an uncontrolled criticality of a nuclear reactor. An out-of-control reactor could exceed design power and thermal limits, damaging reactor fuel assemblies and possibly causing an explosion that allows radioactive material to escape from the immediate area of the reactor. The Chernobyl disaster was an extreme uncontrolled criticality that destroyed most of the reactor's fuel assemblies. Fission products became airborne after the steam explosion and fire in the reactor's graphite moderator. Over half of the total radioactivity was spread with the winds beyond the territory of the Soviet Union, escaping to the environment because the Chernobyl power plant had no containment structure built around the reactor complex.[21] A submarine reactor accident would likely be much less severe because of the smaller size of the reactors concerned, their lower power history, and because much of the radioactivity released from the reactor could be contained within the submarine hull. A localized problem could be caused by rain or other sources of water spreading contamination into the surrounding landscape from improperly stored spent fuel and other radioactive components. This would cause a difficult environmental cleanup problem if not a hazard to life in the immediate vicinity.

Proliferation

Un-fissioned enriched uranium (U 235) and plutonium (Pu 239 and other isotopes — the products of U 238 absorption of neutrons) are contained in spent fuel assemblies and can be recovered by chemical reprocessing procedures.[22] With sufficient uranium enriched to greater than 90 percent U 235, the construction of a nuclear weapon would be made much easier for a possible proliferator. Hence, spent fuel assemblies are a proliferation concern. According to Bellona, two fresh fuel assemblies were stolen from Andreeva Bay in 1993 (although later recovered) and in 1995 from a storage facility in Rosta, near Murmansk.[23] Concern for the loss of submarine nuclear fuel is greater than commercial fuel because the highly enriched uranium used in Russian submarines and icebreakers, reported to be greater than 90 percent in some cases, could be more readily converted to bomb use.

The radiation danger of spent fuel tends to lessen the proliferation problem because potential thieves would have real difficulties handling "hot" spent fuel. Some have expressed concern, however, that the Russian submarine spent fuel assemblies stored for decades have lost much of their radiation hazard and may therefore be more likely targets for theft. Another reason to be concerned about older fuel assemblies is that they may produce more plutonium. The lower the enrichment of uranium, the more plutonium may be produced during reactor operations, which might make older, less highly enriched fuel assemblies a target for proliferators as well. A workable nuclear weapon requires less plutonium than enriched uranium.

Decommissioned Russian Submarines

The Soviet Union built 235 nuclear submarines, almost twice as many as the United States. The focus on numbers was a reflection of the great importance given submarines by Gorshkov's maritime strategy and perhaps an attempt to use quantity as a way to make up for the early qualitative inferiority of Russian submarines to their American counterparts. During the 1970s and 1980s, however, production slowed down and the Russian Navy and submarine design and construction enterprises seemed to put more emphasis on quality. But even as more capable ships were being put in service, older ones were kept operational well past their useful lifetimes.[24] Shore and ship-borne facilities were developed to refuel submarines and to keep them at sea, but not necessarily to take them out-of-service. Decommissioning and defueling were done on an ad hoc basis with little long-term planning and with few resources devoted to the needs of the vessels placed out-of-service. Most were just tied to a pier with their reactors still intact; the ships were minimally manned and maintained, with little preparation for defueling and dismantlement.

The end of the Cold War caught Russian and many other military organizations by surprise. The Berlin Wall, perhaps the most powerful symbol of the Cold War, came down in 1989 and the competition between East and West was declared over in November 1990 at the Paris Peace Conference. Soviet and (after 1991) Russian fast attack submarines did not need to contest the seas with US carrier battle groups anymore nor to worry about interrupting the sea-lines of communications between North America and Europe and the number of allowed ballistic missile submarines was reduced by nuclear arms control treaties and proposals. War was no longer expected and the West became a virtual ally of Russia in the early post–Cold War period. There were just not enough missions or threats around to justify the great expense of manning and operating a large fleet of submarines.

The extent of the submarine spent fuel problem took a while to sink in among Russia's leadership. Like the rest of the Russian fleet reduction, submarine decommissioning has been haphazard and idiosyncratic. According to Georgi Kostev, a retired Russian Rear Admiral and organizer of the Committee for Critical Technology and Non-Proliferation, there was no systematic and purposeful research into the dismantlement problem, no appropriate scientific-technical or technological services created, and hardly any production base developed to accomplish the task.[25] From the late 1980s onward, submarines began to pile up at Russian bases in the Northwest and Pacific regions. The Russian Navy uses the term *Otstoj* for those submarines no longer in operation but awaiting funds for overhaul, conversion, or scrapping. As of late 1998, 95 submarines in the Northern Fleet were in a laid-up status and only 26 of these had been defueled; in the Pacific Fleet, 26 had been decommissioned and 16 were defueled.[26] Hence there is a backlog of well over 100 reactors, with probably greater than 20,000 spent fuel assemblies, still installed on submarines in the Northern Fleet. Several more submarines could gain *Otstoj* status within the next few years as well and with a continued refueling cycle of operational submarines, the spent fuel inventory could swell even more. Yet in the period between 1988 and 1995, only ten Northern Fleet submarines were defueled.[27]

The Northern Fleet's decommissioned nuclear vessels, either with or without fuel, are located at bases like Polyarny, Iokanga, and Murmansk on the Kola Peninsula and at the immense shipyard facilities of Severodvinsk. The Pacific Fleet has a holding site for decommissioned submarines in Palovsky Bay.[28] *Otstoj* submarines are sometimes moored in groups reminiscent of the diesel submarine nests of both Allied and Axis fleets during World War II. They are manned at about 40 percent of a normal crew, with those on board charged primarily with preventing the submarine from sinking and with keeping the reactor safe. In another twist to the country's terrible economic crisis, decommissioned submarines are used to provide sailors with a place to stay because of the acute housing shortage in the Russian Navy.[29]

Lay-up Concerns

Managing so many submarines in a lay-up condition is a problem for Russia. Even at reduced manning per ship and comparatively low operating costs, a large number of Russian Navy personnel and considerable expense are tied up with these unproductive vessels. Proper pier space and electrical power must be provided and routine maintenance kept up. Some are worried about the durability of various types of Russian reactor fuel and believe that their cladding or fuel mixtures may fail after water immersion of more than twenty years.[30] This is particularly true with reactors that have aluminum as part of their fuel assembly construction. Even if the fuel elements do not have cladding failure, they may corrode, warp, or expand such that removal by normal procedures at a later time becomes very difficult if not impossible.

Safety Culture

Others are worried more about Russia's nuclear "safety culture." Safety culture describes "an assembly of characteristics and attitudes within organizations and individuals whereby a deep-seated commitment to safety issues and safety procedures is demonstrated." It requires a commitment at all phases of nuclear equipment design, management, and operation and extends to the proper handing of Radwaste, where the extra mile of effort goes into the operation and maintenance of nuclear activities.[31]

The Soviet Union's emphasis on production resulted in what many consider to be a poor safety culture within its nuclear manufacturing, operation, and Radwaste management activities. According to former US Nuclear Regulatory Commission Chairman Ivan Selin, the three most important elements for shoring up a strong safety culture are:

1. Technical excellence and operational safety enforced by a tough, independent regulator, and supported by timely plant operator wage payments and payments to utilities for electricity produced.

2. A sound economic climate that allows for a sufficiently profitable nuclear program capable of underwriting first-rate training, maintenance and equipment and incorporates a new energy pricing mechanism to encourage energy conservation.

3. Solid organization and management including high-quality staffing, training, and responsible leadership.[32]

During the Soviet era at least and probably to the present, many of these characteristics have not been adequately represented in Russia's nuclear programs.

To give Russia its due, one must also acknowledge that Russian industrial activity and engineering operations have a style that is less rigorous and perhaps more practical than Western counterpart activity. The differing reactions to the *Mir* space station's numerous crises in 1997 were illustrative. While the media coverage was sensational and Western leadership sometimes critical about the circumstances that led to a fire and collision in the spacecraft, Russian officials were matter of fact and methodical in their approach to problem-solving. They seemed confident that they would eventually work through the difficulties, as indeed they did. Nuclear waste may be a parallel circumstance.[33] Russian facilities and procedures may sometimes be "good enough" to get the job done while still falling short of highly developed Western standards. On the other hand, NASA was surprised to learn how close *Mir* came to disaster during the February 1997 fire — only fully understanding the true danger after the US astronaut onboard the spacecraft returned to earth.[34] Without doubt, the West also has ample cause for concern about nuclear practices in Russia.

Past nuclear safety culture problems are now aggravated by Russia's economic and organizational dislocation. Under conditions where soldiers and sailors are often not paid and where nuclear workers must demonstrate publicly for back benefits, supervision and training of personnel and the proper operation, maintenance, and security of submarines and their reactor systems may be reduced or neglected altogether.[35] In December

1995 and again in February 1997, employees at the Polyarny shipyard blocked a nuclear submarine from leaving port; on October 1997, workers at a Russian Navy shipyard blocked an access road and demanded payment of back salaries.[36]

A terrible tragedy occurred near Murmansk that highlighted the potential dangers within today's Russian military. In September 1998, Sasha Kuzminykh — a 19-year-old torpedoman attached to an *Akula* class fast attack nuclear submarine SSN — had just returned from patrol. For reasons yet unknown, early one morning he killed the sentry on duty topside and seized his assault rifle; going below decks on the submarine, he killed another seven crew members and then barricaded himself in the torpedo room. Kuzminykh threatened to detonate a torpedo and destroy the ship, nuclear reactor included; only his suicide ended the standoff. Some speculation followed that the tradition of violent bullying within the enlisted ranks of the Russian armed forces was the root cause of the incident, although the economic calamity of contemporary Russia may have also contributed. According *The Guardian* (London): "As scores of officers commit suicide, mired in poverty and debt because of unpaid salaries, with monitoring of the mental health of servicemen primitive, and with a culture of savage beating, humiliation and degradation endemic among half-starved conscripts, there are reasons to fear that, while Russia's nuclear weapons are not going to blow up of their own accord, the men looking after them are."[37]

Organizations like Bellona and Greenpeace are concerned about the potential for a disaster caused by mismanagement of submarine spent fuel. If a significant portion of the radioactivity contained aboard the submarines or in storage locations is released, contamination to the immediate area and perhaps to the Arctic Ocean environment and adjacent countries could occur. Because of the large amount of spent fuel stored in the Northwest region of Russia, accidents leading to international repercussions are a particular concern. Significant radioactive contamination could result from two general types of accidents: a loss of cooling accident and an uncontrolled criticality. Other hazards, such as sinking and collisions of laid up submarines, are concerns as well because they could conceivably contribute to reactor accidents such as these. Although discussed in general terms below, the potential and consequences of Russian submarine reactor accidents can not be understood precisely by Western analysts because the technical information about the reactors concerned is not available.

Loss of Cooling

Coolant flow is crucial to reactors operating at power to remove the heat generated from fission and to allow the power production process to continue. It is required for non-operating reactors as well to remove the heat generated by the decay of fission products. Loss of cooling could allow heat to build up to the extent that fuel assembly cladding fails and the release of radioactive material to the environment becomes possible. The 1979 Three Mile Island disaster in the United States was a very severe loss of cooling accident that led to partial destruction of the reactor fuel, although little environmental contamination resulted. Operator error, equipment malfunction, loss of electrical power, collisions, or explosions could all result in a loss of cooling accident. Circumstances that could conceivably lead to a loss of cooling on Russian submarines were highlighted in September 1995 when the electricity at several Northern Fleet naval bases was cut off because of a dispute over unpaid bills.[38] Without shore-based electricity, the circulation pumps of the reactor system may not work and the fuel assemblies could overheat and be damaged.

As time passes since their last at-sea operation, it is conceivable that the need for even occasional circulation of reactor coolant will pass. Although the design of Russian submarine reactors is not fully understood, there may be enough natural circulation of water and transfer of heat to other reactor components and the surrounding sea water to prevent fuel assemblies from exceeding their thermal limits. The problem might then be to keep the coolant from getting too cold; it could freeze in the cold Arctic winter or perhaps create damaging stress to some of the reactor's structural components.

Inadvertent Criticality

Nuclear reactors achieve criticality when sufficient U 235 in the fuel assemblies is uncovered by withdrawing control rods; once critical a reactor can be used to meet the power demands placed upon it. An uncontrolled criticality might result from an operational or maintenance error, from deliberate action, or from a severe electrical or mechanical malfunction. It could cause a power excursion that exceeds the reactor structural design limits, perhaps damaging reactor fuel assemblies and causing a steam explosion that allows radioactive material to escape from the immediate area of the reactor. The Chernobyl disaster of 1986 was a very severe uncontrolled criticality and explosion, resulting in many deaths and injuries and enormous economic and environmental consequences.

The Chazhma Bay submarine reactor accident in 1985 was another example of an uncontrolled reactor criticality.

Operator or electrical malfunction-caused criticality on decommissioned Russian submarines could conceivably be made nearly impossible if appropriate safety measures are taken. According to Nikolai S. Khlopkin of Russia's RNRC Kurchatov Institute, a number of precautions have indeed been put in place for submarines taken out of service. These include removing safety fuses and cutting 1.5 to 2.0 meters of power supply cable from the control system mechanisms.[39]

Sinking and Collision

Compared to surface ships, nuclear submarines have far less reserve buoyancy (the amount of watertight volume of a ship above the waterline — essentially the safety margin that keeps ships floating instead of sinking) because they are designed for optimum performance and space while operating underwater. This means that they will sink after taking on relatively less water than a similarly sized surface ship.[40] Water can enter a submarine through the access hatches and through piping or other seawater component failure. Submarines can also lose buoyancy through their main ballast tanks. These are the tanks built around the pressure hull that are flooded to submerge the submarine and blown dry to surface. Welding over the flood ports at the bottom of the tanks can help prevent the unwanted ingress of water; so can pumping low pressure air into the ballast tank to keep the water out. Both practices are apparently common on Russian *Otstoj* submarines.[41] The Russian Navy also places their decommissioned submarines in dry-dock periodically for inspection and maintenance to ensure they remain seaworthy.[42]

If a decommissioned submarine sinks, sea water could cause electrical malfunctions and perhaps damage reactor components. Fears have been expressed that sinking might also cause an uncontrolled criticality. This seems highly unlikely for pressurized water reactors already filled with pure water.[43] An uncontrolled criticality may be a greater possibility for submarines with a liquid metal reactor because of the additional neutron moderation introduced by seawater. The possibility that submarines in close proximity to each other will have a "cataclysmic chain reaction should one suffer a meltdown [uncontrolled criticality]" must also be very small.[44] The conditions for this to happen would seem impossibly unique. Submarines have indeed sunk, however. In May 1997, a moored nuclear submarine sank in Avachinski Bay near the Pacific Fleet naval base at Kamchatka; according to some reports (denied by Russian officials), it had been struck by another vessel.[45] The submarine had not been operating for four years and reportedly caused no immediate contamination hazard. Collisions are a concern because they might sink the submarine and also breach the integrity of the reactor system, making environmental contamination with radioactive material a greater possibility.[46]

Spent Fuel Storage

Spent fuel retained on board decommissioned nuclear submarines is at least in the surroundings for which it was designed, with provisions for adequate cooling and shielding and with containment pre-installed should an accident occur. The same can not be said for Russian spent fuel already removed from submarines and stored in inadequate land- and sea-based facilities. Spent fuel has been stored in Northwest Russia almost since the beginning of the Russian nuclear submarine program. During the Cold War the spent fuel came primarily from ships being refueled for continued use, not from decommissioning, but the need for adequate storage was the same. Spent fuel assemblies from Northern Fleet submarines are stored either on service vessels or at land bases near waters connected to the Arctic Ocean. From 25 to 30,000 spent fuel assemblies were placed at several sites along the Kola Peninsula and White Sea coast, including Zapadnaya Litsa, Gremikha, and Severodvinsk. In the Pacific, about 10,000 fuel assemblies are stored at locations such as the Shkotovo Waste Site near Vladivostok and the Kamchatka Waste Site near Petropavlovsk.[47]

The most notorious spent fuel storage site is at Andreeva Bay in the Zapatnaya Litsa Fjord, only 30 miles from Norway. In the 1980s a significant leak developed in a wet storage tank and allowed substantial contamination to enter the environment.[48] The spent fuel was moved to dry tanks originally constructed for liquid waste storage. Since 1984, approximately 21,000 spent fuel assemblies have been stored in these tanks less than a quarter mile from the fjord even though the tanks were scheduled for only three or four years of use.[49] Other fuel assemblies at the site are stored outdoors in containers that have been exposed to the harsh Arctic climate for decades. An emerging requirement is remediation of a small stream undercutting contaminated areas and taking quantities of radioactive liquid into the fjord. For detailed coverage of the history and problems of Andreeva Bay, see Bellona's 1996 publication *The Russian Northern Fleet*.[50] Significant quantities of spent fuel are also stored at Gremikha, a submarine base located near the eastern end of the Kola Peninsula. It has a variety of spent fuel in storage, including 95 spent fuel assemblies that are damaged and not suitable for reprocessing plus 812 others that will not be accepted for other technical reasons. It also has five liquid metal reactor cores with fuel assemblies installed.[51] At the Zvezdochka shipyard in Severodvinsk, there are three storage barges filled to capacity with fuel assemblies (1,680 each); all are more than 25 years old and reportedly in very poor condition.[52]

Damage to fuel assemblies held in temporary storage has already occurred and caused radioactive contamination of the immediate vicinity. To affect significantly an area greater than the storage facility itself and to cause cross-border contamination, a radiological accident involving spent fuel would probably require an explosion of some kind. An uncontrolled criticality as describe above is conceivable in a storage location if enough uranium bearing material, such as a number of spent fuel assemblies, is brought together along with sufficient neutron moderation. According to Bellona, there is a particular danger at Andreeva Bay because some of the fuel elements are stored only 25 cm apart that, with deteriorating concrete caused by the effects of snow and ice, may move even closer together towards a possible critical mass.[53] Rather than an uncontrolled criticality, perhaps more likely is a conventional explosion of some kind that damages a great number of fuel assemblies stored in close proximity to one another. Although apparently not related to nuclear spent fuel storage, in January 1998 a gas explosion onboard a nuclear submarine at Zapadnaya Litsa caused one death and four injuries.[54]

Long term water-cooled storage of Russian spent fuel assemblies may also be problematic due to corrosion of the support structures holding the fuel assemblies in place and to deterioration of the fuel assemblies themselves. The facilities in use were not designed for long term storage so their construction material corrodes with time, leaving (according to the *Phase II CCMS Report*) a "heap of high-level waste rubble that is very difficult to handle."[55] Bellona also believes that some of the fuel assemblies at Andreeva Bay and Gremikha may be stuck in their storage cells.[56] Even these inadequate storage facilities are essentially full, creating another bottleneck for the beginning of wholesale defueling operations. In the final analysis, keeping fuel assemblies onboard submarines — although not the ideal interim storage location — may be a preferred option to moving them to inadequate facilities on shore.[57]

Why the Backlog?

Too many submarines and not enough money are the root causes for the current backlog of decommissioned submarines. In the immediate here and now, Russia's prolonged economic crisis is preventing the Russian Navy and other Russian organizations from making more progress with defueling and dismantling the submarines it no longer needs. Russia's Minister of Atomic Energy Viktor Mikhailov remarked that $50 million per year will be needed to dispose of the existing 1.5 billion curies of nuclear waste in Russia by the year 2000, but that only $20 million was actually spent in 1996.[58] Scrapping Russian submarines may cost about $3–4 million per unit[59]; getting rid of all of them and cleaning up the resulting radioactive waste may cost at least $1.5 billion, according to Russian Deputy Atomic Energy Minister Nikolai Yegoreov.[60] A later estimate by various Russian scientists estimates $3 billion will be needed to address waste and spent fuel issue in the northwest, a figure Christopher Watson of AEA Technologies of the United Kingdom considers conservative.[61] The final resolution of the Russian decommissioned submarine dismantlement, spent fuel, and associated Radwaste problems will undoubtedly cost several billion dollars — in a country where a billion dollars is still real money.[62]

The project is expensive but has also been mismanaged. For one, the Russian government was very slow to recognize the extent of the problem. As late as 1994, decommissioned submarines received little attention at the highest levels of the Russian government. The Ministry of Defense and other parts of the Russian government have a traditional sympathy with the Army, not surprising considering the Army's role in defeating Germany in World War II and the Russian Navy's patchy record in the war. There is a tendency to depreciate the Navy's needs and, according to one report, the Navy is financed by whatever funds are left over from the other services. With its reduced budget, the Russian Navy has not been anxious to pay for ships it no longer uses — despite the hazards.[63] According to Kostev:

> The sweeping reduction of naval ships is only one of the deleterious effects of the economic and political crisis in Russia. The high command of the four Russian fleets and the Caspian flotilla hardly have a clear view of the state foreign policy concept and each fleet's role in this policy. The high level of the Navy's combat effectiveness is not properly maintained. Naval ships are being neither equipped nor updated at all. The shipbuilding industry is in a critical condition.

The manpower resources of the shipbuilding enterprises and design bureaus are being scattered. Generally speaking, Russia is currently in position to lose the industrial base, which would allow the country to build modern ships of major classes.[64]

There are bottlenecks at virtually every phase of the defueling process, preventing rapid progress in alleviating the backlog and in pursuing a consolidated plan, in addition to the interim storage problem already discussed. Adequate funding could remove or mitigate many of the problems, but deciding on the best way forward is difficult because of the complex interrelationship of technical, environmental, and political considerations.

Service Ships and Shipyards

Russia's defueling procedures often used special service vessels to help remove and to serve as temporary storage for fuel assemblies. Some vessels were also employed to carry the fuel to other facilities, such as for transfer to railheads for shipment to the Mayak reprocessing facility, while others were used to store liquid waste and to dump liquid and other Radwaste at sea. This was particularly useful at remote bases such as those on the Zapadnaya Litsa Fjord where rail connections were incomplete and roads very primitive. Russian service vessels varied in size and capabilities, but were generally about 200 to 400 feet long and displace from 3,000 to 14,000 tons. In other words, they were small to medium size ships. Most of those previously used are now old and outmoded, although some of the so-called "floating technical bases" are still used to store submarine spent fuel.[65]

Submarine defueling and dismantlement capabilities ashore also face problems. Dismantlement includes cutting out contaminated reactor compartments and then completely cutting apart the rest of the submarine. The infrastructure of lifting cranes and railheads and the general condition of the shipyard shops and equipment needed to support submarine maintenance procedures have become decrepit and more difficult if not dangerous to operate. Five shipyards in the Northern Fleet have been involved in the decommissioning process: Sevmash and Zvezdochka at Severodvinsk and Nerpa, Pala Guba, and Rosta near Murmansk.[66] In the future, most of the dismantlement work may take place at the Severodvinsk shipyards where plans have been made to build new dry docks and to modernized facilities for rail transshipment of fuel assemblies to Mayak.[67] On the Pacific coast, Bolshoi Kamen near Vladivostok is the designated shipyard and can reportedly handle 1.5 submarines a year; Severodvinsk at present can handle only one.

Even if the capacity were available, without money to pay for the work, the Russian Navy can not entice these or other facilities to accelerate the dismantlement process. According to Susan Kopte of the BICC, with the end of the Cold War the Russian Navy–shipyard relationship became fractured as shipyards were no longer dependent on orders from the federal government (which were rapidly shrinking anyway) and became free agents to contract for more profitable commercial work elsewhere.[68] Because of their greater profit and prestige, building ships was always a more enticing enterprise for Russian government authorities than ship repair and dismantlement.[69] These days Russian shipyard new construction is usually done for cash-paying foreign customers, not for the credits or promises of Russian government agencies. The shift to a market economy clearly has had winners and losers.

As the decommissioned submarine problem began to emerge in the early 1990s, some in the Russian government and elsewhere hoped that the scrap metal obtained from dismantled submarines would fund the labor and capital expended during the process — and perhaps even allow for some profit. Shipyards and other enterprises were authorized to put the scrap metal up for sale as a source of income.[70] This turned out to be a false hope and a meager source of revenue at best. After cutting up its first submarine in 1993, the Zvezdochka shipyard at Severodvinsk suffered a loss of 311 million rubles. Although sixty tons of copper, 100 tons of lead, and 20 tons of aluminum were salvaged from the submarine and sold, the labor required to extract the material was much more expensive than the value of the scrap itself.[71]

Solid and Liquid Waste

Spent fuel assemblies are a significant hazard because of the very high levels and long life of the radioactivity they contain. Maintenance and operation of nuclear reactors and particularly defueling evolutions generate significant quantities of other Radwaste, both liquid and solid. These range from the potential or low contamination on clothing worn by radiation workers to the very high-level wastes produced during defueling operations. Significant planning and infrastructure is required to ensure the waste does not become a severe environmental and personnel problem.

In the 1960s, the Soviet engineering enterprise VNIPIET designed and built facilities and equipment to process radioactive waste for a number of naval repair facilities. At the time, however, the Soviet Union did not conform with the London Convention 1972 banning the dumping of certain categories of nuclear waste at sea and Soviet authorities found that disposing of its marine Radwaste could more easily and cheaply be done in bordering seas and oceans. The VNIPIET equipment was not utilized and subsequently either corroded or disappeared.[72] In September 1994, Russia announced that it would honor a voluntary commitment to the strengthened London Convention that banned the dumping of all radioactive material, including low-level liquid and solid waste, into the oceans.[73] An unintended consequence of this decision, however, has been an overflow of nuclear waste on land and in afloat storage facilities, adding another impediment to Russia's ability to conduct defueling operations.

Liquid Radwaste can be stored, purified, or reduced in volume and solidified. Volume reduction is usually done by evaporating most of the water to the atmosphere through filter media, then treating the filters as solid radioactive waste and the remaining material as a radioactive sludge. The sludge can be solidified and permanently fixed in either bitumen (asphalt) or cement. For highly radioactive wastes, vitrification (encasing in glass) is often used.[74] The resulting asphalt, concrete, or glass units can then be catalogued and place in storage facilities as solid Radwaste. Thousands of cubic meters of liquid Radwaste are now stored in Northwest Russia because of the paucity of facilities for purification or solidification. About 70 percent of the liquid Radwaste in Northwest Russia was generated and accumulated on the Kola Peninsula and 30 percent in the vicinity of Severodvinsk and Archangel. Liquid waste from Northern Fleet nuclear ships is stored in floating tanks, in shore-based tanks, and onboard service ships and tenders. The combined capacity of all Northern Fleet storage facilities amounts to about 10,000 cubic meters, although 30 percent of the facilities can not be used because of their poor condition. Approximately 2000 to 2500 cubic meters of liquid radioactive wastes are generated annually, with obvious concern about where to put all the waste to be generated in the future.[75] There is a need for liquid waste purification facilities and for "special tanker ships" that could transport liquid waste from the various storage sites to a central storage or processing facility.[76]

Solid Radwaste is a similar concern. It can sometimes be reduced in volume by compacting or incineration, with the remains again placed in bitumen or cement, inventoried, and put in storage. Much of the Radwaste is stored at the military or civilian facility that generates it, but some is also transported to dedicated facilities like the RADON complex southwest of St. Petersburg. About 8000 cubic meters of solid radioactive wastes are stored in Northern Fleet facilities, with an annual production of approximately 1000 cubic meters. There are currently six land-based facilities for storage on the Kola Peninsula and four in the Archangel region. An incineration plant for burnable radioactive waste is in operation at the Zvezdochka shipyard. Considering the volume of radiological work anticipated once decommissioning submarine defueling and dismantlement work begins in earnest, the quantity of Radwaste generated each year could easily double.[77]

Current Radwaste storage facilities in Northwest Russia are inadequate by international standards; contamination of surrounding areas and loss of control of the material has already occurred. Developing and improving facilities that handle liquid and solid Radwaste and properly disposing of excess material are integral parts of moving forward with defueling and dismantling out-of-service Russian submarines.

Transportation to Mayak

The Mayak Chemical Combine, located in the southern Ural Mountains about two thousand miles from Northwest Russia's naval facilities, has reprocessed nuclear spent fuel from military and civilian nuclear reactors since the 1950s. During the Cold War special trains from Murmansk or Severodvinsk transited to Mayak several times a year, made up of rail cars and TUK-11 and 12 containers specially designed to carry spent fuel. The trains stopped running in 1993 when the Murmansk Shipping Company (the icebreaker operating enterprise) and the Russian Navy ran out of money to pay for the newly enforced freight charges.[78] Problems developed with shipping equipment as well. In 1993, GAN (the Russian nuclear regulatory agency) banned the use of TUK-11 and 12 spent fuel shipping containers because of their vulnerability to low temperatures, their potential for rupture during a head-on rail collision, and also because of the poor quality and worn-out condition of the containers, railcars, and other railway equipment.[79]

Shipments must now be made with the newer TUK-18 containers. Russia has about fifty of these formidable stainless steel units, each weighing forty tons and designed to survive a head-on train collision. The containers have seven compartments, with each compartment designed for five to seven fuel assemblies. Specially designed TK-VG-18 railway cars can each carry three TUK-18 containers, but Russia only has four of these.[80]

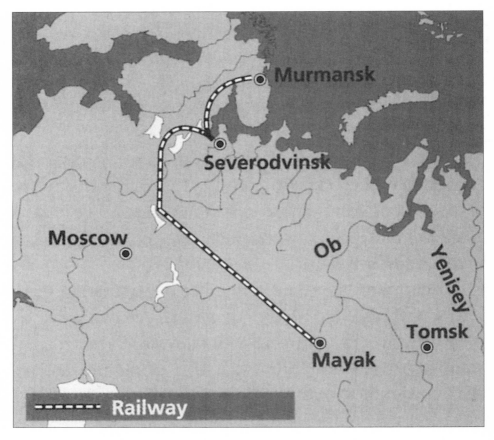

Figure 5. Rail transport route for submarine reactor fuel assemblies from Murmansk and Severodvinsk in Northwest Russia to the RT-1 reprocessing facility at Mayak in the southern Ural Mountains, a distance of approximately 2000 miles (courtesy the Bellona Foundation, from Bellona's *The Russian Northern Fleet*).

The Murmansk Shipping Company began shipping icebreaker spent fuel to Mayak again in 1995 and both the Northern and Pacific Fleets have been able to ship limited amounts of spent fuel since 1997.[81] According to former MINATOM head Viktor Mikhailov, six shipments were made in 1995 and eight in 1996.[82] A trip from the Northwest Russia takes about 30 days while one from the Pacific Coast at least 40 days, meaning that at most the spent fuel from five to six submarines a year can be moved to Mayak with existing equipment.[83]

Reprocessing

Naval spent fuel has been reprocessed at the RT-1 chemical separation plant at the Mayak Chemical Combine (also known as Chelyabinsk-65) in the Ural Mountains since 1976. The plant has three lines of production: one for some types of Soviet-designed commercial reactors; one for naval and other marine reactors; and, a third for research and other highly enriched uranium reactors. Mayak also has facilities for short-term storage of spent fuel, Radwaste storage and treatment facilities, storage facilities for recovered plutonium and uranium, and a number of other support functions.[84] Mayak's other nuclear activities are discussed in more detail in Chapter 4.

The RT-1 plant was designed to reprocess standard uranium-aluminum and uranium-stainless steel naval reactor fuels, but cannot reprocess fuels containing zirconium, damaged fuel assemblies, or fuels from liquid metal reactors. [85] During reprocessing, spent fuel assemblies are chopped into small pieces and then chemically and mechanically dissolved and separated into constituent components. Current Russian reprocessing procedures are reportedly similar to the PUREX process (Plutonium Uranium Recovery by EXtraction process) used in the West.[86] According to a US Department of Energy document, the PUREX process consists of:

> ... dissolution of the irradiated material in nitric acid. An organic solvent is introduced and the uranium and plutonium nitrates transfer into the organic solvent while the fission products remain and are removed in the aqueous phase. The desired materials — plutonium, uranium and sometimes others, notably neptunium — are extracted and concentrated together in an organic solvent and then purified by chemical scrubbing with dilute nitric acid. Two further cycles of solvent extraction and scrubbing each result in separate, concentrate, and purified aqueous solutions of plutonium nitrate and uranium nitrate.[87]

The recovery of enriched uranium and plutonium for recycling into other nuclear requirements has become a controversial issue in the post–Cold War period. There is an oversupply of fissile material available for commercial or other use because of nuclear weapons dismantlement, so the need to reprocess for additional fissile substances is questionable.[88] Keeping the amount to a minimum is desirable to minimize the possibility of proliferation of nuclear bomb-making material. Reprocessing is also a potentially hazardous process that produces large quantities of highly radioactive and poisonous chemical wastes in the form of solutions and sludges; much of the high level Radwaste produced in the world comes from reprocessing. Some chemical components are potentially flammable or explosive, adding to the radiation hazards associated with the waste.[89] The Chelyabinsk region, where Russia's Mayak reprocessing facility is located, has a long and sometimes calamitous nuclear history — discussed in more detail in the next chapter. It is sufficient to note that the region has been labeled "the area of the world most severely afflicted by radioactivity."[90] According to a MINATOM official, safety at Mayak has been compromised by the legacy of Soviet-era emphasis on production rather than safety and by the deteriorated discipline among the plant's operators.[91]

In early 1997, GAN (Russia's Nuclear Regulatory Commission) revoked Mayak's reprocessing license because of problems with high level Radwaste disposal. Maintaining the operating license was based on the condition that the high level Radwaste created by reprocessing could be vitrified for safer storage. An interim Mayak vitrification plant began operation in June 1991 with an estimated three year operational life, but GAN finally revoked Mayak's license two-and-a-half years beyond its limit. Construction of replacement vitrification facilities is stalled for lack of funding.[92] Mayak's current inability to conduct reprocessing operations is a significant bottleneck to proper and accelerated management of Russian submarine spent fuel.

Even if brought back into full production, Mayak would not be the entire answer. It has a capacity of about 1000 fuel assemblies a year (equivalent to perhaps four or five submarine reactors), which is insufficient to move forward quickly to resolve the backlog, and its storage facilities are almost full.[93] Mayak has also been moving away from government reprocessing towards profit-making ventures. It is increasingly influenced by its customer base, including nuclear facilities in other countries of the former Soviet bloc and in Finland — countries with Russian designed reactors in operation and the ability to pay hard cash for services. Mayak prefers to reprocess only a few submarine reactor cores per year because they disrupt its assembly line for other easier and more lucrative reprocessing opportunities. In 1995, the Murmansk Shipping Company finally paid Mayak $4.5 million to reprocess its icebreaker spent fuel.[94] The Russian Navy may be unable or unwilling to follow suit: according to Mayak director Viktor Fetison, as of mid–1996 the Russian Navy owed Mayak $1 billion.[95]

Damaged Fuel and
Fuel from Liquid Metal Reactors

Solving the Russian spent fuel problem will require addressing some special problem areas, including damaged fuel and fuel from liquid metal reactors. The fuel from two submarines in the Northern Fleet (one *Echo* and one *Alfa*) and four in the Pacific Fleet (three *Echos* and one *Victor*), as a minimum, has been damaged by past reactor accidents. Type I submarine nuclear power plants like those on the *Echo* class may have been particularly susceptible to coolant leaks in the reactor system, causing damage to the reactor fuel. The reactors on the icebreaker *Lenin*, which probably resembled Type I submarine designs, may have had similar problems.[96] The fuel assemblies in the submarine reactors listed above are so damaged that they cannot be removed by available means — although Russia is reportedly developing specialized equipment to do so.[97]

Liquid metal reactors are a comparable concern. A *November* class submarine used to test the liquid metal reactor concept was severely damaged when one of its reactors overheated. The first *Alfa* class submarine had numerous mechanical and operational problems and was finally dismantled; its reactor and nuclear spent fuel were covered with inert material and stored at the Zvezdochka Shipyard in Severodvinsk.[98] The liquid metal reactors and their fuel assemblies have been concentrated for storage at Gremikha on the eastern Kola Peninsula, including the damaged reactor from the experimental *November* class and the four *Alfa* submarines that were defueled there. One *Alfa* has its reactor compartment filled with a fixing agent (furfurol) making fuel assembly removal all but impossible; another has its fuel assemblies stuck in the solidified liquid metal coolant of the reactor.[99] According to Bellona, work is in progress to build containers suitable for transport of the spent fuel assemblies from liquid metal cooled reactors.[100]

Reactor Compartments

Submarine reactor compartments remain radioactive even after removal of the spent fuel from the reactor complex because of contamination from corrosion and wear particles left in the reactor system piping and from components made radioactive by the high neutron levels of reactor operations. Cobalt (Co 60) is a major contributor to radioactive contamination levels in reactor systems. It has a half-life of about five years, meaning that 25–50 years after operations the radiation levels should be reduced sufficiently to allow the compartments to be dismantled and the resulting scrap stored as solid waste.[101]

Over the past several years, Russia has been cutting reactor compartments and the adjacent compartments on each side free from the rest of the submarine during dismantlement. The whole structure has then been welded shut and effectively sealed. With a greater percentage of reserve buoyancy than the submarine as a whole, the bizarre complexes are less likely to sink. They are currently moored in nests at Sayda Bay for the Northern Fleet and at the Pavlovsk Naval Base near Vladivostok for the Pacific Fleet.[102] If one of these configurations sink — as feared by Bellona — it could nonetheless contaminate the surrounding Arctic or Pacific waters. Long term land-based storage similar to US storage in the desert of the Hanford Site in Washington would resolve this hazard. Russian officials have considered using tunnels originally designed to conceal nuclear submarines at Ara Bay on the Kola Peninsula for reactor compartment storage, but these could flood and will probably not be used for this purpose.[103] Novaya Zemlya is a possibility as well. With no one permanently living on the island, storage would be more politically acceptable to Russians than a mainland repository and perhaps also to residents of nearby countries.

Chapter 4

Russia's Other
Nuclear Problems

When another Chernobyl occurs, trillions [of rubles] will be needed to clean up the mess from something that will put a "fat cross on humanity."[1]

— Alexander Lebed
Russian Minister of Defense

The Russian submarine spent fuel problem is only one of many nuclear worries in Central and Eastern Europe and the former Soviet Union. Even in Northwest Russia, with its hazardous spent fuel storage facilities and large number of submarine reactors, the operational safety at the Kola Nuclear Power Plant and the Radwaste buildup of the Russian nuclear icebreaker fleet are often greater public concerns. In the West, civilian nuclear power plant safety and weapons-useable nuclear material accountability in the former Soviet bloc command much greater attention than submarine spent fuel. The host of nuclear issues in the region require a coordinated understanding and attention from Russian and international participants to approach each in a cost effective and timely manner.[2]

This chapter highlights several of the non-submarine nuclear hazards in Russia and other parts of the former Soviet bloc. Much more information on these issues is available from the footnoted references and particularly from Don J. Bradley's *Behind the Nuclear Curtain: Radioactive Waste Management in the Former Soviet Union*. Because of this book's focus on international cooperation, where appropriate I emphasize the international initiatives and institutions associated with the various problems noted.

RBMK Nuclear Power Plants

Russian RBMK nuclear power plants are perhaps the greatest concern for policy makers and populations in Western Europe. A total of 17 were built in the Soviet Union of which 14 are still capable of operation. These are the Chernobyl-style nuclear reactors, very large and efficient producers of electrical power, but also burdened with unusual and potentially unsafe operating characteristics and construction design. The reactors themselves are massive, with a cylindrical core about 23 feet tall and 46 feet in diameter, located in a huge gallery containing built-in refueling equipment and water pool storage for spent fuel. Adjacent spaces contain steam turbine and other electrical generation equipment. RBMKs are water-cooled, but unlike most pressurized water reactors rely on graphite moderation. This means that charcoal-like graphite rather than water is used to slow down neutrons and to increase the likelihood that they will be absorbed by U 235 and cause further fissions. The graphite is installed in blocks, leaving room for over 1600 fuel assemblies and for the operating and monitoring equipment necessary to conduct critical operations. During power operations, six circulating pumps of the eight available push water through the reactor to steam generators which in turn direct steam to turbine generators to produce electrical power.[3] RBMK fuel assemblies are made of uranium dioxide ceramic pellets enriched to about 5 percent U 235 and clad with zirconium.[4] They are produced from reprocessed spent fuel from other Russian VVER commercial power plants and submarine reactors and were to be part of a closed reprocessing and fuel production cycle.

Because of graphite moderation and other design decisions, coolant water in an RBMK tends to reduce the ability of the reactor to produce power rather than to increase it as in a conventional pressurized water reactor. The water's capacity to absorb neutrons and hence to rob U 235 atoms of a greater chance to fission has a larger effect than the water's neutron moderation capacity because the neutron moderation or slowing-down in an RBMK is done primarily by graphite. If a power level increase produces sufficient steam in the fuel channels, the neutron absorbing capacity of water could decrease dramatically because of the greater distance between water molecules — causing reactor power to increase even further.[5] This inherent instability of RBMK reactors is apparent particularly while operating at lower power levels and is not found in most water-moderated reactors.

There are other problems associated with the design. According to a 1995 study by the Center for Strategic and International Studies (CSIS), RBMK nuclear power plants have the following additional shortcomings:

1. They lack a containment structure to act as a barrier against large releases of radiation in the event of an accident.

2. They have inadequate reactor protection and control systems.

3. Fire protection systems are inadequate.

4. Emergency operating procedures and operator training programs fall short of acceptable standards.

5. The quality and condition of welds in the pressure tubing are of concern.[6]

A nuclear scientist from the Russian State University of Nizhny–Novgorod noted that: "Even at the time they [the scientists] were drawing the plans for that plant [Chernobyl], they knew it wasn't safe."[7] Concerns about RBMK reactors were multiplied many fold by the events of April 26, 1986 at Chernobyl, the world's worst nuclear reactor accident.

Chernobyl Disaster

Russian nuclear scientists and engineers had been concerned about the effects of a loss of cooling flow on an RBMK reactor. Under the wrong conditions, a loss of flow could cause the reactor to overheat and possibly damage the fuel assemblies. The circulating pumps that force water through an RBMK reactor were driven by the electrical energy provided by the turbine-generators of the nuclear power plant itself and would stop operating if steam were lost to the turbines. Diesel generators would start to provide emergency electrical power for pumps to operate but only after a gap of several seconds — during which core damage might occur. Previous testing had found that the turbines-generators would continue to spin for several minutes after steam was secured, but that electrical power output decreased at a much faster rate. To capture more electric power for a longer period of time and hence to have prolonged circulating pump operation after a loss of steam flow, a magnetic field regulator was installed on one of the turbine generators at the Unit 4 reactor of the Chernobyl Nuclear Power Plant to see if electricity could be extracted from the generator's magnetic flux for a longer period after steam was lost.[8] A plan was developed to test the regulator by securing steam to the turbine generators. Chernobyl was a complex of four RBMK reactors and electrical generating equipment located about 80 miles north of Kiev in the Soviet republic of Ukraine.

Whatever the merits of the test, its planning and conduct were deeply

Figure 6. The author standing on one of the Leningrad Nuclear Power Plant's RBMK-1000 Chernobyl-style reactors, located southwest of St. Petersburg. Note the windows in the background, a vivid reminder of the design's lack of containment structure.

flawed. The emergency cooling system and an emergency shutdown device, among the reactor's primary safety features, were immobilized for the procedure. Over a period of several hours prior to beginning the test, plant operators placed the reactor in a precarious condition by allowing an imbalance in the coolant steam-water mixture to develop and by withdrawing reactor control rods to a point where they could not ensure reactor safety if a power excursion occurred.[9] According to one source, many of the preparations were made by electrical engineers and not by the nuclear engineers or scientists more familiar with the reactor's operating and safety characteristics.

When steam was secured to the turbine generators for the test and circulating pump coolant flow lost, the temperature of the reactor rose rapidly. Because of the unstable conditions that had developed in the reactor, the added heat caused water to change to steam and hence to provide less water absorption for neutrons. This led to a surge of power hundreds of times the rated capacity of the reactor, immediately destroying fuel assemblies and coolant channels throughout the reactor core. Steam also began to react with zirconium to generate more heat and hydrogen; according to some sources, a steam-graphite reaction also occurred that generated hydrogen and carbon monoxide.[10] Because of the added heat additional water in the reactor system flashed to steam and caused an enormous increase in pressure, blasting apart the reactor and sending the 1000 ton reactor shield cover crashing to the side. Another explosion followed as the mixture of graphite and hydrogen came in contact with the atmosphere; according to Viktor Haynes and Marko Bojcum, "the exploding materials broke through the floor, walls and the roof, and shot up into the night sky."[11] The graphite burned fiercely and the winds carried the billowing cloud of contaminated steam and smoke for hundreds of miles and beyond, with significant quantities of radioactivity falling on Poland, Sweden, and Finland — in addition to the Soviet republics of Ukraine and Belarussia.

Heroic efforts were required to put out the flames. Water had no immediate effect because of the flame's intensity so helicopters dropped tons of boron carbide, limestone, lead, clay, and sand on the smoldering ruins. This probably helped to cool the reactor and to keep it sub-critical, and also to trap some of the radioactive material inside the remains of the reactor structure.[12] Two people died immediately from the explosion and another from a presumed heart attack. It took until 2 May to cap over the reactor with dumped material. Because of the possibility of further explosions or a meltdown, authorities waited until 11 May to declare that the immediate action phase of the disaster had passed.[13]

The health and environmental effects of Chernobyl were widespread and long-termed. Reportedly 134 people were diagnosed with "acute radiation syndrome" of whom 28 died within the first 3 months, with several more dying over the next few years. By the end of 1995, approximately 800 cases of thyroid cancer in children under 15 had been diagnosed, primarily

in Ukraine and Belarus.[14] In Ukraine, large tracts of land near the accident remain uninhabitable and unsuitable for farming; in Belarus, fully
one-fifth of the land area was significantly contaminated. Thousands of
people who lived in the affected area were evacuated and still await permanent resettlement. Radioactive material from the accident was
detectable over most of the Northern Hemisphere, although usually at
very low levels.[15] Since the disaster, radioactive contamination levels in the
region have decreased significantly because of the relatively rapid decay of
the main contributing fission products; recovery of the natural environment in some of the most heavily contaminated areas has begun.

Civilian Reactor Safety

Nuclear power generates about 17 percent of the total electric power
production in Russia with 29 or so reactors in operation, compared to 21
percent power production and 110 reactors in the United States. Russian
reactors are located at nine major power stations nationwide with a total
labor force of 40,000.[16] Because of the Chernobyl disaster and the widespread concern it generated about Soviet reactor design and the safety culture of the Soviet nuclear industry, officials and polities in Western Europe
began to focus a great deal of attention on Russian nuclear power plants
and those of similar design in other countries of the former Soviet bloc.
The Leningrad Nuclear Power Station at Sosnovy Bor, for example, has four
RBMK 1000 reactors and is located only a few miles southwest of the
sprawling St. Petersburg metropolis, close to the border with Estonia, and
just across the Gulf of Finland from Helsinki, Finland. Europe is particularly concerned about the operation of the remaining reactors at Chernobyl and the two prototype RBMK reactors in the Tomsk region.[17]
Lithuania, even closer to Western Europe than the Russian and Ukrain-
ian power stations just mentioned, has the dubious privilege of operating
two RBMK 1500s at Ignalina — among the world's largest reactors. Shutting down the Ignalina Nuclear Power Plant reactors would be extremely
difficult for Lithuania because they are a major source of revenue, producing electrical power well in excess of the country's own requirements
and hence available for export.

Subsequent to Chernobyl, Soviet and Russian authorities introduced
a number of programs to improve the safety of RBMK reactors. These
included installing more fixed neutron absorber rods, increasing fuel
enrichment to reduce the problem of power increase with steam formation,

quicker insertion times for control rods, and more containment. Training and safety requirements were increased as well and additional monitoring capabilities established.[18]

RBMK reactors are not alone with their problems, however. Core monitoring systems were inadequate on other Soviet reactor designs as well, making it difficult for operators to receive adequate information on reactor operating status. Emergency cooling water systems were sometimes not separated from the main feedwater system, making it possible for a single failure to remove two cooling capabilities.[19] The Kola Nuclear Power Plant in Northwest Russia has four conventional pressurized water reactors, i.e., not graphite-moderated like the RBMKs, but with a very poor safety reputation. The two older-generation VVER 440/230 reactors are of particular concern.[20] According to the CSIS study:

1. They only have partial containment available and the protection offered is inadequate.

2. No emergency core-cooling system is installed, although the much larger volumes of cooling water provided in the reactor design gives substantial assurance of keeping the reactor core covered.

3. Fire protection systems and plant instrumentation and controls are far below Western standards.

4. Emergency operating procedures and operator training programs are inadequate.

5. Pressure vessel embrittlement must be continually evaluated.[21]

In 1991, the IAEA investigated the Kola Nuclear Power Plant and determined that the chances of a reactor meltdown at the two VVER 440/230 plants was 25 percent over the course of the next 23 years.[22] The two newer VVER 440/213 reactors at the Kola plant still lack containment structures but at least have systems for emergency core cooling. Embrittlement problems (a concern on both 230 and 213-type reactor plants) mean that the reactor vessel containing the core and reactor coolant — a massive steel structure — is subject to hardening with age due to neutron bombardment, with a possibility of catastrophic failure under the wrong conditions.[23] The Kola reactors are located relatively close to the Norwegian border and are consequently a major concern for Norwegian officials, environmental groups, and the population at large. Norway has committed $13.5 million since 1993 to improve reactor safety at the Kola Nuclear Power Plant as part of a Barents Regional Cooperation project.[24]

The West is also concerned about possible shoddy construction methods and the use of poor material in the construction of other Soviet-built reactors. Between 1986 and 1992, there were 118 fires at Russian nuclear power plants.[25] Although the newer VVER-1000 design generally meets international standards, the West would like to see the VVER 440/230 reactors permanently shutdown — in addition to the RBMKs. These designs, however, provide a significant percentage of the generating capacity to the countries of the former Soviet Union. Shutting them down would be particularly difficult because nuclear plants in Russia were often built as "strategic hubs for economic and industrial development" and have become major centers of population and employment.[26] The Kola Nuclear Power Plants, for example, provides 60–70 percent of the electrical production in the Murmansk region and can not be easily decommissioned. Russian officials estimate that running their nuclear power plants requires only one-third of the operating expense of comparably sized fossil-fuel power plants.

The current financial crisis has added to Western concerns about Russian reactor safety. Russia's industry and other electricity consumers often can not or will not pay for their electricity. In the St. Petersburg region, officials of the electrical distribution companies and the local governors do not pay for the electrical power they receive from the Leningrad Nuclear Power Plant at Sosnovy Bor.[27] In Russia, customers owe about $1 billion to the nuclear power plants which in turn owe almost as much to their nuclear fuel suppliers.[28] As a consequence, reactor workers go months without being paid and maintenance and spare parts acquisition might be neglected.[29] There was considerable concern about the year 2000 computer dilemma (Y2K). While civilian reactors in the former Soviet Union were much less dependent on computers than those in the West, there was also very little money and research going on to determine potential hazards if the computers in use responded improperly to the new millennium. According to a former director at the Chernobyl Nuclear Power Plant:

> If you are in an airplane when this happens [Y2K], there is a likelihood that you will crash. If you happen to be in a submarine, you might drown. If you happen to be in a nuclear power plant, we hope that the worst that can happen is that the reactor will simply stop running. But then again, we really don't know what will happen.[30]

Incredible as it may seem, conditions in Russia are better than in Ukraine. Ukraine has its own severe economic and political crises and is suffering a "brain drain" of nuclear workers leaving for Russia, making Ukraine short of nuclear talent.[31] Also unexpected, MINATOM head Viktor Mikhailov's claim in 1997 that the safety record of the Russian civilian nuclear power industry had joined the ranks of Japan and Germany as the world's best — ahead of France, the United Kingdom, Canada, and the United States.[32] This was apparently based upon a comparison of the number of emergency stoppages per generating unit per year as tallied by the World Organization of Nuclear Operators (WANO).

NUSAC, EBRD, PHARE, and TACIS

Because of the perceived clear and present danger from the many Soviet-designed civilian nuclear reactors in operation, the West was quick to begin a program of engagement and assistance once the political barriers of the Cold War were lifted. By 1992, a nuclear safety program under the G-24 [the Organization for Economic Cooperation and Development (OECD) countries, minus Turkey] was put in place to coordinate aid to the countries of Central and Eastern Europe and the former Soviet Union. This was called the G-24 Nuclear Safety Coordination mechanism (G-24 NUSAC). It was conceived as a forum to bring together aid-giving and aid-receiving countries and to coordinate ways to improve the safety of the region's reactors. NUSAC has a small secretariat, hosted DG XI of the European Commission in Brussels, that tracks projects and prepares reports to inform the members and the public at large of its activities.

NUSAC emphasizes the several reactor safety priorities established by the major industrial and economic powers, specifically the G-7 countries. The priorities, listed below, were institutionalized at the 1992 G-7 summit in Munich.

1. Operational safety improvements.
2. Near-term technical improvements to plants based on safety assessments.
3. Enhancing regulatory regimes.
4. Examination of the scope for replacing less safe plants by the development of alternative energy sources and the more efficient use of energy.
5. Examination of the potential for upgrading plants of more recent design.[33]

Under Western programs, the Kola and Leningrad Nuclear Power Plants will eventually be replaced by new generation reactors while the current reactors receive extensive technical and operational assistance to improve their safety as remedial measures.[34] As of October 1998, approximately $1.8 billion had been allocated by G-24 countries to Russia and other countries of the former Warsaw Pact for NUSAC related safety projects. In Russia, funds have also gone into the operating budget of GAN, its nuclear regulatory agency.[35] By accepting NUSAC grants, the aid recipients agreed to maintain essentially Western guidelines to improve their operational reactor safety.

Some NUSAC funding has been coordinated through the Nuclear Safety Account (NSA) of the European Bank for Reconstruction and Development (EBRD). The EBRD was established in 1991 to help the countries of Central and Eastern Europe and the former Soviet Union make the transition to societies based on "democracy, pluralism and a market economy." Areas of emphasis for the EBRD include privatization, reform of the financial sector, development of productive and competitive private sector, and improvement of infrastructure.[36] Russia has been the largest recipient of EBRD funds.

The European Union countries have been the most important contributors to nuclear reactor safety assistance programs in the East through NUCAS, the EBRD, and their own programs under the G-7 recommendations of the Munich summit already discussed and the London summit in 1991.[37] The European Commission–run PHARE program (French for lighthouse or beacon), begun in 1989/90 to help Central and Eastern Europe adjust to the systemic changes taking place in their countries, also has a substantial nuclear safety assistance component. TACIS (Technical Assistance to the Commonwealth of Independent States) provides assistance to most of the former Soviet Union and addresses nuclear safety issues as well. TACIS initiatives are designed to support and speed-up domestic safety enhancement programs in the following areas:

1. Operational safety improvements, mainly through the on-site assistance program at 6 sites in Russia, 3 sites in Ukraine, 1 site in Kazakhstan, and 1 site in Bulgaria.

2. Near-term technical improvement to plants, including design safety studies and equipment deliveries to nuclear power plants.

3. Enhancing regulatory regimes.[38]

The "on-site assistance program" is a particularly important initiative, where European Union member-country utilities assign their own personnel to Russian nuclear power plants.[39] Between 1991 and 1997, over $900 million was allocated to the East for nuclear safety issues as part of the PHARE and TACIS programs.[40]

Additional programs include the International Nuclear Safety Centers founded in 1996 by MINATOM and the US Department of Energy.

Made up of scientists and engineers from East and West, these are funded in association with the Gore-Chernomyrdin Commission to support changes in the nuclear safety culture in Russia and elsewhere. Their purpose has been to carry out independent and collaborative research and development to help improve and ensure the safety of civilian nuclear reactors.[41] The United States has made a number of other commitments to reactor safety in eight countries of the former Soviet bloc, including Russia and Ukraine, originating from its G-7 commitments of 1992. Key programs include operator exchange visits, reactor simulator development, training centers at nuclear power plants, emergency operating instructions, maintenance technology and training, engineering and technology improvements, fuel cycle safety, and the Chernobyl Center for Nuclear Safety, Radioactive Waste and Radioecology.[42]

Chernobyl Sarcophagus

Within weeks of the Chernobyl disaster, work began to encase Unit 4 in a concrete and steel structure to contain the radioactivity and to keep remaining reactor material cool with appropriate ventilation. Now in place for over a decade, the hastily constructed shelter (sometimes called the "sarcophagus") is beginning to fall apart. Western aid to enclose the reactor in a new structure and to remediate other potential dangers at the Chernobyl site are being coordinated through the G-7–sponsored Shelter Implementation Plan (SIP).[43] By September 1998, most of the contracts for the first phase of the program had been awarded by officials of the EBRD who administered the program. The new sarcophagus and supporting work will cost about $700 million and may take nine years to complete.[44] Some of the potential players in the Chernobyl project are also significant to the Russian submarine spent fuel issue, such as the nuclear firms SGN Réseau-Eurisys (SGN) of France and AEA Technology (AEA) of the United Kingdom.

The relationship between international participants and host country has sometimes been stormy. Ukraine has complained that the West has only pledged $300 million for the new sarcophagus.[45] It has threatened to keep other Chernobyl RBMK reactors in operation for longer than planned unless additional assistance is provided. The shelter project at Chernobyl is also absorbing much of Europe's discretionary funding on nuclear issues and could affect international commitment to Russia's submarine spent fuel problem.

Radwaste from Civilian
Nuclear Power Plants

Most of the spent fuel assemblies being generated by civilian power reactors in Russia is stored on site, but the space available is diminishing.[46] Spent fuel from RBMK reactors, for example, is stored in specially designed on-site cooling ponds because Russia does not have the capability to reprocess zirconium-clad fuel. A new facility at Mayak to reprocess RBMK fuel had been planned as part of Russia's closed nuclear fuel cycle, but was canceled because of the fallout from the Chernobyl disaster. For VVER-440 commercial power reactors, spent nuclear fuel was previously stored on-site for a three-year period prior to shipment to Mayak for reprocessing, but is now stored for extended times because of the various difficulties being encountered with shipment and reprocessing.[47] Spent fuel from VVER-1000 reactors can be stored on-site or shipped to a large storage facility at the Krasnoyarsk-26 site in preparation for disposal at a new reprocessing plant, designated RT-2, that was under construction.[48] In late 1998, however, the RT-2 project was canceled, creating an even greater need for permanent spent fuel storage (discussed below). Because of the delays and expenses incurred while waiting for reprocessing or permanent storage, the capacity of some on-site storage facilities has been increased by building new facilities or by modifying existing ones by adding boron components to the storage racks. Boron absorbs neutrons and allows for a higher spent fuel loading density.[49]

Some power stations have facilities for evaporation and solidification of their liquid wastes; solid waste may be compacted or incinerated, but is often stored on-site. There are no vitrification facilities for high level Radwaste available at civilian nuclear power plants, but some make use of deep-well injection (discussed below).[50] Purified liquid waste meeting international standards is usually discharged to the nearest large body of water, such as the Gulf of Finland in the case of the Leningrad Nuclear Power Plant.

Russia's civilian power reactor spent fuel storage problems are not unique. An IAEA and OECD sponsored international symposium on storage of spent fuel from power reactors was held in Vienna in November 1998 to discuss the worldwide implications of Radwaste storage. An important conclusion of the symposium was that the frequency of interim storage was likely to increase as the availability and conduct of reprocessing declines and as permanent geological storage solutions remain elusive. The symposium also emphasized IAEA initiatives related to Central and Eastern Europe and the former Soviet Union, such as:

1. Assisting Central and Eastern European Countries with problems related to the storage of spent fuel and establishing adequate spent fuel storage facilities.

2. Continuing the exchange of information, data and experience (from licensing to operation) on spent fuel storage technologies and public acceptance matters.

3. Organizing peer reviews in the subject of spent fuel storage and management upon request of member states.

4. Continuing discussions on regional spent fuel storage for which countries with small nuclear programs demonstrate interest.[51]

Nuclear Weapons

The greatest Radwaste problem in Russia, and probably the United States as well, concerns the highly radioactive residues remaining from nuclear weapons production processes, particularly the large-scale reprocessing of uranium and plutonium-bearing spent fuel. Mayak, Tomsk-7, and Krasnoyarsk-26 were all plutonium production centers during the Cold War and had a total of 13 plutonium production reactors in use at the height of the conflict. These were fueled with natural uranium but spiked with highly enriched uranium to help sustain the fission process. The reactors shared some design characteristics with the RBMK reactors, including the lack of a containment structure.[52] A few of the reactors were dual purpose, designed to produce plutonium while also generating electric power for the communities that supported the nuclear weapons production. While some of the Radwaste was discharged directly to the environment, much of the high level Radwaste is still stored in tanks awaiting vitrification or other disposal.[53]

Mayak

The Mayak Chemical Combine (Ozersk) was brought into operation in 1949 to produce plutonium and later tritium for nuclear weapons. It was a complete nuclear materials production site, with five graphite reactors for plutonium production and two pressurized water reactors (one using heavy water) for the production of tritium and other isotopes, plus reprocessing and waste management facilities. In the course of the nuclear arms reduction process, the production of military plutonium was gradually halted and the plutonium production reactors shutdown over the period of 1987–1992.[54] The RT-1 reprocessing plant started operation in 1976 and was designed to reprocess spent fuel from VVER-440 and BN-600 fast neutron power reactors, marine propulsion reactors (Soviet Navy surface ships and submarines, plus civilian icebreakers), and research reactors. Over the years, the Soviet Union and Russian have tried to integrate the fuel cycles of their various nuclear operations as much as possible, including plutonium production, research, naval, and civilian power reactors, so that the spent fuel from one type could be reprocessed and converted into fresh fuel for another type of reactor.[55] Technical and economic problems in recent years have kept Russia from fulfilling this ambition to the extent originally planned. The closed cycle goal is an almost ideological belief within the Russian nuclear establishment, as is the desire to use spent fuel assemblies as sources of plutonium for the production of fresh reactor fuel — instead of disposing it as Radwaste.

According to one estimate, each ton of reprocessed spent fuel generates some 600,000 curies of waste, and Mayak can reprocess about 250 tons of spent fuel each year.[56] Spent fuel reprocessing accounts for over 95 percent of all radioactive waste released to the environment in the former Soviet Union.[57] Hundreds of millions of curies of liquid Radwaste are still stored in stainless steel tanks underground at Mayak, with some producing substantial heat and gas residues.[58]

Mayak is in the Chelyabinsk region, home to 1.5 million people. The operation of Mayak and the several incidents and decades of problems with its nuclear waste have resulted in potential hazards to its more than 450,000 residents and in contamination of the lakes, forest, and agricultural lands of the region.[59] Two major radiological disasters have occurred in Chelyabinsk. In 1957, a container of highly radioactive liquid chemical waste exploded and sent a cloud of dangerous substance over an area about 60 miles long and 5 miles wide. The "Kyshtym Disaster" forced over 10,000 people to evacuate and released about 2 million of the 20 million curies stored in the tank. Some of the liquid Radwaste had apparently evaporated allowing highly explosive nitrate salts and acetate to collect on the surface where a spark detonated the mixture.[60] Part of the contaminated territory has subsequently been converted into a nature reserve that studies the effect of radiation on fish, wildlife and vegetation, giving birth to the Russian term "radioecology." A second disaster occurred when Lake Karachai, an open radioactive dump site, dried up during the spring or summer of 1967. Some of the radioactive material that had settled on the lake-bed was exposed to the atmosphere and became airborne, spreading to the surrounding region and affecting over 60 towns and 40,000 residents.[61] Portions of the radionuclide contamination from Mayak's operation and from the 1957 and 1967 accidents have entered tributaries of the Ob River system and reached the Arctic Ocean.

Through past errors and deliberate choice, at least 130 million curies have escaped to the environment in Chelyabinsk — according to Russian sources. Another disaster could be developing. According to Federal Committee for Nuclear and Radiation Safety (GAN) Chair Yuri Vishnevsky, 100 meters under Lake Karachai a "lens of radioactive liquid salts" has formed. It is about 5 million cubic meters in volume and contains waste of medium level radioactive activity. The lens is moving toward the region's watershed and the Techa River 1.5 to 2 kilometers away at about 80 meters a year. According to Vishnevshky, this could pollute the watershed, Western Siberia, and the Arctic Ocean.[62]

Mayak is trying to become a viable economic enterprise through the production of radioisotopes and several arms reduction related projects, such as mixed oxide fuel (MOX — enriched uranium and plutonium) manufacture and a storage facility for plutonium removed from nuclear weapons.[63] A crucial need is completion of vitrification facilities to reduce the quantity of stored high-level Radwaste and to allow the re-start of reprocessing at the RT-1 facility.

Tomsk-7 and Krasnoyarsk-26

Tomsk-7 (Seversk) began to produce plutonium from production reactors and to reprocess spent fuel in about 1955. It is the site of the Siberian Atomic Power Station, a chemical separation plant, facilities for plutonium processing and blending and nuclear weapon pit fabrication, plutonium storage, uranium enrichment, and nuclear waste management.[64] The Siberian Power Station has five graphite-moderated plutonium production reactors, some of which can be used for civilian power production. A number of accidents have occurred over the years, the worst occurring in 1993 when a tank containing heavy metals and a variety of chemicals exploded — collapsing part of the building around it and causing a fire.[65] Radioactive material contaminated about 48 square miles but with relatively small amounts of radioactivity.[66] Several sites at Tomsk-7 were used as open reservoir dumps for Radwaste. Discharges and accidental releases of radionuclides from Tomsk-7 can enter the Tom River tributary system and eventually reach the Ob River and the Arctic Ocean.

Krasnoyarsk-26 (Zheleznogorsk) has three plutonium production reactors, a reprocessing plant to recover plutonium, the partially completed RT-2 reprocessing plant, and various other support facilities. In 1998, MINATOM decided not to complete the RT-2 facility but to add a new head-end to the RT-1 plant in Mayak to reprocess VVER-1000 fuel. Significant amounts of VVER-1000 fuel continue to be stored at Krasnoyarsk, however.[67] A number of other defense and nuclear enterprises are located in the region, including a uranium enrichment plant.[68] Krasnoyarsk-26 is unique because most of its operations are located in a vast complex at the end of a three-mile long tunnel underneath a mountain, designed for protection against a nuclear attack by the United States. One of the plutonium production reactors remains in use to provide electricity and heat to the facilities and supporting community.[69] Like Mayak and Tomsk-7, Krasnoyarsk has used open reservoir storage. Some of its facilities and operations have contaminated portions of the powerful Yenisey River that flows north to the Arctic Ocean.[70]

With the end of the Cold War, both Tomsk-7 and Krasnoyarsk-26, as well as other weapons production facilities, suffered greatly from a lack of mission and a shortage of government funding. According to a featured article in the *New York Times*, "these days it [Krasnoyarsk-26] is an impoverished ward of the state, and a vexing worry for Russian and American officials who fear that Russia's best scientists will leave for aspiring nuclear powers like Iran and Iraq."[71] Although not nearly the radiological disaster area of Mayak, Tomsk-7 and Krasnoyarsk-26 have significant Radwaste problems. Both have also made extensive use of the troubling practice of deep-well injection of high level Radwaste.

Deep-well Injection

In the late 1960s, the Soviet Union began the large-scale use of deep-well injection as a means for Radwaste disposal. Liquid Radwaste of various contamination levels was pumped under pressure into layers of permeable rock. Surrounding the permeable rock were layers of low permeable material like clays that make any movement of Radwaste to other permeable layers unlikely.[72] A total of three injection wells remain in use, one each at Tomsk-7, Krasnoyarsk-26, and Dimitrovgrad (a nuclear research center pursuing a number of projects, such as fast neutron and MOX technology).[73] Deep-well injection of Radwaste was considered by the US Oak Ridge National Laboratory, but was never implemented by the Department of Energy. At Krasnoyarsk and Tomsk, the process "has been going on at a scale far beyond anything DOE ever imagined," with about 1.5 billion curies injected to this point.[74]

A recent evaluation of the radiological consequences of deep-well injection at Dimitrovgrad by the British firm AEA concluded that the practice was acceptably safe.[75] It remains controversial, however, because of the extremely large amounts of radioactivity involved, the remaining uncertainty about its long-term effects, and because there is little remedial action that can be taken should it prove hazardous. Residents of Tomsk seven have expressed concern about the safety of their water supplies and even about the possibility of a nuclear criticality from the fissile material contained in the injected Radwaste.[76] At Krasnoyarsk, Alexander Bolsunovsky of the Institute of Biophysics worries that the Radwaste might move through layers of coal and contaminate the environment.[77] Despite the concerns and uncertainties, Russia seems committed to this relatively inexpensive means of Radwaste disposal. Alternative procedures and technologies like vitrification are expensive or have their own environmental drawbacks, such as the surface storage of Radwaste in tanks and reservoirs.

Nuclear Weapons Material

The Soviet Union manufactured about 55,000 nuclear weapons between 1949 and 1992, deploying tactical weapons throughout its 15 republics and strategic warheads to Belarus, Kazakhstan, Russia, and Ukraine.[78] With the end of the Cold War, the implementation of comprehensive arms control agreements, the fragmentation of the former Union, and the precipitant financial and organizational crises, control of these weapons became a priority concern for both Russian and Western policy-makers. After a difficult negotiation and implementation period, the non–Russian republics of the former Soviet Union have transferred all of the nuclear weapons on their territory to Russia as the sole custodian. Russia however does not have in place adequate facilities and security to store the nuclear weapons and weapon-useable material resulting for disassembly. The continued economic crisis has created funding shortfalls at Russian nuclear weapons research institutes, production plants, and storage facilities.[79] The "loose nucs" problem is another clear and present danger for the West, this time over the possibility of the proliferation of weapons of mass destruction from the former Soviet Union to countries or groups considered dangerous by the West.

Concern turned into real program development and to the creation of a major US collaborative effort with Russia, the Nunn-Lugar Program — known also as the Cooperative Threat Reduction (CTR) initiative. CTR was designed to facilitate "the transportation, storage, safeguarding, and destruction of nuclear and other weapons in the Soviet Union" and (after later amendments) to promote environmental restoration at military sites and to house former military personnel.[80] It has commitments to help eliminate strategic weapons, establishing better fissile material controls, and other projects in Russia, Belarus, Kazakhstan, and Ukraine. CTR and appropriate Russian agencies are co-financing the construction of a $250 million facility to store fissile material from dismantled nuclear weapons at Mayak. When the first wing is competed in 2002, it will hold the fissile material from 6250 nuclear weapons.[81] CTR projects related to the Russian submarine spent fuel issue are discussed in Chapter 6.

Associated with CTR is the "Materials Protection, Control, and Accounting (MPC&A) program developed by the US Department of Energy and MINATOM. Over $300 million has been committed to help prevent the theft or diversion of nuclear material.[82] With France and Germany, the United States is also exploring the possible construction of a mixed plutonium-uranium (MOX) nuclear plant at Mayak to convert weapons-grade plutonium into fuel for civilian power plant use. "The idea behind the plant is to make sure that weapons-grade plutonium does not fall into the hands of rogue states," said an official from the American Embassy in Moscow.[83] In addition, both sides agreed in principle at a US–Russia summit in September 1998 to convert 50 tons apiece of plutonium recovered from dismantled nuclear warheads into material unusable for weapons. This is about half of the declared US plutonium stocks; Russian stock are estimated at about 160 tons.[84] The United States is also poised to begin the transfer of weapons-grade plutonium from locations in Kazakhstan that are close to Iran and other volatile regions of the former Soviet Union to a more secure site in eastern Kazakhstan. The more than 6,000 pounds of high-grade plutonium produced in a breeder reactor will be moved 1,500 miles at a cost of tens of millions of dollars. The project will take several years to complete.[85]

Nuclear Icebreakers

With its long Arctic coastline, Russia has a vital need for icebreakers to ensure access to remote settlements and to keep commercial and military ships in operation during the long months of the Arctic winter. Nuclear power is a logical propulsion for ships that conduct months-long deployments and that run the risk of becoming trapped in pack ice until the spring thaw. The *Lenin* was the Soviet Union's first icebreaker and used two pressurized water reactors for propulsion and a third for maintenance and research purposes. In 1966 *Lenin* suffered a major accident in one of its nuclear reactors, killing up to 30 crew members, damaging much of its nuclear fuel, and keeping the ship out of service for several years.[86] *Lenin* was returned to duty with a two reactor design in 1975 but ultimately retired in 1989. The defueled ship remains tied to a pier in Murmansk.[87]

Russia's eight nuclear-powered icebreakers of the *Arktika* and *Taimyr* classes are homeported and maintained at the RTE-Atomflot base on the northern outskirts of Murmansk. The *Sevmorput*, a nuclear powered containership with some icebreaking capability, is based at the same facility. *Sevmorput* and the two *Taimyr* class icebreakers (intended for river duty) each have one KLT-40 reactor, while the six ocean-going *Arktika* class ships have two reactors. [88] All of these vessels are owned by the Russian Ministry of Transport and operated by the Murmansk Shipping Company, a quasi-private corporation. RTE-Atomflot has shore facilities for storage and treatment of solid and liquid Radwaste and several service ships for spent fuel and other Radwaste storage. The location of the base in Murmansk prompted a visiting correspondent to report: "In no other city in the world where the authorities care, if only a little, about the health of their citizens can one see a nuclear icebreaker being repaired in the dock practically next to the city center."[89]

Because the icebreaker operation has access to funding other than the Russian government, its financial and operational conditions do not seem quite as desperate as those of the Russian Navy. Nonetheless, the icebreaker fleet has generated substantial spent fuel and other Radwaste problems that it can not easily resolve. "We don't have the technology to solve the problem," said Andrei Zolotkov, chief engineer at Atomflot. "We just put the [waste] in containers and fill them up and fill them up some more. There is no storage site where all of this can be sent forever. As long as we don't have this, there will be a problem."[90]

Lepse

The *Lepse* may be the single greatest radiological hazard in Northwest Russia. Located at the RTE-Atomflot base in Murmansk, *Lepse* is a service ship used to store spent nuclear fuel — primarily from nuclear icebreakers. It was build in 1936 as a salvage vessel but converted to an icebreaker service ship in 1962. *Lepse* is about 270 ft long with a displacement of 5,000 tons. It contains two sections for storing spent fuel, with separate cells available for each fuel assembly and provisions for water cooling in each section. One of the sections contains the damaged fuel assemblies from the reactor accident on the icebreaker *Lenin*.[91] The great hazards of damaged spent fuel were compounded when workers tried to force the deformed and swollen fuel assemblies into protective containers using sledgehammers, shattering fuel assemblies and scattering radioactive fragments throughout the ship. Concrete was poured over the fuel assemblies to contain the contamination as much as possible, making the ship top-heavy as a consequence. If *Lepse* were moved, it could conceivably capsize from the instability.[92]

Lepse is in a poor state of repair and is no longer in active use to support the icebreakers. According to one report: "Because there is no access any longer to the holds of the barge, all maintenance has been carried out on the exterior of the vessel. So they have been adding layers of paint to the outside of the hull, but have done nothing about the inside. As a result, the vessel is rotting from the inside out."[93] Yet it still contains 634 fuel assemblies, a great many of which are damaged. There are an estimated 750,000 curies of radioactivity onboard the *Lepse*—located close to the 470,000 residents of Murmansk; if the ship should sink, a significant release of nuclear contamination to the surrounding water could occur.[94]

The hazards of *Lepse* were pointed our as early as 1992 by the Bellona Foundation. The organization has continued to press for Russian and international action to alleviate the threat. US Ambassador to Norway Thomas Loftus toured the ship in 1997 and called it "an environmental disaster waiting to happen." After his visit, a Russian icebreaker captain joked that Loftus would never again need to change the batteries in his watch![95]

Sunken Reactors and Submarines

In 1993, Russia released the document "Facts and Problems Related to Radioactive Waste Disposal in Seas Adjacent to the Territory of the Russian Federation," commonly called the "Yablokov Report," that documented Soviet/Russian nuclear waste dumping in the Arctic Ocean since 1959. It confirmed that several marine nuclear reactors had indeed been dumped into the Arctic Ocean: from icebreakers, six reactors with fuel installed; from submarines, four reactor compartments containing seven reactors (six with damaged spent fuel), two reactor compartments with four reactors with no fuel, plus two reactors without fuel.[96] All had suffered some form of reactor accident during operation. Most are located in the shallow fjords of the Kara Sea east of the island of Novaya Zemlya. Large quantities of other solid and liquid Radwaste had also been dumped in the Arctic by the Soviet Union and Russia. Another reactor is located in the Arctic Ocean (the Norwegian Sea) between Norway and Bear Island as a result of the sinking of the Soviet *Mike* class submarine *Komsomolets*. *Kom-*

somolets went down on 7 April 1989, taking nuclear weapons to the bottom as well as its nuclear reactor. Tragically, 42 crew members were lost in the accident.

The revelations about reactor dumping had much to do with the flurry of international interest about Russian nuclear contamination of the Arctic that developed in the early 1990s, leading directly to many of the initiatives and reports cited in this book. Subsequent investigations, such as a joint Russian-Norwegian 1992–94 survey and other studies cited in Chapter 6, revealed that the reactor dumping has had little effect on the general radioactivity level of the Arctic Ocean — although radioactivity could filter into the ocean over the longer term as the protective material around the reactors corrodes away.[97] Recent analysis by NNC Limited (NNC) of the United Kingdom reaffirmed that there was little environmental danger posed by the dumped reactors and considered remedial action unnecessary.[98] In the opinion of some analysts, the Soviets/Russians did a reasonable job of preparing the reactors for dumping: the reactor compartments were cut out of the submarines and closed at both ends; in the case of the reactor compartments still containing spent fuel, the compartments were filled with steel, cement and polyester to prevent radioactivity seeping out into the marine environment. According to Russian sources, this protection should last up to 500 years.[99] Fission products like Cs 137 and Sr 90 are probably the main constituents of radioactivity contained in the dumped spent fuel; over the longer term, actinides like Pu 239 and Am 241 will become significant.

In addition to the danger of radioactive material release due to corrosion, there has been concern about the possibility of the dumped reactors going critical or super-critical in their watery environment. According to a number of sources, the risk of re-criticality appears negligible since much of the fuel was damaged in the first place, making the geometry no longer optimal for reactor operation. In addition, some of the nuclear fuel was presumably removed before dumping. Re-criticality may be more likely in the case of the two dumped liquid metal cooled reactors which could be affected more dramatically by the entry of water into the reactor.[100] If criticality is attained, the reaction is likely to proceed slowly and at extremely low power levels. A severe power excursions seems unlikely unless the complexes are subjected to a sudden and large increase in reactivity, conceivable if attempts are made to recover the reactors and to expose them to vibrations or other mechanical actions.[101]

Chapter 5

Russian Actors and the Defueling Chain

The Soviet state left behind only administrative and economic rubble, devoid of the judicial accounting and police procedures necessary for a modern society.[1]

— Martin Malia
University of California, Berkeley

Since the re-emergence of Russia at the end of 1991, restructuring Soviet-era institutions to conform with the country's changed economic and political realities has taken much of the new leadership's time and energy. Organizational lines of authority and communications that were once relatively unfettered are now muddled or broken. The loss of territory from the dissolution of the Soviet Union, where an integrated military industrial system had factories and service facilities throughout the 15 republics, has been costly and difficult to resolve. Russian ministries and other government entities are reorganized often, creating additional uncertainty and confusion. Many functions have become subject to market pressures as Russian agencies now bill each other for their work. This also puts the government at a disadvantage when competing with private enterprises for facilities and services. The poorly funded Russian Navy has had little capability or incentive to move forward with a significant program of submarine defueling and dismantlement.

The Russian submarine spent fuel problem is also hindered by the sheer number of governmental entities involved. These include the Navy, MINATOM, various industrial and regulatory groupings, plus multiple regional and local political administrations. Although communication takes place among these organizations, it does so under the shadow of a competition for scarce resources and productive employment.[2] Interagency cooperation was not a natural outgrowth of the centralized Soviet system, so environmental issues and policy have become just another battleground in a continued struggle for influence. Some also believe that close advisors of President Yeltsin, such as former First Deputy Prime Minister Anatoly B. Chubais, have been unsympathetic to allocating scarce resources for environmental projects. Russian environmental groups have become players as well and are certainly a positive development for the country, but also a possible impediment to problem-solving in the short term. Former Minister of Atomic Energy Viktor Mikhailov complained about the stridency of domestic opposition to the Russian nuclear industry, comparing environmental extremists to centuries-old religious inquisitions.[3]

Russian Navy

Navies throughout the world are conservative organizations held together by methods and hierarchies that are slow to evolve. The routine and dangers of naval service have changed over the years, but sailors and officers at sea still have much in common with their forebears of long ago. With a monopoly on internal information and a high degree of autonomy, the Russian Navy seems especially hidebound and slow to open itself to scrutiny — perhaps reflecting too closely its Soviet predecessor.

The Navy is particularly sensitive about its nuclear operations. Dr. Elizabeth J. Kirk of the American Association for the Advancement of Science (AAAS) noted that the science and technological cooperation characteristic of the post–Cold War period is much more intrusive than the arms control regimes that preceded it. To help with Russia's Radwaste cleanup effort in Northwest Russia, Western governments and companies want access to design data and on-site conditions and also want to track how their money is being spent. The Russian Navy is unwilling to divulge too much information, both for security reasons and perhaps because it is unwilling to expose itself to criticism for past and present practices. None of the world's nuclear naval forces, of course, are particularly forthcoming with sensitive information nor should we expect them to be.

The Russian Navy's xenophobia is not confined to international actors. According to Georgi Kostev, severe nuclear accidents during the Soviet-era were covered up for fear of punishment by higher authorities.[4] The Bellona Foundation documents several major accidents in its 1996 publication on the Russian Northern Fleet, including a primary leak on a *Hotel* class in 1961, an uncontrolled criticality on a *Yankee* in 1968, and the explosion on the *Echo II* at Chazhma Bay discussed in Chapter 3.[5] The Russian Navy also resists regulation and monitoring by other Russian governmental actors. In 1994, President Yeltsin declared that GAN should control radiation safety for all nuclear facilities — including those of the military. The Navy strongly resisted, denying access to inspectors and lobbying against the decree so effectively that Yeltsin was forced to cancel its implementation.[6] Since 1995, GAN has shared monitoring functions with the Ministry of Defense's own nuclear regulatory authority.

The Russian Navy produces 70–75 percent of the Radwaste in Northern and Far-East Russia.[7] Until very recently, it had sole responsibility for the storage of fresh fuel, refueling and defueling operations, interim storage of spent fuel, and for loading fuel into shipping casks for transport to Mayak.[8] The Navy controlled defueling operations up to the point that fuel assemblies were removed from the submarines and placed on railway cars — with MINATOM taking control after that point. Within the Navy, the Department of Radiation Safety controls the operations and maintenance of nuclear submarine reactors and the Radwaste they produce.[9] Its Murmansk-based Technical Department has day-to-day responsibility for Radwaste storage and for the security of the nuclear submarines on the Kola Peninsula, whether in service or inactive. The Navy also operates some of the shipyards in Northwest Russia that service and maintain nuclear submarines, such as Sevmorput and Shkval, while other shipyards are run by civilian ministries.[10] The Flag Officer of the Naval Staff Mechanical Engineering Service is responsible for quality assurance and carries out periodical inspections on the status of nuclear submarines in lay-up status.[11]

The Russian Navy has been literally overwhelmed by the buildup of out-of-service submarines and has adopted a caretaker perspective. With its much reduced budget, it would much prefer to concentrate on operations and on maintaining front-line units rather than to fund the disposal of old ones. It also wants new equipment and continues to push for construction of *Akula* attack submarines and the first units of the *Severodvinsk* and *Borey* classes.[12] Proposals have surfaced in the past to move the funding for defueling and Radwaste management out of the Navy's general funding budget. This change may be effectively implemented with a shift in authority over decommissioned nuclear submarines from the Navy to MINATOM.

MINATOM

The Ministry of Atomic Energy (MINATOM) is by far the most important Russian state authority dealing with nuclear issues. It was formed in 1992 out of the Soviet-era Ministry of Atomic Power Engineering and Industry (MAPI), itself the merger of the Ministry of Medium Machine Building with the Ministry of Nuclear Power.[13] MINATOM has remained reasonably coherent and stable during the post–Cold War period and perhaps favors its Soviet heritage more than most new Russian government entities. It is a giant and powerful organization, employing more than 1 million people directly and having connections with a host of allied research, operations, and production enterprises that may keep a total of 3 million workers employed. It also maintains good relationships with the nuclear ministries of some of the other countries of the former Soviet Union which were also parts of the former Medium Machine Building Ministry.[14] According to the *OTA Report*, MINATOM is somewhat analogous to the US Department of Energy and the US commercial nuclear industry rolled into one.[15]

MINATOM's activities can be broken into five complexes: nuclear arms; nuclear fuel; fundamental and applied science; machine and instrument building; and, construction and installation work.[16] It is involved in performing research and development on reactors and fuels, civilian nuclear power plant operation, nuclear weapons production, managing reprocessing facilities, and storing and transporting nuclear materials throughout Russia. It is also working with GAN to develop a regulatory framework for fuel management.[17] In nuclear submarine issues, MINATOM has responsibility for producing naval nuclear fuel, shipping spent fuel casks and transporting them to Mayak, and for spent fuel reprocessing and storage. In the post–Cold War period, MINATOM has given considerable attention to diversifying its domestic assets.[18] It has directed some of its research efforts toward microelectronics, fiber optics, and supercomputers and has used its technology for the mining and processing of diamonds and other precious minerals. Military programs now occupy only 10 percent its activities, down from 30 percent a decade ago, but any profits from civilian production has lagged well behind the government budget cuts for military products and services.

Despite the hard times, MINATOM is somewhat unique among Russian government organizations because it can finance part of its activities from export earnings.[19] In 1997, MINATOM received only 48 percent of its budget from the government but made $2.2 billion from its export activity. Its business has grown because of an increase in nuclear fuel deliveries, services for fuel enrichment, and sales of equipment.[20] All of this makes it a more independent agency than most other Russian government entities. It is precisely these export activities that have created the difficult relationship MINATOM has with the West and particularly the United States. MINATOM is an aggressive exporter of Russian nuclear technology, with important relationships with Central and Eastern Europe, the countries of the former Soviet Union, plus Iran, India, and China. Particularly under the leadership of Viktor Mikhailov, MINATOM energetically pursued its own interests and did not bend appreciably to assuage US preferences and sensitivities. This is particularly true with regard to MINATOM and other Russian involvement in the Bushehr nuclear complex in Iran, an $800 million contract for Russia to complete the several reactor commercial power station. United States officials are adamant that the project will assist in creating a nuclear infrastructure in Iran and hence contribute to the country's development of nuclear weapons.

With the accession of Yevgeny Adamov as Minister of Atomic Energy in March 1998, the atmospherics may have changed for the better but the basic Mikhailov policies seem still to be in place. A nuclear engineer and scientist turned administrator, Adamov is also known as a tough negotiator and hard liner for Russian interests — including exports and the RBMK reactors he helped design.[21] MINATOM would certainly like to see its international business grow and is investing in improvements to its reprocessing cycle in hopes of selling such services to the rest of the world. With the accession of the Green Party as part of the coalition government in Germany in 1998, among other reasons, MINATOM officials believe they have a good chance of capturing some of the Western European market for commercial reactor spent fuel services. Russian law must be changed to do so, however, because the import of Radwaste — a term that includes spent fuel — is not currently allowed. MINATOM would also like to take back the highly-enriched uranium it sold to other countries for research reactors in years past, for a fee of course.[22] The United States has recently been doing much the same thing.

For all of its influence, MINATOM has had little authority over submarine nuclear matters on the waterfront because the Russian Navy has been unwilling to compromise control over its assets. In 1998 Adamov described as inappropriate "the current situation where experts of the Atomic Energy Ministry cooperate with shipbuilders and the navy at the phase of building of nuclear-propelled ships and are excluded from decommissioning and disposal."[23] This is in the process of being changed. On 28 May 1998, President Yeltsin signed a decree that will transfer the functions of "general contractor" in the decommissioning of nuclear submarines from the Russian Navy to MINATOM. Procedures are apparently being developed to transfer decommissioned submarines, shore and floating storage locations of spent fuel, and other Navy Radwaste to MINATOM. On 1 January 1999, MINATOM began the process of taking over facilities such as the spent fuel storage sites at Andreeva Bay. During the next two years, decommissioned submarines are to be transferred to MINATOM in batches so that by the end of 2001 all will be under MINATOM control. The Sevmash shipyard at Severodvinsk (the State Nuclear Vessel Building Center) will act as MINATOM's principle agent and will have effective control of the submarines.[24] Civilian companies are constructing various facilities for defueling and dismantling operations and MINATOM is creating a "specialized civil industrial enterprise" to manage the decommissioning and waste disposal process.[25] Integral to this will be coastal storage complexes on the Arctic and Pacific coasts with storage pads to hold spent fuel assemblies in metal-concrete containers until they can be reprocessed at Mayak. Chapter 6 provides further information concerning the metal-concrete/storage pad system of spent fuel management, one of the important links in the developing defueling chain. MINATOM has indicated that it wants to defuel the reactors quickly and to place the spent fuel in interim storage, and then move toward dismantlement of the submarines.[26]

MINATOM has promised to spend $250 million by 2005 to solve the most immediate problems of decommissioning.[27] With MINATOM's clout in government and its independent earning potential, improvement to the currently bleak submarine spent fuel situation seems likely. In the final analysis, the Russian Navy must be pleased to give up a thankless task for which it is ill-equipped and under-funded.

GAN

A developing player in Russian nuclear waste issues is the Federal Department of Nuclear and Radiation Safety (formerly Gosatomnadzor or GAN, a name still widely used). GAN was established in 1991 from a predecessor Soviet organization as a supervisory authority to regulate the safety of nuclear energy by licensing procedures. It has licensing competence over "production and/or application of nuclear materials, nuclear energy, radioactive substances and products," and Radwaste.[28] It is also charged with developing nuclear and radiation safety rules and standards, supervising nuclear safeguards, inspection of nuclear installations, and coordinating and supporting safety-related research.[29] GAN has grown to an organization of about 1500 people, divided into a central headquarters and seven districts; it has an inspection presence at all major Russian nuclear enterprises and complexes.[30]

According to its current leadership, GAN deals with virtually all questions relating to the use of nuclear energy except for nuclear weapons.[31] The organization reports directly to the Russian president and is roughly equivalent of the US Nuclear Regulatory Commission (NRC) and similar regulatory bodies in other Western countries. It has had some notable successes: GAN closed down the Murmansk RADON Radwaste storage facility because of poor facilities maintenance and practices; it also halted reprocessing operations at Mayak in March 1997 because the license of the vitrification facility had expired. On the other hand, Russian legislation and decrees on the management and regulations for Radwaste are complex, underspecified, and often go unfulfilled. The confusion of authority between the various government ministries and between the government bureaucracy and the *Duma*, plus the controversial nature of nuclear issues themselves has hindered GAN activities.[32] Funding constraints are also a problem and, according to GAN Chairman Yuri Vishnevsky, have hampered the development of new legislative and regulatory documents and restricted the travel of GAN inspectors.[33]

GAN's involvement with submarine nuclear fuel management includes interactions with transport agencies, reactor fuel cycle facility, radiation safety, and material control and accounting.[34] As discussed earlier, since 1995 GAN does not have responsibility for facilities involved with nuclear weapons and has never had much input into the nuclear activities of the Russian Navy. According to GAN's chief, "We simply do not know what's going on there."[35] Efforts to strengthen the role of GAN, including new laws and regulations, will take time to change the nuclear safety culture of Russia in a significant and positive way. Exactly how GAN will engage with the Russian submarine spent fuel problem once MINATOM takes charge has probably not yet been fully worked out.

Environmental Protection

The environmental protection and enforcement regime within Russia is embryonic. Articles in the Russian constitution speak to the rights of citizens for a "favorable environment, to reliable information about its conditions, and to compensation for any loss caused by ecological damage to his health and property."[36] The State Committee on Environmental Protection is the primary agency enforcing environmental laws. It is, however, the result of a downgrading of the Ministry of Environmental Protection and Natural Resources (itself established in 1988 under *perestroika*), with Natural Resources now spun-off as a separate entity. Hence environmental issues may be given even less of a hearing in government decision-making processes than they were only a couple of years ago. Federal environmental agencies have little enforcement authority on nuclear safety issues and little funding to carry out any programs approved. Regional authorities on the environment are evolving but have yet to exert much influence.

Basic concepts such as property rights and a stable judicial system must develop further in Russia; as a consequence environmental decisions are difficult to enforce.[37] Another problem is that the environmental data that does exist in Russia may not be reliable, yet little money is available for more research. Russia has been trying to streamline its approval procedures for Radwaste projects, but the interjection of environmental concerns — however desirable — has added to the processing bureaucracy. No nuclear waste facility can now be built unless it is part of a federal plan and all such projects must go through a detailed environmental evaluation.

Defense Industry

The military industrial complex of the Soviet Union was enormous. Weapons and other military equipment were produced under the authority of several powerful industrial ministries that employed millions of citizens, supporting in turn a major percentage of the Soviet economy. Excessive spending on defense was certainly one of the reasons the Soviet Union collapsed; too great a percentage of GDP was concentrated in uncompetitive military production and too little on other aspects of modern economic life, like consumer products and civilian research projects.[38]

Since the end of the Cold War, the defense industry has suffered gravely from the predicaments left over from the Soviet system of government and reflects the difficulties encountered by Russia as a whole. The loss of territory from Soviet dissolution meant that the previously integrated defense production system had to be revamped. For example, Ukraine manufactured Soviet strategic missiles and maintained the large shore-based infrastructure used by the Soviet Black Sea Fleet. These are no longer available to Russia. Kazakhstan contained a multitude of Soviet defense installations and also the Baikonur space launch facility, still used by Russia but with appropriate deference to the host government.[39] In Latvia the immense Skrunda radar site was a key part of the Soviet early warning and air defense system, but continued Russian use was a source of continuing antagonism between the two countries. This was settled for good in August 1998 by the Russian withdrawal, but replacing major facilities such as Skrunda will be expensive and time consuming.

The Russian defense industry lost almost 2.5 million employees from 1991 to 1995. Its decline varied with industry sectors, but was certainly greater than a 50 percent drop overall. Pay levels have fallen in the defense industry relative to other industries, with the nuclear and shipbuilding industry most successful in maintaining their levels of pay — although wages are not always paid with regularity.[40] According to Bellona, the shipyards of the Northern fleet region were operating at only 5 percent of capacity in 1996 and 1997.[41] Efforts to diversify Russian defense industry have had mixed success. The Severodvinsk shipyard complex has begun production of equipment for the development of offshore oil and gas resources in the Pechora and Barents Seas using equipment previously devoted to submarine construction.[42] Another project is the construction of a high-speed rail line between St. Petersburg and Moscow, reducing the current dilatory journey to 2.5 hours. Many defense companies are involved in the project, such as the Rubin Central Design Bureau of St. Petersburg — a principal Russian design organization for nuclear submarines — which is creating the concepts for the 200 mph high-speed train.[43] Elsewhere, however, the drive to make competitive consumer or industrial products out of outmoded and decrepit factories has not fared well — the victim of inadequate funding from the government and the sometimes hopeless reality of the task.

The Russian defense industry was first controlled by the weak Committee for Defense Industry. In 1993, it was upgraded to a state committee (Goskomoboronprom) and in May 1996 to a full ministry (Minoboronprom).[44] The new Ministry for Defense Industries was put in charge of various facilities and projects associated with the dismantlement of nuclear submarines, including the Sevmash and Zvezdochka shipyards at Severodvinsk and the Nerpa shipyard near Murmansk. It coordinated the work of preparing nuclear submarines for temporary storage afloat, dismantlement, the construction of floating facilities and special rigging necessary for unloading reactor cores, the storage and reprocessing of solid and liquid Radwaste, and the work related to burying reactor compartments.[45] According to former US Deputy Secretary of Defense Gloria Duffy, the

Ministry for Defense Industries enjoyed a good working relationship with the officials running the US Cooperative Threat Reduction (CTR) program[46]— apparently a better one than MINATOM.

In 1997, however, the Ministry of Defense Industry was eliminated and its functions transferred to the Ministry of Economics.[47] The reorganization meant that those responsible for much of the submarine defueling and dismantlement process no longer had a sponsor or direct representation at the highest levels of government. Other government players in the submarine spent fuel issue include the Ministry of Transport, responsible for the nuclear icebreaker operations of the Murmansk Shipping Company, and the Ministry of Railways that participates in the transport of spend fuel assemblies and other nuclear waste. The RADON Radwaste processing and storage facilities are generally under the Ministry of Construction.[48]

Duma and Regional Administrations

The Russian parliament or *Duma* is another complication. Although its power is relatively limited, the political and economic conflict between the *Duma* and the Yeltsin government slows down almost all initiatives — including proposed nuclear safety and Radwaste regulations and programs. Regional government authorities, including those in Murmansk, are involved as well and increasingly a factor in environmental issues. Similar to the rest of the developed world, the state's right of eminent domain has eroded in Russia; individual and group rights are becoming easier to defend but can also create roadblocks to controversial projects that might lead to a greater good.[49] On the other hand, according to Igor Korolyov, head of the Murmansk regional government's health committee, the secrecy of nuclear activities prevents studies on the effect of Russia's many such industrial installations on the health of the country's people.[50]

Examples of political and environmental conflict among the various power centers abound on nuclear issues. Officials in Murmansk and Archangel are opposed to the development of an underground storage facility for Radwaste in their regions. "The technical engineering problem of building the sites is solved," according to Nikolai Melnikov, Director of the Kola Mining Institute, but "the social, political and financial problems remain."[51] In Bolshoi Kamen on the Pacific Coast, local residents opposed its status as a nuclear defueling facility and forced the government to change its plans for a liquid Radwaste purification facility. In Krasnoyarsk, opposition by regional authorities and local citizens may have influenced the Russian decision to cancel plans to complete the RT-2 reprocessing plant.[52] Although MINATOM will be in greater control of submarine defueling operations beginning in 1999, it will still have to work with the *Duma*, the Murmansk and Archangel regional authorities, and with various environmental groups.

Radwaste Plans and Regulations

The transition from the Soviet Union to the Russian Federation in 1991/92 required a restructuring of the country's nuclear plans and regulatory framework. The Radwaste regulations of the former Soviet Union, called SPORO-85, were initially recognized as binding. This document was approved by the State Sanitary Doctor-General of the Soviet Union in October 1985 and covered all enterprises, institutions, and laboratories that made use of radioactive material. Those activities that generated Radwaste were responsible for waste collection and for preparation and delivery of the waste to storage and disposal sites. They also had to ensure that adequate interim storage was available at their own facilities. According to the *Phase II CCMS Report*, the main differences between SPORO-85 and current IAEA recommendations on Radwaste are that, "SPORO-85 does not include a system for public participation and acceptance, the long term safety assessment is based only on the design of the disposal facility, SPORO requires no real segregation of the waste and, finally, the liquidation of accidental contamination is based on obligatory decision."[53]

A 1991 law "On Environmental Protection" has a number of articles dealing with Radwaste, including requirements for proper storage and treatment of wastes and for limited releases to the environment.[54] In July 1994, the *Duma* adopted a law to ensure "safety for present and future generations, and protection of the environment as radioactive waste is collected, transported, treated, and stored." It was designed to stop waste discharges to open water sources (including oceans) as well as the injection of liquid wastes underground, although injecting of solidified wastes was permitted. On October 23, 1995, Russian Prime Minister Chernomyrdin approved the law, called "On the Federal Targeted Program Handling of Radioactive Waste and Spent Nuclear Materials and their Salvage and Burial for the Years 1996 — 2005" or the "Federal Program." Two other laws related to radioactive waste management were approved in 1995, "On Utilization of Atomic Energy" and "On Radiation Protection of the

Population."[55] According to Don J. Bradley, the "Federal Program" law detailed a number of important points concerning submarine and other maritime Radwaste. This includes plans to:

1. reconstruct existing and develop new installations for conditioning and storage of radioactive waste at the nuclear fleet refit depot, the ship-repair yards of the Russian Federation State Committee for the Defense Sectors of Industry, and Navy facilities;

2. develop equipment for processing radioactive waste produced during the dismantling and decommissioning of onshore engineering facilities and auxiliary nuclear maintenance ships, and also ensure their recovery;

3. devise technologies and develop equipment for recovering the reactor compartments of nuclear submarines and reactors of nuclear-powered ships;

4. reconstruct existing and construct new spent nuclear fuel dumps at Russian Federation Transport Ministry and Navy facilities; and,

5. complete the cleanup following the nuclear accident in Chazhma Bay.[56]

Russia is also working to finalize its Radwaste management plan, presumably with more specific procedures and designated infrastructure to implement the listed requirements. In addition, a "Federal Waste Management Concept" was developed and approved in early 1998 and a "Regulation on Accounting and Control of Radioactive Substances and Waste" was developed by MINATOM and GAN for gradual implementation by the end of 2000.

Defueling Chain

A specific sequence of operations or "chain" of events and facilities must be decided upon and implemented before the wholesale defueling of Russian Northern Fleet submarines can begin. No doubt considering the goals of the "Federal Targeted Program," the Russian Navy and MINATOM came up with a list of 20 priority projects for dealing with military and civilian nuclear waste issues in Northwest Russia (see Appendix A)— first vetted to the international community at the second meeting of the IAEA Contact Group on International Radwaste Projects in September 1996. Key items for the defueling and dismantlement of submarines include:

1. improved land transport to the Mayak reprocessing facility;
2. construction of interim storage facilities for spent fuel at Mayak;
3. constructing interim storage facilities for spent fuel in Northwest Russia;
4. construction of specially designed service ships and barges to remove and transport submarine spend fuel; and,
5. adequate provisions for liquid and solid Radwaste processing and storage.

Restoring Mayak's reprocessing capability, permanent storage of spent fuel, and removing spent fuel from Andreeva Bay are significant needs as well and should be considered as part of the defueling chain, although not specifically addressed on the Russian list. Requirements and priorities are still being debated within and among various Russian agencies, but the priority list has become an important starting point for international dialogue on Russia's submarine spent fuel problem.

Transport to Mayak

The Mayak Chemical Combine, located in the southern Ural Mountains about two thousand miles from Northwest Russia's naval facilities, has reprocessed spent fuel from military and civilian nuclear reactors since the 1950s. During the Cold War special trains from Murmansk or Severodvinsk traveled to Mayak several times a year, made up of rail cars and containers specially designed to carry spent fuel. Since then, the trains have run only intermittently because of insufficient or inadequate equipment and because of funding difficulties. Although a sufficient number of the mandated TUK-18 spent fuel transport containers may be available, Russia has only four specially designed TK-VG-18 railway cars to carry them — insufficient for wholesale transport to take place.[57] Shipyards with railheads in Murmansk and Severodvinsk have the capability to transship submarine spent fuel to Mayak, but attention is also being given to Nerpichya at the Zapadnaya Litsa Fjord. With so much submarine spent fuel in the vicinity, particularly at Andreeva Bay, having the capability to load spent fuel directly onto a train at Nerpichya to ship to Mayak, rather than loading it first onto a ship that must transit to Murmansk or Severodvinsk and then to transship the fuel again for the train ride to Mayak, seems a significant advantage.[58]

Determining the transport needs of the Fleet would be easier, however, if final destinations were known: will spent fuel go to Mayak for reprocessing or to destinations on the Kola Peninsula for interim storage, or directly to the island of Novaya Zemlya for permanent storage? If interim or permanent storage on the Kola Peninsula is selected, railway car and rail line improvements may not be required on the scale anticipated because the defueling might be conducted in the vicinity of an interim storage location or service ships that would deliver the spent fuel to storage sites directly. Despite the uncertainties, problems with rail transport seem relatively straightforward although potentially expensive compared to other links in the defueling chain. They could be resolved rather quickly.

Interim Storage

In addition to continuing operation as a reprocessing center, Mayak and MINATOM officials hope to build a new interim storage facility for spent fuel at Mayak or to complete one begun there previously. Interim storage at Mayak would provide the capacity for schedule changes and would allow spent fuel to be moved out of the Arctic region in a timely manner. A number of designs are available and in use in other countries. Finland, for example, has a spent fuel storage facility available that could be constructed for about $40 million.[59] In June 1998, BNFL put forward a plan that would transport spent fuel to Mayak and build a new storage facility there within two years, costing $50 million.[60]

MINATOM and the Russian Navy are also considering construction of an interim storage facility in Northwest Russia to be close to likely defueling and transshipment locations. This would allow spent fuel to become less radioactive and [during storage] hazardous for transport and could also help to empty current hazardous storage sites. Like the proposed Mayak facility, it would provide a surge capacity for delays in transporting spent fuel to reprocessing or permanent storage locations. The Murmansk Shipping Company (MSC) that runs Russia's several nuclear powered icebreakers has proposed building a facility to store both icebreaker spent fuel and Russian Navy nuclear fuel at its Atomflot base in Murmansk. This could be developed from an earlier project that was halted short of completion because of problems with safety standards.[61] Construction would cost about $48 million, but has not yet gone beyond the discussion stage.

With more redundant transport and available interim or permanent storage elsewhere in Russia, any pressing need for an interim storage location in Northwest Russia could presumably be overcome, although some surge capacity that meets accepted safety standards seems a good idea. This might be accomplished at less expense by using metal-concrete containers and concrete pad storage at the needed locations (discussed in detail in Chapter 6).

Defueling Ships

Russia has often used auxiliary surface ships to assist in submarine defueling operations and for temporary storage and transport of spent fuel assemblies, in part because of the relative isolation of its advanced bases in Northwest Russia and the primitive nature of road and rail transportation. The ships previously used, however, are in poor condition and can not carry the newer TUK-18 shielded transport containers now mandated for spent fuel use. Russian officials want to convert or build one or more merchant ships as specialized spent fuel transport vessels. The ships would move from submarine to submarine and from port to port conducting defueling operations; the spent fuel would be placed in twenty to thirty TUK-18 containers onboard the ships. The vessels could then deliver the containers to centralized transshipment locations, such as Murmansk or Severodvinsk, where the containers would be loaded onto rail cars for shipment to Mayak or perhaps placed into interim storage.[62] A related priority is the construction of one or two floating barge-like facilities specially outfitted with cranes and other equipment for defueling the submarines. After removal of their spent fuel, the ships would be placed in a naval or civilian shipyard for removal of their reactor compartments and for dismantlement of the remainder of the submarine.

Because so little Russian funding is available, the international community has been invited to participate in the project. Norwegian policymakers consider the ships a good option and a better course of action than the potentially hazardous practice of towing decommissioned but not defueled submarines along the Arctic coast.[63] Policy and financial obstructions have delayed its involvement, however. In 1996, Norway's Prime Minister complained that Russia was still building new nuclear submarines while at the same time not adequately tending to funding projects such as taking care of those submarines already decommissioned.[64]

Solid and Liquid Waste Management

Operating and maintaining submarines creates considerable quantities of liquid and solid Radwaste, with the defueling process in particular generating large amounts of highly radioactive liquid waste. The volume of radioactive material has been building up since Russian acceded in the early 1990s to the anti-dumping restrictions of the London Convention 1972. According to MINATOM, Russia needs at least three dedicated facilities for treatment and packing of solid radioactive waste in the Northwest: one at the icebreaker base in Murmansk, one for the Kola Peninsula naval bases, and another for the region's civilian nuclear reactors. Various projects are progressing to address both solid and liquid waste requirements, including a Novaya Zemlya facility for disposal of solid low-level waste.

Reprocessing and Permanent Storage

Nuclear spent fuel is reprocessed by chopping up the assemblies, dissolving them in acid, and then separating the constituent components. Enriched uranium and plutonium can be recovered and recycled for other nuclear requirements. The Mayak Chemical Combine has the ability and capacity to meet the reprocessing needs of the Russian Navy, with the exceptions discussed below, and is the only Russian facility that can do so. Mayak's RT-1 reprocessing facility is currently shutdown because its vitrification facility lost its license; reopening the RT-1 plant is essential to moving forward with submarine spent fuel disposal, at least as far as most Russian officials are concerned.

The defueling chain should also address possible locations for permanent storage of submarine spent fuel assemblies. This has not been a public priority because Russia is still committed to reprocessing and to a nearly closed cycle of fissile material usage. A permanent site seems inevitable in any case because of Mayak's inability to reprocess damaged fuel, fuel from liquid metal reactors, and fuel containing zirconium. These exceptions may amount to as much as 30 percent of the Russian spent fuel inventory. Because reprocessing creates highly radioactive wastes and is also a proliferation concern, permanent storage of other submarine spent fuel might also be advisable, ending up less expensive, kinder to the environment, and just better policy than reprocessing. Permanent storage locations must remain safe and secure for thousands of year, however, and require very detailed study and political support prior to implementation.

Russian officials are not clear on where permanent storage for spent fuel might be located, but several sites could be considered. A permanent storage facility may already exist at Krasnoyarsk, for example. Despite its environmental and technical problems, Mayak could be a strong candidate because of its substantial nuclear expertise and capability. Storing spent fuel at Mayak would be a form of nuclear triage; it makes some sense to store highly radioactive material in a region that already has substantial contamination.

There has been a Russian attempt to concentrate non-spent fuel Radwaste storage on Novaya Zemlya.[65] Much work has already been completed or is in progress for storage of various types of Radwaste on the island. Storage could be either at Matochkin Shar (near the channel split between the north and south parts of the island) or on the southern half of the island. Some geological studies have been completed, including the boring of 10 wells to 800–2000 m depth, various wells drilled at the repository (Bashmachnaya Inlet), and a number of technical studies. The tunnels already created for underground testing of nuclear weapons may be convertible to Radwaste storage as well if they can be improved to standards acceptable to the IAEA. If not, new tunnels at another site would have to be constructed.[66] The project seems to involved trenches and wells cut into the permafrost about 15 km from pier location on the coast at Bashnochnya Bay. The permafrost is 300 m thick and there is geological evidence it has been so for at least the last 1 million years.[67] This should make it virtually impenetrable to environmental changes like global warming; the Russians seem to believe that it would require almost an extinction level event to disturb the storage. But Norway remains nervous about the project and there has yet to be a detailed environmental impact assessment.[68]

According to a MINATOM official, Novaya Zemlya looks promising as a potential storage site for icebreaker and Navy spent fuels as well, although the idea is only at the stage of a proposal. Russian officials also hint that foreign wastes might eventually be welcome at Novaya Zemlya. Use of the island as a storage site could depend on acceptance of the permanent nuclear test ban treaty because Novaya Zemlya was where much of the Soviet Unions nuclear testing took place.

Andreeva Bay

Because of the enormous quantities of spent fuel stored at Andreeva Bay under inadequate and potentially dangerous conditions, moving fuel from Andreeva Bay has become a priority item. Norway is a primary funding source and facilitator for international aid on the decommissioned submarine issue, so its well publicized concerns for Andreeva Bay are heard in Russia. Andreeva Bay could be one of the first facilities emptied of spent fuel as funding and alternate storage become available. The spent fuel could be shipped to Mayak or to an interim storage facility; it could also be moved to another storage location on the Zapadnaya Litsa Fjord.

Chapter 6

International Projects and Initiatives

The Russians have more to think about than the nuclear pollution all around them. Their main concern is where their next meal is coming from. If you are in charge of a laid-up submarine and you are now into the fifth month of not being paid, your mind is not on the job. To make the current crisis worse there has been a bad potato harvest in the rest of Russia. Potatoes are now better guarded than nuclear material.[1]

—Nils Bohmer
Bellona Foundation

International interest in environmentally related issues in the Soviet Union grew enormously after the Chernobyl disaster of 1986. It continued into the late 1980s and early 1990s as sensitive information previously withheld by Soviet authorities began to filter out to the country's general population and to an attentive world audience. Ruinous practices by the Soviet military and heavy industries and the severe ecological problems they caused over the years were identified; the safety and Radwaste disposal problems of Soviet nuclear reactors were apparent for all to see. The Siberian nuclear weapons production archipelago became widely discussed and stimulated a desire for more information, while concern about radiological contamination of the Arctic by Soviet and Russian military and civilian nuclear activity grew as well. Ecological problems in the far North were particularly worrisome because of the common Arctic Ocean boundary the Soviet Union shared with several Western nations.

The Russian submarine spent fuel problem was late to emerge as a separate issue of concern, in part because it was associated with sensitive national security projects. When it entered the public eye in the mid–1990s, the first priority for both Russian and international actors was to identify the scope and severity of the problem — a task akin to investigative reporting. As the extent of Russia's economic and political crisis became more

125

evident and the potential hazards of Russian submarine spent fuel more defined, international attention shifted from fact-finding and criticism to exploration of ways to mitigate the problems. Programs of assistance began to develop as Western self-interest and potential profit became more apparent. According to Georgi Kostev, Russian and foreign partners began to cooperate in nuclear powered submarine defueling and dismantlement projects for three reasons: to create joint ventures for mutual gain; to develop technologies useful for other needs; and, to establish technology centers that would be useful for environmental projects as well as for submarine dismantlement.[2] Altruism and concern for the global commons were also motives, as was the possibility of achieving better relations with a large and recently unfriendly neighbor.

The Russian submarine spent fuel problem is worthy of analysis beyond its environmental and security aspects. Because of the relatively large amount of international interest and involvement, it is also a case study of emerging and substantive cooperation with Russia on a difficult and important issue. This chapter presents a largely chronological account of the development of international cooperation on Russia's submarine spent fuel problem. A significant amount of policy information and numerous direct quotations are taken from organizational documents and the various studies on Russian submarine spent fuel and related issues so that the character of research findings and established policy are not misinterpreted. A secondary purpose of this approach is to sort through the multitudinous institutions and acronyms associated with the international management of both nuclear and Arctic issues.

Soviet Reactor Dumping

In 1989 the Russian submarine *Komsomolets* sank in the Norwegian Sea due to a fire in one of its after compartments.[3] The *Komsomolets* had one pressurized water reactor (a surprise to analysts who previously thought it had two liquid metal reactors) and carried two nuclear torpedoes.[4] Soon after, a Russian *Echo* class submarine was spotted under tow in the Barents Sea on its way back to Russian waters. Later information suggested the ship had suffered a reactor accident and was receiving water from a service craft as part of the recovery process.[5] These incidents heightened official and public concerns that Russian nuclear submarines could cause radioactive pollution of the Arctic Ocean region.

At about the same time, rumors began to emerge about deliberate dumping of radioactive material in the Arctic Ocean by the Soviet Union. Particularly worrying were reports that damaged nuclear reactors and their enormous quantities of long-lived radionuclides were included among the waste, raising concerns about the potential for large-scale radioactive contamination of the Arctic and perhaps of nuclear accidents should the reactors go critical again. Dumping radioactive material in the world's oceans is regulated by international negotiations and agreements under the London Convention 1972, agreed to by 80 nations (including the United States and the Soviet Union), which prohibits the disposal of high-level radioactive waste such as reactor spent fuel in the oceans.[6] In 1991, the *Washington Post* cited statements by Murmansk legislator Andrei Zolotkov that accused Soviet officials of routinely dumping radioactive wastes into the coastal waters of the Arctic Ocean and not informing anyone about it. Zolotkov said that "the information gulf, especially in regard to radioactive waste, has been so deep that it now will require great effort to overcome the mistrust of the population to everything connected with the word radioactivity." The newspaper also quoted a July 1990 letter by V. Perovsky, a reserve naval officer, who called the Soviet Navy's methods of refueling nuclear submarines dangerous and totally obsolete. "Sad to say," Perovsky noted, "the chief protagonist when cores are being removed from reactors remains the sailor with a sledgehammer."[7]

As a result of similar allegations and suspicions, in January 1991 Norway raised the dumping issue with the Soviet Union at a meeting of the Joint Soviet-Norwegian Commission for Cooperation in the Environmental Sector. In April 1992, a Joint Russian-Norwegian Expert Group was formed to investigate the dumping and to evaluate the radioactive contamination that may have resulted.[8] At about the same time, the environmental group Greenpeace petitioned the standing body representing the London Convention 1972 to look into the issue.

Concern about ocean dumping of Radwaste led to observation and investigation into the physical decline of the Russian Navy and its nuclear ships. Joshua Handler of Greenpeace wrote a number of articles about the poor condition of Russian nuclear submarines and the potential problems associated with their spent fuel. The Norwegian environmental group Bellona began to publish specific information on the status of nuclear submarines and their service bases and ships in Northwest Russia. Bellona stressed the potential dangers of large quantities of spent fuel in a region so close to Norway's border and the Arctic Ocean and alleged that proper security and safety measures were not being taken by the Russian Navy. Despite the self-identification of both organizations as environmental advocacy groups, the data provided by Greenpeace and Bellona has been generally accepted as credible by most of the parties concerned with the Russian submarine spent fuel issue — including many Russians.[9]

A singular moment for Arctic nuclear concerns was the release of the *Yablokov Report* in 1993, formally "Facts and Problems Related to Waste Disposal in Seas Adjacent to the Territory of the Russian Federation." Here Russian officials (the Soviet Union came apart at the end of 1991) openly revealed their record of nuclear waste dumping in the Arctic. It confirmed that several nuclear reactors from submarines and icebreakers, some with spent fuel installed, had indeed been dumped by the Soviet Union into the Arctic Ocean, in violation of its pledge under the London Convention 1972.[10] As transcribed in a US government document, the *Yablokov Report* stated in part that:

1. Between 1965 and 1988, 16 marine reactors from seven former Soviet Union submarines and the icebreaker *Lenin*, each of which suffered some form of reactor accident, were dumped at five sites in the Kara Sea [between Novaya Zemlya and the Russian mainland];

2. Between 1960 and 1991, low-level liquid radioactive waste was discharged at sites in the White, Barents, and Kara Seas; and,

3. Between 1964 and 1991, low- and intermediate-level solid radioactive waste was dumped at sites in the Barents and Kara Seas.[11]

In the Pacific region, similar but smaller quantities of dumping occurred in the Sea of Japan, the Sea of Okhotsk, and the Bering Sea, including two submarine reactors without spent fuel and five reactor-related solid objects.[12]

The report's originator, A. V. Yablokov, was the chairman of the Russian commission appointed by President Yeltsin to do the investigation and has remained a figure of prominence in Russian environmental matters. The nuclear cat was out of the bag and the international community began to follow Russian maritime nuclear affairs much more closely.

IAEA

The IAEA became concerned about Russian nuclear dumping in the ocean and Russian submarine spent fuel problems at an early stage. It is the authoritative body for many of the world's nuclear issues, including how to define radioactive waste in the context of the London Convention 1972. Arctic dumping and spent fuel management were just two of the many nuclear concerns emerging from the countries of Central and Eastern Europe and the former Soviet Union as information about the region was finally becoming available. The IAEA was pushing the newly independent countries to accept its views on a "global nuclear safety culture," made up of at least three elements:

1. Legally binding international safety agreements such as the various conventions, which have been adopted or are still being developed.
2. Non-binding international safety standards which have been developed mainly under the auspices of the Agency [IAEA].
3. Provisions for the application of those standards.[13]

The IAEA also wanted to implement its Radioactive Waste Safety Standards (RADWASS) program in Central and Eastern Europe and the former Soviet Union. A basic document for the program, "The Principles of Radioactive Waste Management Policy," defined the objective of radioactive waste management as "dealing with radioactive waste in a manner that protects human health now and in the future, without imposing undue burdens on future generations." The IAEA hoped to encourage the development of radiological and safety criteria for waste disposal and for the coordination of international radiological assessment projects. It also pushed for programs to improve infrastructures and to develop mechanisms for more effective transfer of technology to improve radioactive waste management.[14]

IASAP

In 1993, the IAEA commissioned a study to look into the potential hazards resulting from Russian nuclear dumping in the Arctic Ocean. This led to the establishment of the International Arctic Seas Assessment Project (IASAP), formed with the following objectives in mind:

1. To assess the risks to human health and to the environment associated with the radioactive wastes dumped in the Kara and Barents Seas.
2. To examine possible remedial actions related to the dumped wastes and to advise on whether they are necessary and justified.

Scientists from a number of countries carried out the IASAP study, although coordinated by the Norwegian-Russian Expert Group for Investigation of

Radioactive Contamination in the Northern Area. The program was partially funded by the United States.

Several portions of the study have become available and will be published in a report titled "Assessment of the Impact of Radioactive Waste
Dumping in the Arctic Seas — Report of the International Arctic Seas
Assessment Project (IASAP)."[15] According to IASAP information released
by the IAEA (abridged):

1. Monitoring has shown that releases [radioactive] from identified
dumped objects [e.g., the Russian nuclear reactors] are small and localized to the immediate vicinity of the dumping sites. Overall, the levels of
artificial radionuclides in the Kara and Barents Seas are low and the associated radiation doses are negligible when compared with those from natural sources.

2. Doses to marine fauna are insignificant, orders of magnitude below
those at which detrimental effects on fauna populations might be expected
to occur. Furthermore, these doses are delivered to only a small proportion of the local fauna populations.

3. On radiological grounds, remediation is not warranted. Controls
on the occupation of beaches and the use of coastal marine resources and
amenities in the fjords of Novaya Zemlya used as dump sites must, however, be maintained. This condition is specified to take account of concerns regarding the possible inadvertent disturbance or recovery of high
level waste objects and the radiological protection of the hypothetical
group of individuals occupying the beaches adjacent to the fjords.[16]

It is of course possible that the protective material around the nuclear
spent fuel will eventually corrode or wear away and that more radioactivity could filter out over the long term.[17] While the reactors could conceivably be recovered or capped over with concrete, the level of risk and
potential danger to the Arctic and its inhabitants is probably too low to
justify the effort, risk, and expense.

AEPS, AMAP, ANWAP,
and the Arctic Council

Other national and intergovernmental fact-finding activities were also
begun. As a result of initiatives by Norway and other countries, in 1991
the Arctic Environmental Protection Strategy (AEPS) was organized to

help coordinate the efforts underway to protect the Arctic environment. It was composed of eight countries, Canada, Denmark, Finland, Iceland, Norway, Soviet Union, Sweden, and the United States, plus representatives of various Arctic native peoples and from a number of NGOs. A major part of AEPS activity was the Arctic Monitoring and Assessment Program (AMAP), sometimes called the "Rovaniemi Process" after the town in Finland where the first Arctic ministerial took place in 1991. AMAP was formed to coordinate research done on all types of contamination in the Arctic region. This included research into contamination from "persistent organics (pesticides and PCB oils), heavy metals such as mercury and lead, (since 1995) acidification issues, and of course radioactivity."[18] AMAP includes over 400 projects, many based on data taken from samples of sediments, water, and animals. The program includes participation from AEPS states, a number of AEPS observer states, plus representatives from organizations of the various indigenous groups in Russia and North America, and cooperates extensively with IGOs like the UN and the European Union.

The AMAP report on man-made pollutants and their effects on the Arctic environment was presented at the 1997 AEPS meeting in Alta, Norway. In early 1998, the data was released and made available to the public as six volumes of information, with a digestible summary available on the AMAP Internet website. The project's conclusions and recommendations concerning nuclear waste issues and radioactive contamination in the Arctic include:

1. The Arctic remains a clean environment in comparison with most other areas of the world.

2. Local sources of radionuclides, such as dumped nuclear waste, nuclear storage sites, accidents and past explosion, have led to local radioactive contamination.

3. A high concentration of radioactive sources exists in northwestern Russia and represents a potential for release of considerable quantities of radionuclides.

4. Exposure to radionuclides is mainly through atmospheric transfer and deposition to terrestrial ecosystems. Particular soil and vegetation characteristics concentrate some radionuclides, enabling high concentrations to develop in plants and animals (reindeer/caribou, game, and mushrooms). Arctic people are generally exposed to higher levels of radionuclides than people in temperate zones.

5. Gaps in current understanding include changes in contaminant concentrations, transformations, and interactions that occur within food web pathways, including dynamics of the transfer of radionuclides into

traditional foods arising from both terrestrial and freshwater pathways.

6. There is a need for actions to clean up contaminants from industrial and military sites and to reduce risk of nuclear accidents and radioactive releases and oil pollution in the Arctic.

7. International recommendations regarding the improvement of nuclear and radiation safety in the nuclear industry, which cover reactor refueling, decommissioning and associated spent fuel storage and disposal operation, should be extended to, and implemented in, all nuclear fleet operations.[19]

Radioactivity levels in the Arctic region actually have decreased in recent years, peaking in the 1960s as a result of contamination left over from nuclear weapons testing. The report encouraged compliance with existing legal instruments and guidance on radiation protection, nuclear safety, radioactive waste management, and emergency preparedness by all Arctic countries to minimize the probabilities and consequences of accidents. A database on Arctic radioactive contamination was added as an AMAP functions in response to requests made at the Nuuk, Greenland AEPS meeting in 1993 and is now maintained by the Norwegian Radiation Protection Authority.

Another effort to identify ecological problems in the Arctic was proposed and initially managed by the United States. Reacting to public and Congressional concerns about the hazards to the Arctic environment posed by Soviet/Russian nuclear dumping, the United States began the Arctic Nuclear Waste Assessment Program (ANWAP) process in 1995. This was a three year environmental study into nuclear contamination of the Arctic seas conducted by the US Navy's Office of Naval Research (ONR). ANWAP was specifically tasked to address the following questions:

1. What is the magnitude and location of the radioactive waste which has entered the Arctic marine environment?

2. How is radioactive contamination transported around the Arctic basin, and what are the present levels away from the various contamination sources?

3. What is the risk to the environment and to human health as a result of this radioactive contamination?[20]

Under a $10 million grant from Congress for each year of the three year project, ONR sponsored about 70 field, laboratory, modeling, and data analysis projects, and various workshops and other collaborations. ANWAP activities were accomplished in association with AMAP and IASAP, and were particularly involved in investigating the contamination that could result from Eurasian rivers that emptied into the Arctic Ocean, such as the Ob and Yenisei. These pass through the Russian nuclear weapons producing areas in Siberia at Chelyabinsk-65, Tomsk-7, and Krasnoyarsk-26. ANWAP also produced the detailed technical publication, *The Arctic Nuclear Waste Assessment Program: Kara Sea Marine Reactors and Russian Far Eastern Seas Source Terms* (UCRL-CR-126279), that estimated the amount of radioactivity associated with dumped Russian reactors and their technical situation. Like IASAP and AMAP, the preliminary reports of ANWAP indicate that Russian dumping of radioactive waste has caused only localized contamination.[21]

The AEPS became the Arctic Council in September 1996 and has continued its environmental advocacy role, with particular emphasis on the welfare of Arctic native peoples (see "Declaration on the Establishment of the Arctic Council" contained in Appendix B). Canada assumed the two-year presidency of the organization in 1997 and expressed hopes of pursuing a more vigorous agenda. Canadian leaders proposed using the organization to promote sustainable development in the Arctic while at the same time acting as a clearing-house for environmental information. In June 1997 an AMAP International Symposium on Environmental Pollution of the Arctic was held at Tromso, Norway, drawing hundreds of specialists from around the world. Prominent on the agenda were papers and panels dedicated to Russian submarine spent fuel and other Radwaste issues in Northwest Russia. Jyrki Käkönen wrote that the Arctic Council can be viewed as part of the shift from a strategic or scientific view of the Arctic region towards one that is a "social domain of concern for its people, environment, and economic development."[22] On the other hand, the organization is likely to have only a limited impact on the Russian submarine spent fuel problem because it lacks strong support from the United States and Russia and specifically declares in its charter that it "should not deal with matters related to military security."[23] The greatest value of the Arctic Council may be in publicizing and making available environmental information and in providing opportunities for scholars, government officials, and industry representatives to evaluate and coordinate activities in pursuit of the common purpose of protecting and preserving the Arctic region.

Barents Cooperation and NEFCO

The Nordic countries have their own intergovernmental bodies to engage with Northwest Russia. These include the Barents Euro-Arctic Council and the Barents Regional Council; the first is an intergovernmental forum of representatives from the national governments of the Barents region (Finland, Norway, Russia, and Sweden) and the second comprises representatives from the various counties and oblasts of the member states, i.e., the sub-national units contiguous or close to the Barents Sea.[24] Together the two organizations form the initiative called Barents Cooperation. Norwegian Foreign Minister Thorvald Stoltenberg originated the idea in 1993 as a means to coordinate assistance to Russia as its society opened up and continued its transition from totalitarian rule.[25] The philosophical rational behind the initiatives was that Northwest Russia and the adjacent or nearby territories could best advance if they were viewed as a single region with a robust process of cross-border coordination on development and problem-solving of regional issues. The area of concern covers 1.23 million square kilometers, has a total population of about 3.5 million people, and includes three Russian regions (Karelia, Murmansk, and Archangel), three Norwegian regions (Finnmark, Troms, and Nordland), two Finnish regions (Lappland and Oulu) and two Swedish regions (Norrbotten and Vaesterbotten).[26] The headquarters and perhaps focal point of Barents Cooperation rests nominally in Kirkenes, Norway — very near the Russian border — where a small secretariat is maintained.

As with many Western initiatives with Russia, Norway has been intimately involved in the workings of Barents Cooperation and has committed $175 million to development in Northwest Russia under the organization's framework. The European Union has emerged as a close partner with the Barents regional organizations and has made about $350 million available for the region in 1991.[27] Countries such as the United States and Japan have participated in Barents Cooperation meetings as observers. Barents Cooperation focuses largely on economic development and is associated with projects such as the Barents Euro-Arctic regional zone and a proposed Murmansk transport corridor.[28] Important initiatives include the development of port infrastructure at Murmansk and Archangel, a rail link between the Russian cities of Ledmozero and Kochkoma, and conversion of the Zvezdochka shipyard at Severodvinsk from military to civilian production. These initiatives should help Russia and its neighbors exploit the gas and oil located under the Barents Sea north of Murmansk.[29] Some successes have been reported, including increased economic activity in the Kirkenes-Murmansk corridor, a vigorous fish trade, a growing numbers of border crossings, and perhaps a more business friendly attitude from Russian regional leaders.[30]

The organizations' mandate includes environmental issues as well. On 15 June 1994 in Bodø, Norway, the Barents Euro-Arctic Council adopted an Environmental Action Programme aimed at preventing radioactive and oil pollution and at strengthening preparedness against nuclear and oil pollution accidents. Concerning radioactive contamination, a "Task Force" of experts was formed and given the following guidance:

1. Available information indicated that current levels of radionuclides in the Euro-Arctic Region are very low and do not at present pose any threat to human health and the environment. However, significant concern exists with regard to the risks of potential releases of radionuclides from sources dumped in the Kara Sea, from inland sources like Mayak in Ural, from unsafe storage of spent nuclear fuel and radioactive waste, and from possible accidents at any of the numerous civil and military nuclear facilities and objects in or near the Barents Region.

2. The Task Force is requested to organize a regional program on prevention of radioactive pollution, based, inter alia, on the inventory of radioactive waste in the Region drawn up by AMAP. The program should include measures of emergency prevention, preparedness and response at all levels of Government, i.a., in connection with possible nuclear accidents, and a review of radioactive waste management practices in the Region. Recommendations on pollution prevention and abatement measures should be made on the basis of a risk assessment.[31]

The Task Force was funded by the Nordic Environment Finance Corporation (NEFCO), a "risk capital institution" that has financed environmental projects throughout Central and Eastern Europe. NEFCO was established in 1990 by the five Nordic countries (Denmark, Finland, Iceland, Norway and Sweden) and is located in Helsinki, Finland, together with the Nordic Investment Bank (NIB). Its purpose is to facilitate the implementation of environmentally beneficial projects in adjacent countries (i.e., the former Soviet bloc) that have potential transboundary benefits to the NEFCO membership.[32] Its efforts have generally favored Poland and the Baltic states, but NEFCO has also been involved in improving water supplies in Murmansk and Archangel and in reducing emissions from paper and pulp factories.

NEFCO, in conjunction with the AMAP project, prepared a list of non-radioactive and radioactive priority investment projects reported at the Second Meeting of Environment Ministers in 1995. The projects associated with nuclear issues were:

1. Mapping, risk assessment and monitoring of dumped radioactive waste and other kinds of contamination in the Northern region.
2. Risk of marine radioactive pollution from reprocessing plants through rivers.
3. Management, handling and storage of spent nuclear fuel and radioactive wastes.
4. Nuclear safety and preparedness against nuclear accidents.[33]

In December 1995, a report on the initial phase of the NEFCO/AMAP program was presented to the Barents Euro-Arctic Council during a meeting of Environment Ministers in Rovaniemi, Finland. It emphasized the extensive funding needed to make a real difference and that most of the in-progress projects were under-financed. In 1996, the member countries decided to double NEFCO's capital to almost $100 million. A report of the Task Force activity was also made to the Third Ministerial Conference of the Barents Euro-Arctic Council in St. Petersburg, Russia, on 9 October 1997. It concluded that pollution prevention and remediation measures should be made on the basis of a risk assessment and that abatement measures or mitigation actions must be carried out with a concern for cost benefit analyses to ensure they are justified.[34] Moving forward with projects such as construction of a nuclear spent fuel transport vessel, emptying inadequate and full waste storage facilities [e.g., Andreeva Bay], and treatment of liquid radioactive waste were given particular attention. The report also concluded that the energy and environmental sectors were closely linked so that close cooperation between the Council's Energy Expert Group and the Environmental Task Force was necessary.

The report also noted that "a number of problems and barriers in the Russian section of the Barents Sea, are currently blocking or hampering the development of economic cooperation and trade with Nordic neighbors and other countries." These include the litany of familiar complaints about doing business in Russia, including inadequate commercial legislation, a high level of taxes, and uncertainties over the ownership of natural resources.[35] The 1995 report on these issues concluded that the most pressing task in the near future was to establish a solid legal and practical foundation for project implementation, including exemption from taxes and duties, and solving the nuclear liability question. These might help projects like Russian submarine defueling and dismantlement and spent fuel management initiatives gain approval from various sources of intergovernmental finance, such as NEFCO, the European Commission, and the European Bank for Reconstruction and Development (EBRD).[36]

European Union and NATO Studies

Concern for the Arctic environment also reached some of the most successful and powerful international organizations in the world. In the early 1990s the European Union began a cooperation program with Central and Eastern Europe and the countries of the former Soviet Union to improve the safety of the region's nuclear power plants and other nuclear facilities. This included the management of radioactive waste and various aspects of the nuclear fuel cycle. To determine the extent of the radioactive waste problem, the European Commission tasked CASSIOPEE (a group of Radwaste management agencies from the various European Union countries) to work with Russian counterparts, such as the Kola Mining Institute, to compile an accurate inventory.

The first phase of the inventory project was completed in 1996 when the European Commission published its findings in a document titled *Nuclear Science and Technology; inventory of radioactive waste and spent fuel at the Kola Peninsula region of North West Russia* (EUR 16916). The report gave a detailed accounting of nuclear spent fuel and other radioactive waste in the Murmansk and Archangel regions of Russia and suggested a management plan to improve conditions. It also provided information about key Russian actors, existing Russian regulations, details about the Kola Nuclear Power Plant, and a number of other issues relevant to Russian nuclear problems.[37] The report has become one of the common tools of reference used to increase understanding and to guide action towards remediation of Radwaste issues in Northwest Russia. The second phase of European Union cooperation with Russia is focusing on developing practical solutions to the problems identified.[38]

At NATO there was a similar desire to understand the environmental problems of the countries of the former Warsaw Pact, particularly as they might affect NATO member countries. In 1992, Norway proposed a study of cross-border defense-related environmental problems in Europe. The NATO-backed Committee for Concerns in Modern Society (CCMS) was the sponsoring agency, a group of countries from both NATO and the former Warsaw Pact. CCMS was formed as an outgrowth of the cooperation on security and security-related issues that was emerging between East and West in the immediate aftermath of the Cold War's end. This was reflected in various forums and initiatives, such as the North Atlantic Cooperation Council (NACC) and later the Partnership for Peace (PfP), and in the greatly revised NATO military and political strategy for the post–Cold War period approved at the Rome Summit in 1991. The new strategy emphasized cooperation instead of competition with the countries of the former Warsaw Pact and helped to establish an atmosphere in which collaborative efforts such as CCMS could develop.

In association with the NATO Science Committee, CCMS initiated a "Pilot Study" on both nuclear and chemical contamination caused by defense related activity. Phase I was conducted between 1993 and 1995 to gather and assess available information, meaning it did not commission very much original research. The report looked at the sources and levels of radioactive contamination in various regions including the Arctic, at the movement of radionuclides in the Barents Sea, and at a variety of assessments about the hazards identified. Original research was commissioned for a risk assessment of the sunken Russian submarine *Komsomolets* because so little information was available on the ship's condition. Research was also done to determine the different sources that contributed to radioactivity in the Arctic seas. The report gave particular attention to Russia's spent fuel handling procedures and its defueling and spent fuel problems. Edited by researchers from the Norwegian Defence Research establishment, the *Phase I CCMS Report* (formally *Cross-Border Environmental Problems Emanating from Defence-Related Installations and Activities, Final Report, Volume 1: Radioactive Contamination*) provided an extremely useful assessment of spent fuel hazards while attempting to increase the perception and reality of cooperation among new and old NATO associates.[39] Because of CCMS' diverse representation and NATO's defense orientation, the report appears to take great pains to be inclusive of both East and West, to be non-accusatory in tone, and not to stray too deeply into sensitive defense-related areas.

The *Phase II CCMS Report* (formally *Cross-Border Environmental Problems Emanating from Defence-Related Installations and Activities, Subtopic 3: Management of Defence-Related Radioactive Waste*), commissioned under Norwegian leadership as well, was completed in early 1998. It also relied on information made available by other studies and provided another opportunity for participants to cooperate and to assess the extent of problems associated with defense related waste. The report encouraged further technical cooperation among the concerned parties:

> Although very small, the highest risk of cross-border contamination due to radioactive waste is found at heavily contaminated sites where both soil and groundwater or surface water is contaminated with long-lived radionuclides. It is recommended that experience in stabilisation and restoration of contaminated territories be communicated between countries, and that questions related to such contamination be addressed openly and in cooperation with neighbouring states.[40]

OTA Report

Reports of Russian dumping of highly radioactive material motivated the United States to actions in addition to ANWAP. The US Arctic Research Commission and the Interagency Arctic Research Policy Committee (IARPC) issued statements of concern and the US Congress also began to mobilized. In 1993, Senators Ted Stevens, William V. Roth, and John Glenn, asked Congress' Office of Technology Assessment (OTA) to investigate the issue of nuclear waste in the Arctic. The *OTA Report* (formally *Nuclear Waste in the Arctic: An Analysis of Arctic and other Regional Impacts from Soviet Nuclear Contamination*) was the result, completed in 1995. It examined the environmental and human health impacts of waste dumped in the Arctic and North Pacific regions, from nuclear contaminant discharge into these environments, and from radioactive release from both past and future nuclear activities in the region.

The *OTA Report* also covered the accident vulnerability of Russian nuclear ships and civilian nuclear power plants in the Arctic and the management of their nuclear waste. Because the report was not an international effort and had little cooperative spin to it, it was perhaps more critical of Soviet/Russian practices and more open in its concern about potential dangers than the EU and NATO efforts. The *OTA Report* noted that "Only minor releases and transport of these radionuclides into the Arctic Ocean have been suggested by recent research, but future migration and impacts beyond Russian borders constitute a plausible scenario and deserve investigation."[41] Congress disestablished the Office of Technology Assessment just as the *OTA Report* was being completed.

Norway's Plan of Action

In 1996 Norwegian Foreign Minister Bjorn Tore Godal said that: "Nuclear contamination in Russia and the Eastern European countries represents one of the greatest environmental and security priority challenges we face today."[42] Norway was among the first countries to become actively engaged with the Russian submarine spent fuel problem and has continued to lead international commitments ever since. It shares a common border with Russia and has an extensive Arctic Ocean coastline that might suffer from a significant radiological accident on the Kola Peninsula; it is also an advanced and prosperous country that can no doubt afford to help out, particularly since Russia is in real trouble on this issue.[43]

Tore Gundersen of the Ministry of Foreign Affairs stated categorically that Russia cannot possibly deal with the problems related to its nuclear activity on its own.[44] To operationalize its concern, Norway developed a framework of bilateral and multilateral initiatives to cooperate with Russia on Radwaste and associated issues. Norway cites Agenda 21 of the UN Conference on Environment and Development in Rio in 1992 as a basis for its focus on the Arctic region, that "states undertake not to store or dispose of radioactive waste near the marine environment, unless they determine that scientific evidence shows that such storage or disposal poses no unacceptable risk to people and the marine environment."[45]

Based on a report on "nuclear activities and chemical weapons in areas adjacent to our northern borders" made to the *Storting* (the Norwegian parliament) in April 1994, the Norwegian government drew up a draft proposal for its engagement. The original "Plan of Action" became effective in April 1995 and gave priority to cooperation on safety issue involving the Kola Nuclear Power Plant, to investigations and evaluation of pollution in the northern areas and of possible sources of pollution, and to reviews of cost-effective measures to alleviate the situation in key areas.[46] It also encouraged the transfer of expertise that would enable Russia to use improved technology and to find its own cost-effective solutions to its problems, with the hope that additional international approval and funding would follow. The plan was revised for 1997–98 and continued to focus on four areas of particular concern: safety measures at nuclear facilities; management, storage and disposal of radioactive waste and spent nuclear fuel; radioactive pollution of northern areas; and, arms-related environmental hazards (see Appendix C for excerpts from the Plan of Action).[47]

In addition to technical assistance on the Kola Nuclear Power Plant and other reactors in the region, the safety measures initiative under the plan included studies of possible accidents at the Kola Nuclear Power Plant, support to close down the Chernobyl Nuclear Power Plant in Ukraine, investigation of the sunken submarine *Komsomolets*, and increased collaboration between Norwegian and Russian regulatory agencies. The Norwegian Radiation Protection Authority (NRPA) is working with Russia's GAN on technical cooperation and the exchange of information on the safe utilization of nuclear energy, for example. This includes collaboration on nuclear power plants, decommissioned ship reactors, service vessels, research reactors, and Radwaste storage. In a joint effort with Sweden, the Norwegian agency is providing GAN with computer equipment, software, and training courses to help improve assessment of Radwaste facilities.

Key projects to push forward the Russian submarine spent fuel problem are contained under the "management, storage and disposal of radioactive waste and spent nuclear fuel" category. The multilateral Murmansk Trilateral Initiative and the *Lepse* and AMEC projects mentioned in the plan are discussed separately below. Other initiatives of importance to the defueling chain for Russian submarines include:

1. To construct a specialized vessel for safe transport of spent nuclear fuel, and possibly other radioactive waste from decommissioned Russian nuclear submarines on the Kola coast to a transfer terminal on the mainland. The ship will have independent propulsion machinery, double hull, and other safety features.

2. To fabricate specialized railway rolling stock (railway cars) for the transport of spent nuclear fuel from decommissioned nuclear submarines (and possibly the *Lepse*) from Murmansk or Severodvinsk to the Mayak reprocessing facility.

3. To upgrade storage tanks for liquid radioactive waste at the Zvezdochka shipyard in Severodvinsk.

4. To empty and discontinue the spent fuel storage facility at Andreeva Bay. This will include an assessment of alternative management of the fuel, such as safe interim storage in the region or transport out of the region. It will also be possible for the project to include assistance in the establishment of the necessary infrastructure for emptying and closing down the storage facilities.

5. To participate in the completion of an environmentally safe interim storage for spent nuclear fuel at Mayak.[48]

Another priority area is "radioactive pollution of northern areas," addressing the various Norwegian information gathering efforts completed or in progress. Since 1992, Norway and Russia (in association with the IAEA and the European Union) have undertaken three joint expeditions to chart the radioactive waste dumped in the Kara Sea and in the fjords off Novaya Zemlya.[49] Norway has encouraged various multilateral frameworks for the investigation already discussed, such as IASAP, AMAP, and the European Commission and CCMS studies and is also involved in studies to determine the danger of radioactive pollution from reprocessing and other activities at Mayak, Arctic pollution from rivers and streams, and pollution of the Kola Fjord. The "arms-related environmental hazards" portion of the Plan includes a survey of the pollution left over from nuclear testing, gathering information useful to the verification and control of nuclear weapons under the Comprehensive Test Ban Treaty, safe destruction of chemical weapons, control of fissile material, and participation in the International Science and Technology Center (ISTC) in Moscow (also discussed below).

Despite the great variety of nuclear-related projects, Norwegian attention is most focused on the problems associated with Russian submarine spent fuel. This may be part of a de facto division of labor among the Nordic states: Norway concentrates on Russian submarine spent fuel while Sweden and Finland give more attention to nuclear safety at Russian civilian power plants and to nuclear issues in the three Baltic states.

Many of Norway's nuclear initiatives with Russia have been carried out by the giant Norwegian construction and engineering firm, Kvaerner Moss Technology. Kvaerner is best known for its sea-borne oil exploration work and, along with the Russian rocket manufacturer Energia and the US aerospace firm Boeing, for the Sealaunch project to launch satellites from an at-sea platform near the equator. Kvaerner Maritime is the division normally engaged with Russia, specializing in containment systems for hazardous waste cargoes, maritime operations, and the design of ships and other floating structures. With regard to Russia's submarine spent fuel problem, the company has the Norwegian lead on projects such as the provision of ships and rail cars for nuclear spent fuel transport and an overall evaluation of the spent fuel situation under a Norwegian-Russian agreement.[50] Elsewhere, Kvaerner has a cooperative arrangement with Lockheed Martin Corporation at the Idaho National Engineering Laboratory — the location of much US reactor research and testing.

Kvaerner was also part of a major international initiative to address and solve the Russian submarine spent fuel problem in a comprehensive manner. In November 1995, the company announced that it had reached agreement with Russia's Energia to defuel and dismantle all Russian nuclear submarines by the year 2010 and to take care of the Radwaste generated in the process. After the Norwegian foreign ministry spent nearly a million dollars on the study, the agreement fell apart when disparate Russian enterprises would not support it.[51] Despite the failure, the Kvaerner-Energia initiative was an important first step towards an overall plan and served to enervate participants and observers of the Russian spent fuel problem toward further action.

The Norwegian Ministry of Foreign Affairs was allocated $50 million by the *Storting* to implement the Plan of Action for 1995–97 but has not been able to spend much of it.[52] The Norwegian commitment to fund four TK-VG-18 railway cars to transport spent fuel, for example, was delayed when the *Storting* asked for additional information before providing the needed appropriations.[53] Until early 1998, much of the collaboration between Norway and Russia was stymied by disagreements over taxation and liability.

Norway's Framework Agreement

On 26 May 1998, "The Norway-Russia Framework Agreement on Cooperation Related to Dismantling Nuclear Submarines and Enhancing Nuclear Safety" was signed by Norwegian Minister of Foreign Affairs Knut Vollebaek and Russian Minister of Nuclear Energy Yevgeny Adamov. The ceremony was accomplished as part of the official visit of King Harald V of Norway to Moscow, the first Norwegian royal visit to Russia since 1905. The agreement was perhaps the most significant breakthrough in international collaboration on Russian decommissioned submarine spent fuel since the issue achieved international notoriety. Key was a mutually acceptable settlement permitting Norway to provide free technical assistance to Russia, such as equipment and technology transfer, with a minimum of overhead cost and legal exposure. The agreement clears up important points of specific disagreement including lack of exemption from taxes, duties and fees on technical assistance grants, and lack of indemnification from lawsuits that might arise following a nuclear incident or damage to property owned by the Russian Federation. Article 5 of the Framework Agreement covers tax exemption and states:

1. Equipment and materials which are imported into the territory of the Russian Federation as free technical assistance for the implementation of this Agreement, and which are financed by funds provided by the Norwegian Party, shall be exempt from taxes, customs duties and other fees in accordance with the legislation of the Russian Federation.

2. Exemption in accordance with paragraph 1 of this article shall be granted on terms not less favorable than those accorded to technical assistance provided free of charge by any third party.

Article 9 on liability (included as Appendix D) states in part:

> With the exception of claims for damage or injury against individuals arising from their premeditated actions, the Russian Party shall bring no claims or legal proceedings against the Norwegian Party and its personnel or contractors, subcontractors, consultants, suppliers of equipment or services at any tier and their personnel, for indirect, direct or consequential damage to property owned by the Russian Federation. This paragraph shall not apply to legal actions brought by the Russian Party to enforce the provisions of contracts to which it or a Russian national is a party.[54]

The agreement specifically lists the activities under consideration, essentially the submarine defueling chain projects detailed in the Plan of Action and various initiatives involving the Kola Nuclear Power Plant. The Framework Agreement also provides for the establishment of a Norwegian-Russian Commission that will coordinate and control the implementation of the agreement, approve joint projects, and provide a mechanism for arbitration. The Royal Norwegian Ministry of Foreign Affairs and the Ministry of the Russian Federation for Atomic Energy will represent their governments on the commission. Russian Deputy Atomic Energy Minister Nikolai Yegorev stated that Russia expects to receive about $30 million under the agreement to help with the disposal of nuclear submarines, although the project will cost much more before it is completed.[55] The agreement has a term of five years, with provisions for extension at five-year intervals if the two parties agree.

The joint commission met for the first time in September 1998 and decided to focus Russian and Norwegian efforts on three projects: the *Lepse* pilot-project; construction of a set of railway cars for spent fuel shipment; and, clean-up work at the Radwaste storage site at Andreeva Bay.[56] The Framework Agreement is an important step forward and could serve as a catalyst to remove other bottlenecks preventing significant progress in the defueling chain.

Murmansk Trilateral Initiative

Becoming a good international citizen can have unintended consequences. For decades, the Soviet Union had disposed of its solid and liquid Radwaste into the Arctic Ocean and along its Pacific coast. When Russia ceased dumping radioactive waste in 1992, it faced a dilemma because of the limited facilities available ashore and afloat to store or dispose of any newly generated Radwaste. Defueling operations generate considerable solid and liquid radioactive material, so the decision to discontinue at-sea dumping, however meritorious, created another obstacle to implementing the defueling chain.

During the 1993 London Convention on dumping of radioactive materials, Russia declared its willingness to adhere to the Convention's dumping prohibition, but claimed insufficient capability to do so. This led to preliminary discussions with the United States and Norway on how best to address the Russian dilemma. In September 1994, Russia, Norway, and the United States agreed to the "Murmansk Trilateral Initiative," also called the "Murmansk Initiative." The objective of the project was the creation of modern and reliable means to treat all types of radioactive waste created by the operation and maintenance of nuclear civilian and military ships, as well as to address the waste already accumulated by the Russian Northern Fleet. The most important part of the initiative involved expanding the capacity of a liquid waste treatment plant operated by the Murmansk Shipping Company at its Atomflot Base in Murmansk. The facility purifies 1200 cubic meters per year of icebreaker waste and dumps the effluent into the Murmansk Fjord. Contamination levels of the water are reportedly reduced to below the Russian potable water requirement. The Murmansk Initiative envisages increasing the capacity of the plant to 5,000 cubic meters per year to process submarine waste in addition to icebreaker waste. Russia may later expand the facility to 15,000 cubic meters to accommodate further submarine decommissionings.[57]

The major technical problem in modifying the plant was the high saline content of submarine radioactive waste. Icebreaker waste is apparently relatively pure, but Russian submarines may have their liquid Radwaste contaminated with seawater, probably from storage in onboard holding tanks that are periodically flushed from the sea. According to a US Environmental Protection Agency official, there are three critical waste streams to consider in the design and operation of the modified Atomflot plant:

1. Spent fuel primary coolant containing Cs 137 and Sr 90.
2. Equipment decontamination and laundry wastes containing contaminants such as oils, salts, oxalates, and EDTA.
3. Northern Navy high-salt wastes (brine).

The plant will use a combination of processes and technologies, including electrochemical destruction, mechanical filtration, adsorption, and electromembrane desalination. [58]

The principle American participants are the Environmental Protection Agency (EPA), Department of State, and the Department of Energy, with the project done under the framework of the US–Russian Joint Commission on Economic and Technical Cooperation — more commonly known as the Gore-Chernomyrdin Commission (GCC). GCC is an umbrella mechanism for science and technology cooperation with Russia and includes an environmental working group to address military base contamination. Western organizations and companies such as the Brookhaven National Laboratory and Raytheon from the United States and NKPA from Norway are involved in the project along with several enterprises from Russia and other countries of the former Soviet Union. Russian technology and labor are generally being used, although the project has some technological transfer from the West. Like other assistance programs with Russia, taxation and liability were considerations. The tax issue was resolved by a unique arrangement: the work and funding were channeled through Nuclide, a MINATOM agency, and the US–based International Science Foundation (ISF), entities that already had a special agreement with the Russia government to waive the taxes of concern.[59] For this project, Russia agreed to accept the requirements of the Vienna and Paris Conventions on nuclear liability.

The technical design phase of the project was completed in 1995 and equipment procurement and construction begun in June 1996. The project will have a combined US/Norwegian contribution of $1.6 million, with the Russian government allocating $600 thousand.[60] The entire Murmansk Initiative was conceived of as a 3-year project with a total price of $4– $4.5 million.[61] This has since been raised to $5.6 million and the completion date pushed back. Russian participants have complained about payment delays for equipment already being fabricated and about problems with ordering and delivery of equipment; Western participants have expressed concern about the quality and timeliness of Russian material and workmanship. Construction has also been difficult because it has been carried out at an operating facility, meaning that Radwaste treatment has continued. By August 1997, much of the major equipment had been received; testing may begin in early 1999, with operational status likely later in the year. A possible problem in operation, however, is that MSC intends to bill the Northern Fleet for use of the facility. With the Russian Navy all but broke, the usefulness of the modified plant for defueling nuclear submarines may turn out to be problematic.

Bolshoi Kamen Project

Paralleling the Murmansk Trilateral Initiative liquid waste purification project for the Northern Fleet was a similar initiative in Russia's Far East. The Soviet Union conducted extensive dumping of Radwaste in the seas off its Pacific coast, including two nuclear reactor assemblies (without fuel installed). Under condition that the Russian Navy discontinue ocean dumping, in 1993 the Japanese government promised to support construction of a liquid radioactive waste processing plant to support the Pacific Fleet. After difficult negotiations, the contract was signed on 11 January

1996.[62] Its funding was part of a $100 million dollar package the Japanese government had allocated for use in Russia and other republics of the former Soviet Union to help dispose of excess nuclear weapons left-over from the Cold War.[63]

It was agreed to construct a liquid waste purification facility for use at the Zvezda shipyard in Bolshoi Kamen, near Vladivostok. The plant's capacity would be between 5,000 and 7,000 metric tons per year. This helped to pave the way for Viktor Mikhailov, then head of MINATOM, to pledge that Russia would officially accept the 1993 amendments to the London Convention 1972 that banned the discharge of low-radioactive substances into the world ocean.[64] Because of protests from residents of Bolshoi Kamen against the establishment of a permanent infrastructure for dismantling nuclear submarines in their vicinity, officials from both Russia and the West decided to construct the purification plant on a barge for transportability.[65] Local resistance was due in part to concerns about the disposition of the solid Radwaste remaining from the purification process, but residents may also have reflected on the 1986 Chazhma Bay submarine reactor accident when they were apparently poorly informed about exposure hazards. As in the United States, fierce debates take place in Russia on how and where to handle and dispose of radioactive material; local politicians in both countries generally understand the need for disposal but argue that the process should take place somewhere other than their own districts.[66] The choice of a barge arrangement, however, made the facility more costly and difficult to build than a land-based arrangement.

Construction began in January 1996 with the participation of Japanese, Russian, British, and American firms. The US corporations Babcock and Wilcox (B&W) and ChemNuclear, along with AEA from the United Kingdom, were among the significant contractors, and could work with about $25 million of Japanese funding. The actual construction was performed primarily by the Russian AO Amur Shipbuilding Plant under subcontract with the Tomen Corporation of Japan. The Amur shipyard is located in the city of Komsomolsk, about 150 miles from the Sea of Japan on the Amur River. The purification barge displaces 5000 tons and is about 60 meters long, 20 meters wide, and 5 meters tall.[67] Once in operation, the facility will remove solid waste from water, transferring it to drums for storage, and discharge the purified effluent overboard into the adjacent sea.[68]

The barge complex was scheduled for completion in November 1997 but suffered substantial problems during construction. Russian enterprises again complained about delays in receiving American technical data; Americans complained about changes in the design, delays in settling

financing problems, and construction that did not meet design requirements. The barge project [called *Landysh* (lily) by Russian officials] was
also delayed when officials demanded additional money and held the facility hostage in Komsomolsk, hundreds of miles from its intended destination. The residents of Bolshoi Kamen got into the act and rejected
placement of the barge in their city in a non-binding referendum.[69] The
facility was finally moved to the Bolshoi Kamen area in 1997, just before
the Amur River froze over for the winter, and will probably be tested in
1999. Operational status may follow later in the year, but in December
1998 reports indicated that the facility had defects in its control system;
according to *TASS*, these were the responsibility of Babcock and Wilcox.[70]

Lepse Project

The service vessel *Lepse* has drawn international attention as one of
the most dangerously radioactive sites in Northwest Russia. The enormous
amount of radioactive material in the spent fuel contained on the ship is
located within the metropolitan area of Murmansk, making *Lepse* a specific
and immediate hazard to hundreds of thousands of civilians. Although
filled with primarily icebreaker fuel, *Lepse* is important to the submarine
spent fuel issue because many participants in the various submarine defueling initiatives view it as a test case for whether or not large-scale cooperation between the West and Russia on such a politically sensitive and
potentially dangerous environmental issue — moving nuclear spent fuel —
can actually occur.

In 1994, the Bellona Foundation received funding from the Norwegian government to study the *Lepse* problem and to develop alternatives
for its resolution. An international advisory panel on the ship was established with representatives from Norway, France, the European Commission, the United States, Russia, and NEFCO. At one point, Russia proposed
moving the *Lepse* to Novaya Zemlya for disposal, but the idea was opposed
by most other participants as too hazardous to consider. An alternative
solution emerged that would use international funding to design and build
equipment to remove the spent fuel from the ship and then to store it in
dual-use metal-concrete containers for eventual transport to Mayak for
reprocessing or storage. Following a fact-finding trip in 1995 by Western
experts, European Commission TACIS and DG XI officials provided funding to the companies SGN Réseau-Eurisys of France and AEA Technology
of the United Kingdom for a design study.[71]

Spent fuel on board the *Lepse* is stored in channels inside two very
large tanks. Some of the spent fuel was forced into the storage areas with

sledgehammers and became stuck in the upper parts of the channels. The SGN/AEA feasibility study recommended that the spent fuel be removed remotely using specially designed equipment. The SGN system envisages cutting the channels and spent fuel out of the tank system together with a milling machine and then removing the combined unit with another machine, followed by separation, drying, and canistering operations to be performed on board the *Lepse* itself.[72] The damaged spent fuel will probably be stored and shipped in newly designed RBMK containers modified to take marine spent fuel, as discussed below. Preliminary work will be needed before the actual spent fuel removal process begins, such as upgrading ventilation systems, improving shielding, cleaning out debris, and building a steel shield on the roof of the ship.[73] SGN specializes in fuel retrieval systems and storage technologies and seems to have taken the lead in the project. Removal of the spent fuel would rid the ship of 95 percent of its contamination and its chief hazard; disposal of the rest of the ship could then be done at leisure and by more conventional means.

In June 1997, the *Lepse* Advisory Committee met and recommended dividing the project into segments, including fuel retrieval, management of retrieved fuel, handling of solid and liquid radioactive waste, and conversion of the vessel to an environmentally safe condition. By mid–1998, technical manuals and procedures were prepared and SGN had completed development of the robotic system to remove and collect the fuel and to put it into the storage containers. The next major step would be to test the equipment on a mockup in Murmansk, followed by actually putting the system into service. This, however, has been held up by taxation and liability questions. Even though the Norway-Russia Framework Agreement resolved these issues for bilateral Norwegian and Russian projects, no final agreement had been reached to proceed with the multinational *Lepse* project as of early 2000. Liability is a particular concern for the *Lepse* because so much of the fuel is damaged and because the work must be done in the populated Murmansk region. The millions of dollars of robotic and other equipment were delayed transport into Russia because of the high taxes they would face.[74] On the positive side, the Mayak Chemical Combine has made the decision to accept the *Lepse* fuel, even though much of it is damaged and can not be easily reprocessed.

Approximately $13 million dollars, in addition to Russian funding, has been set aside for the project by France, Norway, the European Commission, and NEFCO, although total costs from wages, transportation, and dismantling will be much higher.[75] Once defueling begins in earnest, the project should take about four years to complete.[76]

European Commission

The European Commission has been playing an important role in Russian nuclear safety and Radwaste issues in addition to the *Lepse* project. Through its TACIS program (administered by the European Commission DG 1A unit) the Commission has given significant funding to various civilian nuclear initiatives in Russia and toward the Chernobyl project in Ukraine. Russia has received about $300 million from TACIS, going primarily to nuclear reactor safety and Radwaste management projects, including:

1. Disposal of radioactive waste, including investigation of sites, designs, and safety assessments.
2. Interim storage, including assessment of safety, capacity, designs.
3. Spent fuel, including assessment of complications with shipping spent fuel to Mayak and of recoverability of spent fuel dumped in the Arctic seas.
4. Regional radioactive waste management initiatives, basically to help the Archangel and Murmansk regions and MINATOM come up with better schemes to meet common policies and guidelines.

Other programs are funded through DG XI, the European Commission's directorate on the environment. DG XI projects completed or in progress include:

1. Inventory of radioactive waste and spent fuel at the Kola Peninsula region of Northwest Russia.
2. Evolution of the radiological situation around the nuclear reactors with spent fuel dumped in the Kara Sea.
3. Interim storage of spent fuel from submarines and icebreakers in the Murmansk/Kola region.
4. Prototype containers for interim storage of both damaged and undamaged fuel.[77]

As discussed in Chapter 4, the European Commission and other European entities and countries are actively engaged in projects to improve the safety of nuclear reactors in the former Soviet Union and to address the contamination created by nuclear weapons production. These include assessments of injection of radioactive liquid waste at Dimitrovgrad, Tomsk-7, and Krasnoyarsk-26, evaluating the radiological consequences of Lake Karachai Radwaste storage, and management and restoration of contaminated areas at Mayak, Krasnoyarsk, and Tomsk. DG XI seems to have considerable discretion in dispersing its funds and is highly courted by the European governments and companies involved in radioactive waste issues. As a symbol of European Union involvement, on 15 May 1998 at the EU-Russia summit in Birmingham, England, European Commission President Jacques Santer, European Union Council President and British Prime Minister Tony Blair, and Russian President Boris Yeltsin agreed to strengthen environmental measures related to spent nuclear fuel.[78]

As the European Union and the rest of the West consider additional initiatives to tackle the nuclear submarine spent fuel problem, we should also take stock of the controversy concerning EU aid to Russia on civilian nuclear reactor safety. This erupted in November 1998 after a report by the EU's Court of Auditors charged that EU programs to improve reactor safety were "wasteful, plagued with muddled strategy and staff shortages, and ineffective." The report noted that only half of the funds earmarked for reactor safety projects had been spent thus far and that some of those funds were likely wasted on "excessive profits" for Western consultants. According to Bernhard Friedmann, the president of the Court of Auditors: "It is particularly worrying that at the end of 1997, it was not possible to judge whether there had been any actual progress in terms of nuclear safety."[79] Russians have long argued that much of the aid they received from the West was swallowed up by US and European firms and the Court seemed to support their allegations, at least in part. Others have argued that Western aid actually exacerbated the Russian nuclear reactor safety problem: with their safety upgrades, Western vendors have encouraged the continued operation of some of Russia's more dangerous plants and the completion of other unfinished Soviet-designed nuclear facilities.[80]

European Commission leader and spokesman Hans van den Broek defended Europe's record, noting that Europe's strategy had been clear and transparent and was proceeded in the following logical stages:

1. The G7 Munich Action Plan of 1992. This plan called for strong regulatory authorities, for improvement in operational safety and for the distinction between reactors that can be upgraded and reactors which need to be replaced by alternative energy sources.

2. The 1993 Commission Communication on nuclear safety in the East which stated the support of the EU to the Munich Action Plan and emphasized the link of the nuclear power sector to the overall energy policy.

3. The Commission's strategy paper of 1995/96 which provided a detailed outline of actions in the nuclear sector which should continue to

be supported through the PHARE and TACIS programs. It also spelled out the relative balance between the various objectives.

4. Agenda 2000 in 1997 which gave a clear indication on the political importance of a high level of nuclear safety for the enlarged Union and indicated which reactors are considered upgradable and which reactors are considered not upgradable.

5. The March 1998 Communication on nuclear activities in the East which gave an overview of actions undertaken by the Community and presented ways forward with regard to programming and program implementation.[81]

Van den Broek also lauded the record of new arrangements between Eastern and Western operators, the new provision of training and training material (simulators, manuals), the delivery of equipment and spare parts, the improvement in regulatory agencies in the East achieved through transfer of methodology and applications, and the number of safety assessments and studies. On the other hand, he acknowledged that measuring the effectiveness of technical assistance and improvement in nuclear safety culture was difficult to do.[82]

AMEC

The Arctic Military Environmental Cooperation (AMEC) program is another important initiative that focuses on the Russian submarine spent fuel problem. Thus far in this report, the lead government agencies for Radwaste projects have been the foreign affairs, energy, or environmental ministries of the countries concerned; in the case of AMEC, the relevant organizations are the defense and military establishments of the participating countries.

AMEC is again the result of initiatives by Norwegian officials. Over the years, Norway has worked to engage the United States more closely with the Radwaste problems of Northwest Russia as part of a preference for multilateral approaches. Because of its superpower status and expertise in nuclear matters, the United States would be an advantageous partner to have when dealing with Russia on this issue. Norwegian efforts bore fruit in September 1996 when the Defense Ministers of Norway and Russia and the Secretary of Defense of the United States established AMEC, "a framework for contacts and cooperation among the Parties on military environmental issues in the Arctic ..." As a starting point, the participants agreed on six AMEC projects: construction of transportable interim storage containers for damaged and undamaged spent fuel, liquid Radwaste treatment technologies, solid Radwaste volume reduction technologies, Radwaste storage improvements, plus two initiatives dealing with Arctic military base cleanup methods and collection/assessment of shipboard waste.[83] In Congressional testimony, US Deputy Under Secretary of Defense for Environmental Security Sherri W. Goodman stated:

> One of the main objectives of AMEC is to help the Russian military address their radioactive and non-radioactive waste problems in the fragile ecosystem of the Arctic. AMEC is a cooperation, not an assistance program. All three parties provide funding for this program and the specific projects. DoD will leverage the United States' expertise, including DOE and EPA, in environmental techniques in radiation and chemical waste associated with nuclear submarines. Importantly, this unique effort helps build trust and understanding among these three militaries.[84]

AMEC has a steering committee of the top environmental officials from the US Department of Defense and the Norwegian and Russian Defense Ministries. In 1998, the Norwegian delegation was headed by Deputy Director General, Department of Defense Resources, Royal Ministry of Defence John I. Laugerud, the Russian delegation by Chief of Ecological Security of the Armed Forces of the Russian Federation, General Lt. Sergie Ivanovich Grigorov, and the US delegation by Under Secretary Goodman. As Goodman implied, AMEC is under military sponsorship but draws on scientists, engineers, and other professionals from various government agencies and sources. All sides have agreed on the six original projects, with an estimated total cost of $17.3 million. The first phase of studies has drawn pledges of $870 thousand from the United States, $620 thousand from Norway, and $500 thousand from Russia.[85] As with other cooperative ventures with Russia, issues such as liability, taxes, intellectual property rights, business confidentiality, and third-party transfer of material and equipment have slowed progress.

Spent Fuel Containers

The most important AMEC initiative is participation in the design and manufacture of a new type of spent fuel storage container. It has the potential to ameliorate significantly the Russian submarine spent fuel problem as well as other Radwaste hazards. This could happen in the very short term with project completion (meaning the construction, testing, and certification of a prototype) by late 1999. The AMEC container program, however, is just one part of a confusing set of container initiatives and interim storage alternatives.

AMEC containers (also called casks, flasks, and canisters) would be part of an integrated system of spent fuel storage. Each container would house a large number of fuel assemblies with multiple containers then stored on a common concrete pad. The pads could be located at a variety of locations, such as naval bases or current spent fuel storage facilities, that have appropriate geological strength and stability plus adequate access and security. The containers would be made of steel and concrete and contain several baskets where the spent fuel assemblies would actually be stored. They may also have neutron-absorbing material installed, such as borated steel, as a safeguard to allow for greater density of fuel assembly installation without concern for an inadvertent criticality. Because of the heat generated by fission product decay, the containers require material strong enough to remain intact at temperatures up to several hundred degrees — perhaps with aluminum fins to help dissipate the heat. However, they must also be able to withstand the extremely cold Arctic climate of northern Russia. The key to the project may rest with the design of the baskets that will actually hold the fuel assemblies: they must be flexible and reliable enough to withstand temperature extremes but also rugged enough to store and transport fuel assemblies of various designs. The AMEC containers are likely to be about 5 meters tall, 2 meters in diameter, and weight 45 tons; they may be capable of holding up to 95 fuel assemblies.[86]

Associated with the AMEC containers would be a concrete "overpack" or outer covering for use while in a storage function. For transportation if so designated, the containers would be provided with a "transport overpack" instead, for added strength and compatibility with transportation equipment. In this capacity, they could supplement the functions of the very expensive TUK-18 transport containers. According to a MINATOM official, AMEC containers will have specifications similar to the TUK-18s but will be cheaper by a factor of 5. Presumably the AMEC containers could also be used to store and transport damaged fuel because of design compatibility and perhaps because of less concern about making them unusable for further transport duty because of radioactive contamination. The containers will be able to accept fuel assemblies from both submarines and icebreakers, another reflection of the similarity of the two reactor types, and will meet international safety standards. According to US officials, funds will be provided for design and siting of a prototype storage pad for placement of 5 to 10 containers.[87]

The AMEC containers involve a number of companies, including AEA Technology of the United Kingdom, NAC International of the United States, and the Special Mechanical Engineering Design Office (KSBM) and Izhorsky Zavod of Russia. NAC has had considerable experience in spent fuel storage issues, having designed the world's first transportable storage container, and will assist primarily with licensing and technology transfer.[88] The concrete container and pad storage system has been used in the United States by commercial electric utilities, such as Virginia Electric and Power Company (VEPCO), for temporary storage of spent fuel from their nuclear reactors pending a decision on permanent storage. In addition to the AMEC participants, DG XI of the European Commission has committed to fund 35 percent of the total costs. The pilot project will cost $1.1 million.

The AMEC containers are a spin-off of work already underway to store spent fuel assemblies from Russian civilian nuclear power plant reactors. Herein lies the cause for some confusion. NAC has also been working with the Leningrad Nuclear Power Plant to develop a container system for managing RBMK fuel, required because Russia decided not to reprocess the zirconium-clad spent fuel assemblies from RBMK reactors. The container design is complete and testing and regulatory review are underway. Like the AMEC design, they are part of a metal-concrete container and pad storage system to be sited in various locales; they also may have a transport option. With apparently little modification, the RBMK containers can be used to store submarine spent fuel as well and hence are something of a competitor with the AMEC project and for new fixed interim storage facilities — like those being considered for Northwest Russia and Mayak. Spent fuel from submarines and inadequate storage facilities like Andreeva Bay could be placed in either RBMK or AMEC containers and arranged in rows on concrete pads at various locations. Some sources indicate that the RBMK containers will be about 10 meters tall and 4 meters in diameter, with a capacity of about 300 spent fuel assemblies.[89] They are 80-ton monsters that would undoubtedly be more difficult to handle than the AMEC containers. Concrete storage pad location selection for such a systems would be crucial because of the significant weights involved, the high radioactivity of the spent fuel concerned, and the potential requirement for further relocation of the containers.

A Russia–US project called "Omega" is working toward using the modified–RBMK containers for storage of submarine spent fuel. Test rigs are being built and a test container constructed; Russia is establishing a training center in Moscow. Although the initial prototype will be expensive, perhaps $5 million, serial production costs of the system would be modest: the 45 ton AMEC containers will cost $160 thousand each while the 80 ton RBMK units will cost $260 thousand. Because the larger containers can hold three times as many fuel assemblies, however, they are effectively half the price of the smaller units. A total of 450 to 500 would reportedly be needed to deal with the accumulation of spent fuel from submarine reactors.[90] The United States has committed to funding the production of 60 to 100 casks in 1999 for distribution to the Northern and Pacific fleets. In August 1998, MINATOM approved the storage of marine spent fuel in the RBMK containers, designated TUK MBK-VMF, and full-scale testing was completed on 23 October 1998.[91] GAN licensing may slow their introduction, however.

The metal-concrete and pad system has great potential. V. Ershov of MINATOM noted that: "When the rate of fuel discharge from submarines exceeds Mayak processing capacity, the metal-concrete containers with fuel will be placed on the accumulating pads or in surface storage facilities."[92] It would be conceivable, for example, to establish a buffer storage area of AMEC or modified–RBMK containers in the Zapadnaya Litsa region and to transfer to them the thousands of inadequately stored spent fuel assemblies from Andreeva Bay. Spent fuel from submarines removed from service could go directly to these containers as well, at least for those that have been out of commission for several years and hence have relatively low heat generation potential. In effect the defueling chain could be diverted from the populated regions of Murmansk and Severodvinsk and from storage and reprocessing at Mayak, to end up — at least in the intermediate term — in the Zapadnaya Litsa region, perhaps at Nerpichya, the current *Typhoon* class SSBN base and potential railhead. This would mean that Zapadnaya Litsa — 30 miles from the border of Norway — would remain a center of spent fuel storage and defueling activity, probably not what Norwegian environmental advocacy groups and policy-makers had envisaged through their leadership in the Russian submarine spent fuel issue. Whatever the final destination of submarine spent fuel, widespread use of the metal-concrete container/pad storage system seems likely.

Other US Initiatives

Despite its obvious expertise in dealing with marine nuclear issues and its muscular economy, the United States is a relatively modest funding source in projects specifically targeted at Russia's submarine nuclear waste and spent fuel problems — at least when compared to Norway. In the context of the substantial financial and political support provided the Russian government, however, the United States has been doing its fair share.

The Nunn-Lugar or Cooperative Threat Reduction (CTR) program is undoubtedly the most important US–Russia initiative.[93] Under the Strategic Offensive Arms Elimination Program, Nunn-Lugar has put hundreds of millions of dollars into Russia and other countries of the former Soviet Union since 1991 with the goal of reducing the possibility of proliferation by helping to control or destroy weapons of mass destruction made available as a result of the end of the Cold War. According to Senator Lugar, over $2 billion has been spent in the effort, facilitating the destruction of 339 ballistic missiles, 286 ballistic missile launchers, 37 bombers, 96 submarine missile launchers, and 30 submarine-launch ballistic missiles. It also sealed 191 nuclear test tunnels and, most notably, helped to deactivate 4,838 warheads taken from strategic launch systems.[94] A centerpiece project is the construction of a $300 million storage facility at Mayak for fissile material removed from Russian nuclear weapons. When the first wing opens in 2002, it will hold the plutonium and enriched uranium from 6,250 nuclear weapons. Although slightly less visible and under some criticism in recent years, Nunn-Lugar has been a cornerstone of the post–Cold War US–Russian relationship. According to Senator Richard Lugar, it has "established a bridge of communication and cooperation for a mutual US–Russian advantage."[95] Reflecting on President Clinton's State of the Union message of January 1999, CTR could be in-line for greater funding and significant growth as a result of additional counter-proliferation initiatives.

Since late 1994, the United States has also been delivering equipment to assist Russia with the dismantlement of its SSBN missile launchers under the CTR program. The projects have provided a total of about $28 million worth of equipment and services, including hull-cutting shears, cable cutters, and other ship-breaking equipment.[96] According to Senator Lugar, seven strategic missile submarines will be eliminated using FY 1998 CTR funds. The program is committed to eliminating 30 more by the year 2003 and will apparently include the first *Typhoon* class to be decommissioned in 1999.[97] Equipment, such as plasma torches and high strength hull cutting equipment, has already been provided to Russian shipyards to assist in the project. The effort has also unfortunately demonstrated some of the difficulties that accompany international cooperative efforts with Russia. One report noted that the Harris-Baylor shear cutting tool (essentially a powerful "jaws of life" mounted on a Caterpillar tractor) can not easily access Russian submarine hulls because the Russian ships have internal structural ribs closer together than American ones. Russians have complained about the cutting blades of the shear as well, which have to be replaced after only seven hours of operation, instead of the expected 70 — 80 hours. Some have estimated that these and other problems limit the equipment's usefulness to 15–20 percent of that expected.[98]

A new land-based dry-dock with special equipment for dismantling submarines is under construction at the Nerpa shipyard north of Murmansk and will be equipped with other machinery manufactured in the Unites States, such as a plasma torch for cutting tempered steel hull plates. The construction began in 1993 and was scheduled to be completed by 1996, but has been delayed by economic problems. Building costs are estimated at about $54 million.[99] CTR has also provided dismantling equipment to facilities on the Russian Pacific coast. According to First Vice-Governor of Maritime Territory Konstantin Tolstoshein and Director of the Zvezda plant Valery Maslokov, "it is not very pleasant to be supported by somebody" but the project will be helpful for the town of Bolshoi Kamen which is in severe economic straits.[100]

CTR has also taken on the funding requirement for an additional four railcars to carry TUK-18 spent fuel transport containers, complementing the four funded by Norway under the Norway-Russia Framework Agreement. In a move impossible to consider only a few years ago, CTR has committed to help pay Russian shipyard workers to dismantle Russian missile submarines. CTR is also funding development of a multi-compartment unit for long term afloat storage of reactor components.[101] A relatively recent initiative involves a plan to unload spent fuel assemblies from the service ship *Lotta*, currently attached to the icebreaker fleet in Murmansk, and to store the fuel in AMEC containers when they arrive. The *Lotta* could then go to the Nerpa shipyard north of Murmansk to be available to accept fuel assemblies from submarines undergoing defueling and dismantlement.[102] Another initiative includes a commitment of $500 thousand toward the construction of a Radwaste storage facility in the Murmansk region, announced by Deputy Secretary of State Strobe Talbott at the 20 January 1998 Barents Euro-Arctic Council meeting.[103] This may include metal-concrete containers for the spent fuel.

The Department of Energy has a number of its own initiatives with Russia under the rubric of the nuclear material protection, control, and accounting (MPC&A) program. The United States has a sophisticated and elaborate control system for storage and use of its weapons useable material, such as the procedures and equipment in place at Los Alamos National Laboratory. The methodologies were less developed in the Soviet Union

Figure 7. Russian submarine being dismantled in Northwest Russia.

where, according to estimates, more than 1,200 tons of highly enriched uranium and 150 tons of plutonium were produced.[104] Because of concern for the accountability of such material in the aftermath of the Cold War, the Department of Energy began a partnership with Russia and other states of the former Soviet Union to improve security—based on US MPC&A concepts. In association with CTR, MPC&A programs to upgrade facilities in the former Soviet Union have been underway since the mid–1990s and include upgrades to sensor and monitoring systems at Mayak and Tomsk-7, improvements to MINATOM's spent fuel transport railcars, and security upgrades at a number of other nuclear laboratories and reactor sites. According to US Secretary of Energy Federico Pena, the Department of Energy is involved at 53 sites in the former Soviet Union to assist with various materials protective control and accounting projects. In 1995, the department initiated a Laboratory-to-Laboratory program whereby US national laboratories would cooperate directly with Russian nuclear institutes to improve MPC&A. There is a nuclear cities initiative as well to help Russian nuclear installations with their conversion from defense production and to help guard against proliferation.[105] For the Russian Navy, the initiative has:

1. completed construction of physical protection annex at a Northern Fleet nuclear fresh fuel storage facility;

2. completed MPC&A designs for fresh fuel storage on the icebreaker refueling ship *Imandra*; and,

3. completed site visit and vulnerability analysis for the Russian Navy Refueling Ship *PM-63*.[106]

In addition, about $55 million has been committed to support programs focused on the environmental and health effects of the long-term operation of the former Soviet Union's nuclear weapons production complex. Of that amount, about $9 million has been spent on studying Russia's possible nuclear contamination of the Arctic region. The Sandia National Laboratory has been providing help to Russia in radioactive material transportation management and the Nuclear Regulatory Commission (NRC) has been working with GAN on issues such as physical security, regulatory development, licensing, and inspection. The NRC is not funded directly for this effort and must work through agreements with the Department of Defense and the Department of Energy.[107]

The NRC/Department of Energy relationship has not always been smooth and is an example of the complications resulting from the large number of US actors engaged with various nuclear safety, security, and Radwaste initiatives in Russia. In addition to the NRC and Department of Energy, other agencies involved with the Russian submarine spent fuel problem include the Department of State, the Department of Defense, and the Environmental Protection Agency, various national laboratories and a number of multinational corporations. Each has its own expectations and agendas that sometimes operate at cross purposes. Interagency cooperation is a developed art-form in the US government, however, so difficulties are usually worked out, if only after some messy negotiations.

In the process of working with Russia on these issues, the United States has developed some influence over Russia's nuclear activities by tying cooperation and aid to specific projects and procedural changes within the Russian nuclear establishment. For example, in keeping with the US policy of trying to reduce the world-wide stocks of fissile material, one of the vitrification plants at Mayak is being constructed by the sale of Russian weapons grade uranium to the United States.[108] Under another agreement, Russia will receive $70–80 million from the United States under the Gore-Chernomyrdin Commission to convert its plutonium production reactors to purely civilian use.[109]

ISTC

An innovative American initiative related to the Russian Radwaste problem is the International Science and Technology Center in Moscow (ISTC). It was established in 1994 by the United States, Russia, the European Union, and Japan, with Sweden, Norway, and South Korea joining later. ISTC was created to help develop appropriate employment for Russian defense sector scientists, engineers, and technicians who would otherwise be unemployed and possibly drawn to sell their skills to unstable countries or terrorist groups. The formal objectives, as defined by the organization's founding agreement, are:

1. To give CIS [Commonwealth of Independent States, i.e., most of the states of the former Soviet Union] weapons scientists, particularly those with knowledge and skills related to weapons of mass destruction and their delivery systems, opportunities to redirect their talents to peaceful activities.

2. To contribute to solving national and international technical problems.

3. To support the transition to market-based economies.

4. To support basic and applied research.

5. To encourage the integration of CIS weapons scientists into the international scientific community.[110]

ISTC currently provides direct payments to the individual accounts of 17,000 Russian professionals to use their talents in peaceful activities.[111] There are about 38 ISTC projects, including work on safe storage of weapons-grade plutonium and uranium, development of a system for computerized nuclear control and accounting, work with laser isotope separation, plus a number of environmental assessment projects. ISTC is a member of the IAEA Contact Group (discussed below) that helps coordinate Radwaste projects in Russia and has also conducted studies to support advanced solutions to Radwaste problems, such as the feasibility of using particle accelerator technology to convert long-lived spent fuel isotopes to shorter-lived elements. Though acknowledged by many as a successful program, ISTC has come under recent criticism from the US General Accounting Office (GAO) because some Russian scientists receiving ISTC subsidies have allegedly continued to work on weapons development programs.[112]

Sweden

Sweden has played a significant role in addressing the nuclear problems of the countries formerly under communist rule. Much of its attention has gone to projects in Central and Eastern Europe dealing with radiation protection and nuclear power plant safety, such as initiatives at the Ignalina Nuclear Power Plant in Lithuania (two RBMK reactors) and (with Finland) the Leningrad Nuclear Power Plant near St. Petersburg (four RBMK reactors). Swedish funds have also gone to Radwaste projects in the Barents region, including studies of radioecology, instruction in general safety and waste strategies, medical radiation training and studies, and project assessments. Under the leadership of the Swedish Radiation Protection Institute, Swedish experts are training personnel from Russian ministries and organization on nuclear safety control and decision-making. Sweden also organized a workshop on nuclear liability with representatives of GAN, helped provide regulatory support in licensing for the *Lepse* project, and assisted with studies of the RADON waste storage facility in Murmansk.[113] In 1994 the Swedish National Radiation Protection Institute (SSI) prepared a summary of waste management problems in Russia that included the Barents region.

Sweden has begun to take a more active role in Russian submarine spent fuel matters. A representative from the Swedish Radiation Protection Institute occupied the presidency of the IAEA CEG on Radwaste for the first two years of its existence and Sweden has been in the forefront of efforts to streamline CEG procedures. Of particular importance to the submarine spent fuel problem has been Sweden's involvement in interim storage projects for spent fuel. These include proposed studies of conditions at Mayak and Murmansk to support the construction of an interim storage facility, involvement in the metal-concrete container project for spent fuel at Andreeva Bay, and studies and seminars on the feasibility of using the island of Novaya Zemlya as a final repository for radioactive waste. Sweden has been promoting so-called "chain analysis" to move forward with the defueling process in a cost-effective and rational way. As of 1997, the country had set aside $1.29 million for Radwaste projects on the Kola Peninsula.

Sweden is often represented in these matter by the firm SKB, the Swedish Nuclear Fuel and Waste Management Company. SKB was formed jointly by the four electric companies in Sweden that operate nuclear power plants to manage the Radwaste from the operation of their reactors. The company has also worked extensively with Estonia and Lithuania to improve the quality of their Radwaste management practices and is a member of

the Industrial Group investigating ways and means to alleviate the Russian submarine spent fuel problem (discussed below).[114] Because the nuclear
industry in Sweden is being legislated out of existence over the next several years, despite operating 12 nuclear reactors and providing 50 percent
of the electric power used in the country, Swedish companies and nuclear
agencies would no doubt welcome significant participation in Russian
nuclear safety and Radwaste projects.[115]

Finland and Denmark

Finland has also been active in efforts to improve nuclear power plant
safety in the Barents and Baltic regions. It has participated in a nuclear
safety culture project with the Leningrad and Kola Nuclear Power Plants
and developed a program of regulatory cooperation between the Finnish
Center for Radiation and Nuclear Safety (STUK), GAN, and the RADON
complex near St. Petersburg. Of direct impact on the defueling chain has
been Finland's support of a portable liquid waste purification facility. The
IVO Company of Finland, with funds from the Finnish foreign ministry,
has developed a modular truck-delivered liquid Radwaste purification system called NURES. NURES successfully purified icebreaker waste at Murmansk and IVO hopes to gain permission to try NURES on high-salinity
submarine waste, perhaps at Zapadnaya Litsa. Finnish companies and
officials have also been involved in resolving environmental problems at
Andreeva Bay. In particular, a small stream has been undercutting part of
the Radwaste storage area and carrying radioactive contamination toward
the Zapadnaya Litsa Fjord.

The Danish government has not been active in the Russian submarine spent fuel problem, despite its involvement with several Arctic environmental organizations. Worth mentioning however is the work of the
Danish "Nuclear Preparedness Group," established as a cooperative project between the Risø National Laboratory, the Technical University of
Denmark, and the Danish Nuclear Inspectorate. The accident analysis of
NATO's *Phase I CCMS Report* on cross-border contamination was based
on work done by the Risø National Laboratory. Professor P. L. Ølgaard of
the Laboratory has published several documents on the Russian submarine spent fuel issue, including the book *Decommissioning of Naval Nuclear
Ships.*[116]

Europe's Great Powers

Both the United Kingdom and France have robust civilian and military nuclear establishments and hence considerable expertise to address the Radwaste needs of Northwest Russia. They also operate several nuclear submarines, are acknowledged possessors of nuclear weapons, have reprocessing capability and, as a consequence of all this nuclear activity, Radwaste disposal problems. In the United Kingdom particularly, nuclear issues have been controversial with much passionate debate and occasional public protest. The Campaign for Nuclear Disarmament (CND) was enormously influential during the nuclear controversies of the 1970s and 80s, such as over NATO's deployment of new nuclear missiles to Europe. In recent years, the British nuclear industry has been subject to considerable criticism for proposals to use mixed oxide fuels (MOX — plutonium mixed with enriched uranium) in British commercial power plants. The Labor government of Prime Minister Tony Blair was also subject to unwanted notoriety when it accepted 5 kg of highly enriched uranium from the Republic of Georgia, acceding to a request from the Clinton administration of the United States.[117] Controversies aside, British Nuclear Fuels (BNFL), AEA Technology, and NNC are large and experienced British firms that have been involved in reactor safety and Radwaste projects in Russia for several years. These include design and analysis of plutonium storage and Radwaste management at Mayak, evaluation of contaminated regions such as Mayak, Tomsk-7, and Krasnoyarsk-26, and participation in the *Lepse* and metal-concrete container projects.

In France, nuclear issues have only recently become controversial. Over 75 percent of the electrical power in France is provided by nuclear reactors and the French nuclear industry is among the most advanced in the world, represented by large corporations like SGN and Cogema. French regulatory agencies are participants in the *Lepse* project, but in general both the French and British governments do not play an active role in the Russian submarine spent fuel issue. They seem to defer to the European Commission on funding for projects and may be sensitive to their own military services in not assisting the Russian Navy in any significant way. British and French nuclear industries seem anxious for nuclear contracts in Russia, however, and are important participants in a number of initiatives.

Germany is a relatively minor player in the submarine Radwaste problem, focusing instead on safety programs for the civilian nuclear power plants of the former Soviet bloc. The German company Siemens, for example, is providing equipment to upgrade the Kola Nuclear Power Plant.[118]

Germany is also funding CTR-like projects in the region to help with arms dismantlement and environmental cleanup, as is Japan.[119] The Green part of the SPD/Green coalition government that took power in Germany in 1998 has an active anti-nuclear agenda that has already caused substantial controversy within NATO and the German nuclear industry, but it is not clear how this might affect the country's participation in Russian Radwaste projects.

Industrial Group and Interim Storage

In 1997 the so-called "Industrial Group" was formed, a consortium of four multinational corporations with nuclear expertise established to bid on projects dealing with Russian Radwaste problems. Industrial Group members are:

1. BNFL Engineering of the United Kingdom, experienced with projects at the Mayak reprocessing plant and Krasnoyarsk.
2. Kvaerner Maritime of Norway, working the ship and rail issues of the defueling chain and conducting an overall evaluation of Northwest Russia Radwaste issues under the Norwegian-Russian agreement.
3. SKB of Sweden, with extensive nuclear experience in the Baltic States and Eastern Europe.
4. SGN, leading the *Lepse* project and engaged at Krasnoyarsk.

VNIPIET, the Russian design and engineering firm based in St. Petersburg, is associated with the Industrial Group. It designed the spent fuel storage facilities at Andreeva Bay and Gremikha and has been active in a number of other nuclear projects.

In September 1997, the Industrial Group was awarded a contract by the European Commission, Norway, and Sweden, to study options available for interim storage of submarine spent fuel in Northwest Russia. Several alternatives are available:

1. Completing the VNIPIET-designed wet storage facility at Mayak.
2. Building a new dry storage facility at Mayak of Western design.
3. Completing the Murmansk Shipping Company wet storage facility at Murmansk.
4. Building a new dry storage facility in Northwest Russian of Western design.

5. Making extensive use of the new AMEC or RBMK metal-concrete containers, perhaps at Andreeva Bay and Murmansk.

Completing the Mayak wet storage facility was an early favorite of Norway and remains the preferred option of Russian officials. The facility would tie-in with Mayak's hoped-for future as a major and profit-making nuclear reprocessing activity. However, Bellona and other groups now argue that transporting so much spent fuel 2000 miles from Northwest Russia to Mayak would be dangerous, would take too long (up to 20 years to get rid of all the spent fuel), and would be prohibitively expensive.[120] There are also concerns about using wet spent fuel storage designs like the incomplete one at Mayak instead of newer designs that would incorporate easier to manage dry storage technologies. Wet storage creates contaminated water that must be managed and monitored and that can escape to the environment under the wrong conditions. Environmentalists and perhaps even official Norway now tend to favor building a dry storage facility on the Kola Peninsula, even though it would retain large quantities of radioactive material within the fragile Arctic region — again counter to a central goal for much of the international initiatives undertaken to this point.

Another part of the Industrial Group study was to evaluate possible ways of treating the spent fuel that cannot be reprocessed at Mayak. The RT-1 plant at Mayak will not accept the thousands of damaged spent nuclear fuel assemblies remaining from past Russian Navy reactor accidents, perhaps 10 percent of the total.[121] It will also not accept fuel from liquid metal cooled reactors and those with zirconium cladding, perhaps another 20 percent of the total spent fuel inventory.

The Industrial Group completed its storage facility study in June 1998. Its findings supported the view that a dry storage facility should be built, preferably on the Kola Peninsula. Much of the reasoning concerned cost rather than hazards: dry storage could be built for about 80 percent less than a new wet storage facility, not including the substantial expense of improving rail transport from the Kola Peninsula to Mayak. Dry storage could also be built at Mayak, but finishing the wet storage facility would cost 20–30 percent more than building a new dry storage facility. The Mayak facility also suffers from "a complete lack of quality assurance standards," according to Industrial Group representatives. Russian officials are likely to continue to push for completion of their Mayak wet storage facility and point out that it is already licensed although the license is old and probably does not meet international standards. Western aid is unlikely to be forthcoming for any facility that is not in line with their environmental expectations.[122]

During the study, the Industrial Group was barred from the Andreeva Bay base where they had hoped to study the various submarine spent fuel storage problems of the site. The Russian Navy was in control of the facilities and did not allow access, perhaps increasingly unwilling to do so. The facility will be transferred from the Russian Navy to MINATOM, perhaps by sometime in 1999, after which foreign access should improve.[123]

Norway and Sweden are prepared to fund the design and engineering work for an interim storage facility and as much as $26 million may be available through the TACIS program of the European Commission to build the facility. Construction of a dry storage facility would take about four years and would probably receive a 40-year license; it could hold 6,750 canisters in the first phase and an additional 6,750 in the second, for a total of 65,000 fuel assemblies.[124] Moving forward with an interim storage facility would be a major step towards alleviating Russia's submarine spent fuel problems. The Industrial Group seems to have the industrial muscle, expertise, and political connections to get things done and is the envy of other Western corporations and groups engaged in Russian nuclear projects, earning the sardonic nickname "the gang of four." The Industrial Group will likely play a key role in any overall defueling chain plan developed by Russia or the international community.

IAEA CEG

International Atomic Energy Agency Contact Experts Group for International Radwaste Projects (IAEA CEG) is the international organization most closely associated with Russia's submarine spent fuel problem. Interest in a dedicated organization emerged as a result of a May 1995 IAEA seminar titled "International Cooperation on Nuclear Waste management in the Russian Federation." The seminar was requested and sponsored by the Nordic countries with the hope that a group could be created to help coordinate information and initiatives related to Northwest Russia's nuclear waste problems. The goal was to avoid redundancy and duplication of effort, to assure that priority needs were understood by all concerned and interested parties, and to identify points of contact to facilitate cooperation.[125] Coordination was clearly necessary because of the proliferation of Radwaste and reactor safety projects over the years, with an obvious risk of overlapping or missing areas of concern without proper coordination. Other contact groups have developed in the post–Cold War period, such as those operating under OSCE auspices to help the international community manage various crises in the Balkans. The objective of the IAEA CEG is to advance international cooperative efforts aimed at resolving Radwaste management issues, such as radiation safety, environmental, technical, legal, organizational and financial matters; a particular focus is to facilitate practical measures to reduce Radwaste hazards in Russia and to deal with the submarine spent fuel problem in Northwest Russia. The IAEA CEG recently expanded its attention to include monitoring and cooperative efforts at Mayak, including environmental and spent fuel and waste management problems.[126] These of course may be crucial to moving forward with resolving the submarine fuel problem.

The IAEA CEG was formally established in September 1995 at a meeting in Stockholm, with its first meeting held in March 1996. The group is composed of twelve members and two observers. The members are Belgium, France, Finland, Germany, Norway, Russia, Sweden, United Kingdom, the United States, the European Union, the International Institute for Applied Systems Analysis (IIASA), and the International Science and Technology Center (ISTC); the two observers are Japan and NEFCO. The ISTC and NEFCO were identified earlier; the IIASA is a research group with a charter to investigate issues of sustainability and "the human dimensions of global change." Its headquarters are in a Habsburg palace in Laxenburg, a small town about 15 km south of Vienna, Austria. Since its origins in 1972, the IIASA has promoted and conducted international scientific collaboration on issues such as energy, water, environment, risk, and human settlement. The group was founded in the midst of the Cold War with a charter to promote East-West scientific cooperation; it still does.[127]

The IAEA CEG maintains a small secretariat in Vienna at IAEA headquarters. The secretariat has scheduling functions, follows up commitments, and ensures members have appropriate documents and reports. It is currently tracking over 150 projects, including many of the studies and engineering projects discussed previously that are aimed at setting up a functioning defueling chain. The Group convenes every six months in a member country; in 1998, for example, it met in Augusta, GA (close to the US Savannah River nuclear weapons facility) in April and in Murmansk, Russia in November. The president of the Contact Group for its first two years of operation was a high ranking member of the Swedish Radiation Protection Institute; in 1998, the members selected the ranking US representative. The vice president has been Viktor Gubanov, Head of MINATOM's Department of Safety, Ecology and Emergency Situations. Despite these formalities, the CEG's level of institutionalization is very low; members contribute time and information because it is in their own interest to do so, not because of any institutional imperative. The Contact Group budget is met by contributions from the membership and is minuscule by international standards. Meetings are run by the host countries and sustained by ample contributions from host organizations and interested industrial activities.

Contact Group meetings vary in attendance, but always include member diplomats, technical experts, representatives from Russian activities, and Western companies that hope to profit from nuclear waste contracts. At the June 1997 CEG meeting in St. Petersburg, Russia, MINATOM, Mayak, the Russian Navy, and a number of other activities represented Russia. Officials from the European Commission's DG XI and TACIS, European nuclear agencies, Norway, and the United States, and personnel from industrial firms in Finland, France, Norway, the United Kingdom, and the United States were also present. The meetings and reports of the CEG provide a public opportunity for countries, international organizations, and companies to trumpet their successes or to confess by silence their lack of participation or progress. The ad hoc nature of the IAEA CEG is a strength because issues can be discussed in an unofficial off-the-record fashion, with a straightforward sharing of information that can and does promote cooperation. On the other hand, the lack of institutionalization means that there is little organizational or moral opprobrium, and certainly no political or economic sanction, if projects go unreported or are not updated. The weak institutionalization also means that the group could disappear overnight if important supporters — such as the Russia, Norway, the United States, and the European Commission — lose interest in using it as a forum. Recent proposals have opened the way to more regularized IAEA CEG procedures along European institutional lines that might help to ensure its continued existence and to increase its influence. Russia has asked that an IAEA CEG representative be stationed in Moscow for closer and quicker liaison with Russian activities.

As with other such grouping, what happens at the margins may be as importance as the meetings themselves. The formal agenda and briefings provide useful updates on significant activities, but the conversations that take place during coffee breaks and after adjournment are where relationships are established and deals made. Overall, the CEG has shown that coordination and prioritization of various bilateral and multilateral programs is possible and can have a positive benefit. It seems effective as a catalyst for project integration within its membership and with other internationally sponsored initiatives. A particular benefit is that Russia is brought into a forum of equals, where Radwaste problems can be discussed in a reasonably collegial and professional environment.

The 7th Meeting of the IAEA CEG, held in November 1998 in Murmansk, was significant in that the group agreed on a list of recommended "highest immediate priority" projects to complement the MINATOM/ Russian Navy list discussed in Chapter 5. The group encouraged those involved not only to continue the projects so designed, but to accelerate them:

1. Modernization of facility for treatment of liquid radioactive wastes at the repair yard RTP Atomflot [the Murmansk Trilateral Initiative].
2. Decommissioning of the floating service ship *Lepse* [the *Lepse* project].
3. Construction and commissioning of an interim storage for spent nuclear fuel at Mayak [the Industrial Group study].
4. Construction of Metal-Concrete Casks for storage & transport of spent nuclear fuel deriving from nuclear submarines [the AMEC and modified–RBMK container projects].[128]

With luck, a long-term plan for Russian spent fuel, supported and funded by both Russia and the international community, will emerge from some future IAEA CEG meeting.

Revolutionary Solutions and Approaches

Despite the obvious defects in Russia's nuclear safety culture and the need for immediate international aid to resolve Russia's submarine spent fuel problem, one should not get the idea that Soviet nuclear technology is crude and unsophisticated. While Russia lags the West in areas such as Radwaste disposal and reactor instrumentation and control, it is a world leader in technologies such as uranium enrichment and reactor design.[129] According to a safety report received by the Norwegian Nuclear Energy Safety Authority, the *Sevmorput* reactor (the nuclear container ship with reactor technology reflective of modern Russian submarines), has fuel tubes containing the exotic metal gadolinium. This can absorb neutrons for a designed-for period and hence interfere with the fission process, but with a diminishing effect with time. This acts as a long-term burnable poison in the reactor fuel that can be used to extend the core's lifetime.[130] Following its experience with the *Alfa* class, Russia is undoubtedly the world leader in liquid metal reactor technology and MINATOM officials have expressed an interest in using liquid metal technology for land-based facilities. There could be some safety advantages to this approach because of the much lower pressures necessary to operate liquid metal reactors as compared to a pressurized water design.

It is also possible that solutions to the Russian submarine spent fuel problem and to other Radwaste dilemma's could take a radical turn from some emerging Russian or foreign scientific initiative. New technologies are in development that have some promise of reducing the time and expense necessary to store and dispose of high level Radwaste suitably. Russian scientists, for example, are working on the transmutation of spent fuel materials through neutron bombardment. Much of the very long-lived radioactivity associated with spent fuel and reprocessing waste comes from actinides, the heavy elements created by neutron bombardment of uranium during reactor operations and subsequent radioactive decay. The principle of transmutation, as stated by the Russian scientists concerned, is to separate actinides, fission products, and/or other isotopes of long half-life and to subject them to high fluxes of thermal neutrons, protons, or lasers. ISTC, working with Los Alamos National Laboratory of the United States, conducted a feasibility study on technologies possible for accelerator-based conversion of plutonium whereby the heavy elements were bombarded with neutrons and converted into isotopes with much shorter half-lives, from tens of thousand of years to only a few hundred. This could have a real impact on the kind of geological or other storage required for spent fuel material. While this area continues to be discussed, its implementation is likely to be far in the future because of the need to develop a credible and practical particle accelerator-driven system.[131]

Another technology would replace current reprocessing technologies and generate much less Radwaste in the process. Babcock & Wilcox has been working for several years on the Electro-Metallurgical Treatment (EMT) process that would reprocess nuclear spent fuel and create less than 1 percent of the radioactive material generated by the conventional PUREX process. According to Congressional testimony, the process would bind together long-lived actinides with plutonium without massive chemical processes, reducing the volume and toxicity of the end products, and separating only low-grade uranium that can then be used for light water reactors.[132] Russia could purchase such a system for about $15 million, twice that if the equipment necessary to "chop up" the spent fuel is included. Construction would take about two and a half years to complete and the entire Russian backlog of spent fuel could be disposed of in another three to four years.

Russia might also look for more affordable and low-tech solutions to its Radwaste problems instead of the gold-plated ones common in the

West, simply because many Western practices are prohibitively expensive to achieve. Russian Minister of Atomic Energy Adamov has proposed "burning" the radioactive waste in Russian fast breeder reactors.[133] Proposals have also been made to build a joint US–Russia spent fuel storage facility on an uninhabited Pacific atoll, such as Wake Island.[134] Because Russia faces special problems with a great deal of damaged spent fuel that cannot be easily reprocessed or stored, the issue of at-sea dumping could be revisited. The cores already dumped have not contributed significantly to the radiological contamination of the ocean because of the preparations made by Russian organizations. According to Povl Ølgaard of the Risø National Laboratory, further dumping of specially prepared damaged reactors might be a cost effective and safe alternative to rid Russia and the international community of a major environmental problem.[135]

Chapter 7

Decommissioned Russian Submarines, Cooperation, and International Theory

> *... although scholarly knowledge can generally be expected to make only an indirect, limited contribution to policymaking, its contribution will nevertheless often be critical for the development and choice of sound policies.*[1]

— Alexander L. George
Stanford University

The initiatives to help resolve the Russian submarine spent fuel problem are examples of successful international cooperative behavior in the post–Cold War era. Western government agencies, intergovernmental organizations, and multinational corporations have been working with Russian organizations on a variety of sensitive and hazardous nuclear safety and Radwaste projects. On the other hand, progress has been difficult and positive gains are measurable on one hand; no comprehensive plan has yet been accepted and no real endpoint to the problem is in sight. The success or failure of international cooperative efforts, not to mention the importance of the submarine spent fuel problem itself, make the issue an appropriate subject for a more systematic and theoretical analysis.

This chapter looks at international cooperation on the Russian submarine spent fuel problem to see if there are useful processes or patterns of behavior and activity that might be identified and generalized for application elsewhere. No grand theory of international relations or foreign policy is intended, given the embryonic and fractious nature of events and progress thus far, but a useful application of facts and events to established

theory that can contribute to an understanding of international cooperation in general and to environmental collaboration in particular. Indeed,
a structure and pattern to the engagement thus far is apparent that is consistent with previous theoretical work.

International Theory and Cooperation

Identifying and explaining the extent to which relations among states
and other world actors can be classified as cooperative is a prominent
fissure within the international relations discipline. A fundamental
assumption of both classical and structural realism is that the international system is anarchic and that cooperation is rare, occurring only when
the self-interest of the powers involved somehow converge or when the
impetus to cooperate is imposed by a more dominant authority. Countries often ally with each other against common enemies that threaten to
dominate the rest and will use warfare if necessary to guarantee their survival. Balance of power coalitions are usually temporary and break apart
once the threat is removed and the normal anarchy of the international
system returns.[2] Anarchy in this context means the lack of a central authority to enforce system-wide order, not continuous war or chaos.

The international system may develop a multipolar arrangement
where a number of great powers keep an eye on each other and shift allegiance to maintain a balance if necessary, or a bipolar one where two rigid
blocs exist under the domination of two very great powers. The Cold War
period of tension and confrontation between East and West was a bipolar
system, with the East dominated by the Soviet Union and the West by the
United States. It was relatively peaceful, at least as far as conflict between
the two superpowers was concerned, as predicted by structural realist theory for a bipolar system. Realists also characterized the Western security
and economic relationships of the Cold War period as hegemonic, meaning that the United States was the predominant state and had the power
and influence to establish the direction and tone of Western policy.
Arrangements such as the NATO military alliance and the various Western economic and financial regimes were developed under US hegemony
and served to anchor the freedom and prosperity of the free world.[3]

Liberalism in international relations takes a more positive view of the
likelihood of cooperation than realism.[4] Taking cues from 16th, 17th, and
18th century scholars like Hugo Grotius, John Locke, and Adam Smith,
liberal international theory considers the anarchy portrayed by realists as

an overstated and flawed assumption about the world condition. Countries are in fact rarely in military conflict with each other and the divisiveness among them, such as over trade or resource allocation, can usually be worked out by negotiations or arbitration under generally accepted rules of the game. Liberal theory also points out that a huge increase in cooperative activities has occurred since the end of World War II representing a sea-change in the way international relations take place. Nation states are no longer the only significant actors in international affairs and must share the spotlight with numerous intergovernmental organizations (IGOs), nongovernmental organizations (NGOs), and powerful multinational corporations (MNCs). Issues like the environment, with vexing problems such as ozone depletion and climate warming, are increasingly recognized as global in character and thereby in need of cooperation and action by almost all the countries of the world in order to succeed.

The internal character of states may also affect the frequency and depth of cooperation. Many liberal theorists now point to the empirically strong proposition that countries with liberal democratic governments and free market economies are unlikely to war with each other.[5] Explanations for this phenomena emphasize the shared values of the democratic polities involved, the number of institutional linkages among democratic countries, and the economic costs of conflict — an unattractive burden for capitalist republics to bear. Whatever the reason, the evidence is about as convincing as any hypothesis can be in the social sciences. The cooperative arrangements that have developed in Western Europe since World War II, particularly under the umbrella of the NATO alliance and the Treaties of Rome that led to the European Union, are perhaps the most important examples of this phenomena. With the end of communist rule in Central and Eastern Europe and the rejection of authoritarian governments in many other places, particularly Latin America, there is hope and occasional fulfillment of the promise that new governments will be less warlike and more prone to get along with each other than their authoritarian predecessors. Liberalism, in other words, finds reason to believe that contemporary international relations will be more pacific than other eras and that it should witness significant and varied examples of cooperation. Even if realists had once held an accurate view of international relations, exemplified by the balancing state behavior of the mid–18th century and the diplomatic legerdemain of Metternich and Bismarck in the 19th century, their model is decidedly "unrealistic" today.

Realists, however, watch the uncertainties and insecurities of the contemporary world with a knowing pessimism. Places like the Balkans, Africa, and the Middle East are by no means pacific, trade disputes between

Western powers are common and may be increasing in severity, financial crises can heighten regional tension, and states continue to measure their economic and military capabilities relative to their neighbors, leading many realists to conclude that the world is as it always was. They would be surprised if the cooperative structures created to confront the Soviet Union, like NATO, the European Union, and the Bretton Woods financial legacy, survive any significant shocks to the international system and whether the benefits of the regimes can be extended much beyond the security and economic interests of the major players.[6]

Other international relation studies, such as James K. Sebenius' 1984 classic analysis in *Negotiating the Law of the Sea*, have analyzed the specific dynamics of negotiations and bargaining among countries.[7] Andrew Moravcsik's more recent work has drawn attention to the power-based aspects of international bargaining — particularly as applied to the development of the European Union.[8] Both Sebenius and Moravcsik point to the great importance of domestic factors in international agreements. United States leadership in cooperative ventures is sometimes a response to the political agendas of domestic ethnic communities, committed political factions, or economic vested interests. Robert D. Putnam pointed out that while participants in negotiations are bargaining with their fellow diplomats in an international arena, at the same time they are looking to their domestic audience — the political, economic, and social groups that eventually must ratify any agreement made. This practice is sometimes called "double-edged diplomacy" or "two-level games."[9] Perhaps surprisingly, the country with the more difficult domestic situation for approval of a particular agreement often has the stronger bargaining position at the international level because its negotiating partners recognize that only limited concessions can be expected. Moravcsik contributed further to an understanding of this phenomena by attempting to unify the domestic and systemic aspects of international decision-making and cooperation.[10] The Russian submarine spent fuel problem presents challenges and gratification to several of these approaches to international cooperation.

Arctic Cooperation

The Arctic region has a number of examples of international cooperation, some long predating the end of the Cold War. One of the first was reached in 1911 with an agreement on North Pacific fur seal hunting among Russia, Great Britain (Canada), Japan, Russia, and the United States. In the security realm, the "Treaty Relating to Spitsbergen" of 1920 settled the international status of the Svalbard archipelago—a group of islands about 500 miles north of Norway. Rival claims to the islands, particularly among Norway, the Soviet Union, and Sweden, were settled with the recognition of Norwegian sovereignty over the region but with resource and personnel access concessions made to the other interested powers. The agreement remains in force, having stood the test of World War II combat and Cold War tension.[11]

International agreement on polar bears, according to Anne Fikkan, Gail Osherenko, and Alexander Arikainen, was a real "ice breaker" for international cooperation on Arctic issues.[12] Polar bears migrated across the Arctic region without regard to political boundaries and were becoming a frequent target for airplane-delivered trophy hunters. In 1973, Canada, Denmark (Greenland), Norway, the Soviet Union, and the United States, agreed to a ban on almost all hunting of polar bears. More recently, efforts have been made to combat the problems of ozone depletion and atmospheric haze, both affecting the Arctic region more than temperate areas. Worldwide concern for the ozone layer resulted in a ban on chlorofluorocarbons (CFCs such as Freon) through a series of agreements in the 1980s and 1990s. Arctic haze is a more difficult problem to solve because of its varied sources.[13] It also makes clear that the Arctic is a peripheral region with relatively few inhabitants and little intrinsic political power. Actions that would limit the activity and energy consumption of the major population centers of the world, as would be needed to reduce Arctic haze, have little political support and would be difficult to implement.[14] This is a northern variation of the core-periphery conflict emphasized by Immanuel Wallerstein in his world system theory.[15]

In addition to agreements and conventions on specific Arctic problems, numerous organizations and regimes dedicated to Arctic issues have developed over the years. Some are significant only as entries in a catalog of NGOs while others have enduring influence, like the International Arctic Science Committee.[16] Oran R. Young and his colleagues of the Institute of Arctic Studies at Dartmouth College and elsewhere have examined various Arctic initiatives and regimes to identify the factors causing their success or failure. As with most issues in international relations, the reasons are complex, interrelated, and subject to interpretation. Power and interest are of course often essential. The dominant members can push a particular agenda and bring along other countries because of their overriding influence. Agreements or institutions may also be created because self-interested participants recognize they can achieve their goals more successfully through cooperation, even if no distinctive power bloc is formed to force a particular agenda. Power and interest are both basic building blocks of the realist view of cooperation. A more liberal notion is the possibility that cognitive-based incentives may also be important, meaning that the scientific and technical knowledge made available by a community of scholars, interested policy-makers, and other advocates can have a significant influence on the decisions ultimately made. Contextual factors might emerge as well, meaning that unique circumstances may be attached to the decision process in a peculiar way. Indeed, Young's group found that collaboration usually resulted from some mixture of incentives.[17]

Collaborating: Finding Common Ground for Multiparty Problems

Another approach to international cooperation was developed by Barbara Gray of Pennsylvania State University and the Darden School of Business at the University of Virginia. She evaluated a number of joint problem-solving efforts, including those to end military conflicts, labor-management disputes, and particularly environmental disputes and concerns. Gray prefers the term "collaboration" over "cooperation" in her work to stress the greater extent of interaction she hopes will result. Collaboration is a more involved process, often characterized by formal rules, pursuit of group instead of individual goals, and multiple linkages among the participants.[18] Gray also identified two types of situations where collaboration might emerge: those where participants were in conflict with one another and those where they have the same essential vision concerning a problem.[19] Nuclear waste in Northwest Russia is an issue where participants share a basic understanding of the problem and desired outcome, specifically that submarine spent fuel is a hazard that should be properly managed and cared for as soon as possible. The consensus comes apart, however, over timing, process, method, and commitment of resources. Because the Russian decommissioned submarine spent fuel problem has not been identified as a crisis, attention from key national leadership has been sporadic so that no really decisive action has been taken. The specific courses of action to follow have not been agreed upon, few resources have been made available, and other priority projects have not been dropped to give more attention to the spent fuel problem.

According to Gray, collaboration is a process where the issues and actors become more organized through the establishment of a negotiated order between various "stakeholders." Stakeholders are the actors that have a real or perceived interest in solving the problem and that are prepared to make significant commitments to do it.[20] In the spent fuel problem, key stakeholders (in addition to Russian participants) are organizations and officials from Norway, Sweden, Finland, the United States, and the European Commission — international actors with approximately the same ends in mind but with often different ideas and priorities on how to get there. Gray also emphasizes the "cognitive and expressive" nature of the process rather than "objective and instrumental" factors — meaning that the act of collaborating itself may be as important as the results. There is a hope and conviction that success in a particular collaboration will lead to new patterns of interaction and encourage a "richer relationship in the future" among the parties concerned.[21] This is a classic liberal framework, mingling the hopes for collaboration with the democratic peace hypothesis and even the spillover aspects of integration theory.[22]

Gray would no doubt accept Oran Young's power and interest hypotheses, but would appreciate his cognitive incentive approach even more. Unlikely coalitions may form "amid a dynamic interorganizational field," meaning that agreement may occur even when substantial discord on various other issues remains among the parties concerned. Such dynamics can occur in situations of great importance and value complexity and help to explain, for example, the 1975 Helsinki Final Act negotiations of the Conference on Security and Cooperation in Europe (the CSCE — now the OSCE). According to US participant John Maresca, "the questions [at the CSCE negotiations] were so complicated, the number and variety of countries and national interests so broad, and the various interrelated negotiating problems so tangled that only the negotiators themselves, on the spot in Geneva, could see through to possible solutions."[23] The Russian spent fuel problem has some aspects of this, with representatives in the field and at intergovernmental meetings trying to resolve complex issues known best to themselves. They can discuss and recommend various courses of action with at least some autonomy and in the process create greater trust and cooperation for the future.

A particularly helpful part of Gray's analysis is her identification of three phases of collaboration and the characteristics attached to each. The phases are "problem setting," "direction setting," and "implementation." While her treatment is generic and frequently focused on circumstances of pressing and divisive conflict among concerned parties, the collaboration developing to manage Russian submarine spent fuel and related issues can also be usefully analyzed with her categories. Applying Gray's paradigm suggests a further elaboration, that the types of international actors engaged in each phase can be identified and her phases further specified: problem setting is primarily the domain of nongovernmental organizations and related environmental advocacy groups; direction setting is dominated by national governments, intergovernmental organizations, and rule-making regimes; and, implementation is where the involvement by private enterprise and multinational industrial alliances may be decisive.

Problem Setting and Russian
Submarine Spent Fuel

The military and commercial applications of nuclear energy are among the most controversial issues of modern times. Since the use of the atomic bomb in World War II, practitioners and opponents of nuclear energy have been debating its terror and promise — though usually talking past each other in the process; arguments are frequently made not face-to-face or in official proceedings, but in the tribunal of public opinion. With the end of the Cold War, the dialogue has shifted from fears of destruction from nuclear attack by a superpower to concerns about nuclear weapons proliferating to rogue countries and terrorist groups and to the potential dangers and enormous expense required to cleanup the residue of nuclear weapons production. In post–Chernobyl Europe significant worry remains over the operation of nuclear reactors used for electric power production, particularly those designed by the former Soviet Union.

The Arctic region has its own nuclear history. Soviet nuclear weapons were tested on the Arctic island of Novaya Zemlya from 1955 until 1990, in the atmosphere and underwater until 1962 and underground thereafter. Nuclear powered submarines, surface warships, and icebreakers have operated extensively in Arctic waters for decades, with some carrying nuclear weapons. The virtually unlimited power of nuclear reactors allowed ships to survive and function reasonably well in the harsh conditions at the top of the world, but also made the region one of crucial importance to both East and West during the Cold War and — according to anti-nuclear activists — a likely place for nuclear accidents. The Chernobyl disaster heightened concerns about radioactive contamination of the Arctic and remains one of the significant contributors to the region's anthropogenic contamination.

As detailed in Chapter 6, in the early 1990s rumors began to circulate that the Soviet Union had dumped highly radioactive material into the Barents and Kara Seas — both portions of the Arctic Ocean. Norway raised the issue with Russia in 1991, leading to formation of a Joint Russian-Norwegian Expert Group to investigate and to provide an assessment of the radioactive contamination in the area.[24] The sensational *Yablokov Report* of 1993 stated that a total of 16 reactors from nuclear vessels had been dumped at five different locations in the Kara Sea. Oran Young pointed out that shocks can set in motion international cooperation on environmental issues.[25] The fact that nuclear reactors containing enormous quantities of radioactivity had been deposited into the Arctic Ocean was viewed with grave concern by many, both in and out of governments, and motivated many actors toward involvement with Russian submarine reactor issues. While subsequent investigations of the dumping seemed to have mitigated the immediate concern, the public admissions by Russia and the issues they raised nonetheless encouraged a more careful scrutiny of other possible problems with the Russian Northern Fleet and the Russian nuclear industry, and to the problem setting phase of the submarine spent fuel problem.

NGOs and NGO-like Activity

According to Gray, problem setting is "getting to the table so that face-to-face dialogue can begin." It has several attributes, including the development of a common definition of the problem, a commitment to collaborate, identification of stakeholders, establishment of the legitimacy of stakeholders, convener characteristics, and identification of resources.[26] International environmental NGOs, such as Greenpeace and Bellona, were particularly important in providing a common definition of the Russian submarine spent fuel problem, the first step of problem setting.

Greenpeace

Greenpeace has long been an opponent of nuclear weapons and nuclear energy in general. In the 1980s, the organization also began to call attention to potential hazards associated with the operation of nuclear powered submarines. Rumors about Soviet dumping of highly radioactive material from maritime reactors into the Arctic Ocean prompted a Greenpeace "submission" to the London Dumping Convention in 1991 and a public airing of the issue.

With the *glasnost* of the times, Greenpeace was invited to tour nuclear facilities in the Soviet Union. In October 1991, Joshua Handler (then-research coordinator for Greenpeace's "Nuclear Free Seas Campaign") and others toured Severodvinsk, a previously closed nuclear submarine construction and repair facility in Northwest Russia, and then went on to Vladivostok on the Pacific coast. Handler published his observations as "More Real Soviet Nightmare: Nuclear-Powered Submarines" in December 1991. He was highly critical of what he saw, detailing "first-hand observations of the deadly legacy left by the Soviet submarine fleet" and that "a solution is necessary to avert a Soviet nuclear disaster of potential global effect." Handler published "No Sleep in the deep for Russian subs" in April 1993 where he argued that submarine nuclear reactors should be considered along with nuclear weapons as part of the hazardous legacy of the Cold War. In 1992, Hans Kristiensen wrote "Nuclear Power at Sea" for Greenpeace, giving further details of the Russian submarine program. Susanne Kopte, former head of Greenpeace's "Disarmament Campaign" and author of the August 1997 paper "Nuclear Submarine Decommissioning and Related Problems" for the Bonn International Center for Conversion (BICC), has continued the legacy of nuclear submarine monitoring and environmental advocacy.

Bellona

Less known by the world at-large than Greenpeace but more directly involved in the Russian submarine spent fuel issue is the Bellona Foundation, a Norwegian environment action and protection group. Founded in 1986 shortly after the Chernobyl disaster, Bellona early-on organized non-violent protests against "environmental culprits," but later developed substantial research and information functions as well. Bellona is based in Oslo and has field offices in several locations, including Washington, D.C. and a number of Russian cities. It obtains much of its approximately $3 million in annual revenue from Norwegian businesses but also accepts a subsidy from the Norwegian government.[27] With a staff of 20–30 individuals, Bellona has gained substantial notoriety for its aggressive investigation of nuclear safety and Radwaste problems with Russia's Northern Fleet and from its involvement with energy policy and industrial pollution issues in Norway. The organization took its name from a vengeful war goddess of ancient Roman mythology.[28]

Bellona has been crucial to pinning down the Russian submarine spent fuel problem and to keeping the issue on the world's agenda. Government officials and private individuals engaged with the Russian submarine spent fuel issue rely on Bellona information and generally consider the organization's scientific credentials and published data very credible.

Virtually all reports on Northern Fleet spent fuel problems, including this one, use Bellona data and opinion; international newspaper articles about the Russian decommissioned submarine problem continue to quote statements by Bellona representatives and to cite the organization's information. The 1994 Bellona report "Sources of Radioactive Contamination in Murmansk and Archangel Counties" by Thomas Nilsen and Nils Bohmer was among the first to analyze closely the status of Russian decommissioned submarines.[29] This was followed in 1995 by "Sources of Radioactive Contamination — Submarine Bases on the Kola Peninsula, Zapadnaya Litsa" (Bellona Working Paper 5: 1995). In 1996, Bellona published *The Russian Northern Fleet: Sources of Radioactive Contamination*, a substantial volume with revealing detail and photographs of many disturbing aspects of Russia's nuclear submarine spent fuel problem.

The organization has its detractors. In Norway, Bellona has a reputation for publicity seeking and has lost some government support because of its controversial public positions.[30] Following the arrest of former Russian submarine commander Alexandr Nikitin, a Bellona representative, the organization's personnel were denied visas to travel in Russia. Some Russian officials now argue that Bellona is not a true NGO and that its findings should not be trusted because of its links with the Norwegian government. Bellona nonetheless remains a key source of public knowledge and policy initiative on the Russian spent fuel and related issues and continues to have significant influence.

NGO Limitations

Often first on the scene and armed with substantial expertise, NGOs like Greenpeace and Bellona can provide real-time information and help to define problems quickly. Without governmental obligations and excessive institutional obligations, they are free to use alternative sources of information and to write sensational accounts of their concerns. According to Thomas Princen and Matthias Finger, NGOs can "exploit transnational opportunities" and, by increasing environmental awareness, act as agents of "social learning."[31] NGOs like Greenpeace and Bellona have a difficult time going beyond problem definition, however. Part of this is cultural: Greenpeace and Bellona have broader goals than just cleaning up Radwaste in Northwest Russia and would no doubt be pleased if nuclear operations were shutdown completely, both in Russia and the rest of the world. Nuclear issues unleash passion and reveal belief system gaps that must be recognized and overcome. According to scholars Mary Douglas and Aaron Wildavsky, the risks that a person or group are willing to take are typically a joint product of their knowledge about the future and their consent over the most desired prospects.[32] People react differently to risk taking and risk aversion largely because of their social relationships. Personnel in environmental advocacy groups such as Greenpeace and Bellona may tend toward egalitarian behavior and therefore weigh risks in very different ways from government bureaucracies and heavy industry managers, who experience hierarchy in their organizational life.

NGOs are free lance institutions as a result, responsible to themselves, their own agenda, and perhaps to certain sponsors — but not to the public at large. In their book on global governance, Thomas G. Weiss and Leon Gordenker pointed out that: "The naive and exaggerated notion that the outcome of NGO efforts is universally worthwhile is, in fact, contradicted by experience and analysis. In particular, efforts that look good and may be effective in the short run are sometimes failures or disasters in the long run."[33] NGOs also lack the necessary political power to enforce and sustain their efforts at change. In Belarus the government of President Aleksandr Lukashenko forced the Soros Foundation out of the country in 1997, allegedly for currency violations. The foundation had supported educational, ecological, and medical programs, but also groups critical of Lukashenko.[34] Governments in Africa have similarly accused NGOs of exercising "power without responsibility" and monitor their work with suspicion.[35]

The desired end-points of environmental NGOs are often vastly different from those of the industrial and governmental establishments of the world — where issues such as nuclear safety and waste problems will have to be negotiated and resolved. Because of the limitations of NGOs it is appropriate for representatives of the people, both elected and otherwise selected, to decide which agenda has the most appeal and is most likely to achieve the greatest public good. Further problem setting, not to mention direction setting and implementation, must necessarily involve nation-states.[36]

Arctic Council

Following initial NGO engagement, it was necessary for stakeholders to identify themselves and the extent of their commitment to Russia's submarine spent fuel problem. This portion of problem setting has taken years to sort out: Russia's internal organization kept changing; Western countries were distracted by higher priority problems; and, confusion remained about exactly which nuclear issues in Russia were most important and where collaboration would do the most good. The Arctic Council was an IGO that helped to identify stakeholders and to advance the problem setting phase.

The Arctic Council began in 1991 as the Arctic Environmental Protection Strategy (AEPS) and evolved into the Arctic Council in 1996. It is an intergovernmental response to concerns about pollution in the Arctic made up of the eight countries that border the Arctic Ocean: Canada, Denmark (Greenland), Finland, Iceland, Norway, Russia, Sweden, and the United States, plus representatives of Arctic native peoples and from a number of NGOs. As discussed in Chapter 6, the Arctic Monitoring and Assessment Program (AMAP) to coordinate research on radioactive and chemical contamination of the Arctic is without doubt the major initiative and achievement of the Arctic Council. Due in part to discussions and presentations that took place under AEPS/Arctic Council auspices and to the research it encouraged, the sunken Russian reactor issue has declined in perception as a major hazard to the Arctic environment while concern for the huge amount of spent fuel associated with decommissioned Russian submarines has simultaneously increased. Attendees at Arctic Council/AEPS conferences began to express interest in the emerging nuclear submarine Radwaste management issue in bilateral and multilateral discussions and to submit research papers on the problem. Nation-states started to make commitments to collaborate and to establish their identities as stakeholders in other fora. The foreign policy, defense, nuclear energy, and regulatory agencies of several Arctic Council countries began to establish their legitimacy as relevant national spokespeople on the issue while additional resources, forums, and initiatives were identified to define the problem further.

NGOs participate in Arctic Council proceedings as well and can vet their concerns and distribute their information. An epistemic community is at work here, where the Arctic Council and its associated activities provide a venue for policy-makers to gain scientific opinion to set priorities for their own limited resources. This knowledge-based grouping of scholars and officials has helped to sort out the submarine spent fuel problem and to focus attention on areas where further cooperation can make a difference. As Don Munton pointed out, there is a give and take between policy-makers and specialists of a particular technology: sometimes science provides the information to meet a demand requirement from policy-makers; at other times, scientists take the initiative and approach policy-makers with their own information, discoveries, and theories.[37] The Arctic Council can provide an environmental imprimatur for the Arctic region not unlike the manner the Helsinki Accords of the CSCE/OSCE are used as moral authority for Western action in the Balkan conflicts of the 1990s.

All of that said, the Arctic Council is not the lead-organization to help Russia with its Northern Fleet Radwaste problem; it is not the "convener" in the sense articulated by Gray. The Arctic Council lacks resources, strong support from the United States and Russia (two crucial stakeholders), and a mandate to investigate military matters.[38] More like an NGO than an IGO, its primary value has been to keep Arctic environmental issues in the public eye and to provide periodic opportunities for scholars, government officials, and industry representatives to meet and evaluate current activities and proposed alternatives.

National Stakeholders and Norway—The Convener

With information from forums like the Arctic Council and advocacy groups like Bellona, national actors became increasingly engaged in the Russian spent fuel issue as their interests were clarified. A series of struggles then took place within various countries over primary stakeholder status. Russia's organizational conflicts between organizations like the Russian Navy, MINATOM, and GAN on the submarine spent fuel issue were readily apparent, but the United States had disputes as well. Views on what to do varied between US environmental and regulatory agencies, such as the Environmental Protection Agency and the Nuclear Regulatory Commission, and those organizations representing actual nuclear operations and management authority, such as the Department of Energy and Department of Defense. The State Department was by mandate and tradition the senior foreign policy organization in the United States, but had difficulty establishing its leadership over other agencies on the Russian spent fuel issue: organizations like the Departments of Energy and Defense had far greater resources and often greater expertise at their disposal to investigate the problem and, if authorized, to do something about it.

Stakeholders can also be judged by their success in dealing with Russian counterpart activities. Reports have indicated that some US agencies did not have a particularly good working relationship with MINATOM during the 1990s and were not very interested in improving them, especially during the stewardship of Russian Minister of Nuclear Energy Viktor Mikhailov.[39] This could be one reason why the United States has not been as vigorous a participant in the Russian submarine spent fuel problem or facilitator in mobilizing action as one might expect, given US expertise in the matter. The United States is not unique in the West with its internal disputes and difficulty in working with Russia. Norway seems to speak to the world with one voice, but the foreign and defense establishments can be at odds over national initiatives concerning Russia. Norway's leadership in the submarine spent fuel issue is unmistakable, however.

According to Gray, the role of convener is to identity and bring legitimate stakeholders to the table and to set the collaboration process in motion. Conveners need power to induce stakeholders to participate, either through established networks or by their political status and skill at verbal and moral suasion. Gray suggests that successful conveners have a sense of timing and the ability to create the appropriate context for the negotiations.[40] The convener for international engagement on the Russian submarine spent fuel issue is unquestionably the government of Norway. Norwegian officials became active on the issue because of their environmental concern in view of the country's close proximity to the Russian submarine spent fuel problem and because they had the resources and expertise at their disposal to make a difference. Norway's early bilateral efforts with Russia, such as the various initiatives to investigate sunken reactors, were successful and probably served to encourage further collaboration. In 1994, the Norwegian government developed a "Plan of Action" to give official direction and sanction to its efforts. The Plan was comprehensive to the region, dealing with safety measures at nuclear facilities, management of Radwaste, dumping of Radwaste in the Arctic, and arms-related environmental hazards.

But dealing with Russia can be intimidating for a small country like Norway. Despite its advance technology and oil-based prosperity, Norway is a minor world power when compared to even a struggling Russia. The population difference alone is striking — approximately 4.5 million in Norway compared to 150 million in Russia. As a consequence, Norway took several steps to heighten the awareness of the problem among other international actors and to encourage their participation in the spent fuel project. The targeted partners included political units of much greater weight, like the United States and the European Union. In 1994, the United States joined Norway and Russia in the Murmansk Trilateral Initiative to increase Russia's liquid waste purification capacity; in 1996, the three countries agreed on the Arctic Military Environmental Cooperation (AMEC) program of defense collaboration to develop spent fuel storage/transport containers, among other initiatives. The European Commission teamed with Norway and France on the *Lepse* project and agreed to fund a substantial portion of it; British, French, and Swedish firms are allied with Norway's Kvaerner in the Industrial Group to bid for Russian nuclear safety and Radwaste projects.

Norwegian officials have self-designated their country as the convener, or "catalytic agent" as they call it, to raise political awareness and support for the various spent fuel projects in Russia. Norway was important in the founding and activities of various intergovernmental groupings, including the Arctic Council, the Barents Euro-Arctic Council and Regional Council, the IAEA CEG, and also in encouraging the involvement of NATO. The powerful alliance has become a strange bedfellow in the problem setting phase with Greenpeace, Bellona, and the Arctic Council, but nonetheless continues to sponsor conferences and publications dealing with Russian submarine spent fuel and other environmental concerns.

Figure 8 — Phases of Collaboration

Barbara Gray's Collaboration Model	*Key Actors Observed in Russian Submarine Spent Fuel Collaboration*
Problem setting • common definition of problem • convener characteristics • identification of resources • commitment to collaborate • identification of stakeholders • legitimacy of stakeholders	— NGOs like Greenpeace and Bellona key to problem definition — Norway as convener, offering good offices, encouraging further discussion and organization, identifying resources — Arctic Council useful for problem definition and identification of stakeholders
Direction setting • exploring options • reaching agreement • establishing ground rules • agenda setting • organizing subgroups • joint information search	— National governments explored options and reached agreement on limited projects: Murmansk Trilateral Initiative, *Lepse* — IGOs like Barents Council and IAEA CEG helped set ground rules and agenda, organized subgroups, established trust and communications — Rule-making regimes (London and Vienna Conventions) important for legal grounding of activities
Implementation • dealing with constituencies • building external support • structuring • monitoring agreements	— Multinational corporations can help with constituencies and build external support; have expertise to accomplish the task — National governments, IGOs, and rule-making regimes to monitor agreements — IAEA CEG seeks support of other IGOs

Direction Setting — Multilateral Initiatives, IGOs, and Regimes

Despite Norwegian and other initiatives, openness and honesty by Russia did not trigger a flurry of international aid on this issue nor a rapid reorientation of Russia's priorities toward greater environmental concern — at least not in the short term. The *glasnost* of the *Yablokov Report* faded rapidly. Although several studies and initiatives were begun to assist Russia with its nuclear safety and Radwaste problems, the West seemed to pocket the revelations about ocean dumping and other nuclear and radioactive contamination issues and to use them as criticism of Russian activities. Nor did Russia divert substantial resources from military and other projects to its Radwaste problems. Bellona officials have argued that by 1994, the old Soviet order — including former KGB officials — had made its way back into positions of influence in the Russian Federation.[41] Severodvinsk was once again a closed city after only a short period of normalcy; a new law on state secrets was in force by late 1997 and seemed likely to restrict information and access to sensitive facilities even further. A more national and perhaps natural posture had returned to Russian foreign policy by the mid–1990s.

Direction setting includes establishing ground rules, agenda setting, organizing subgroups, conducting joint information searches, exploring options, reaching agreement, and closing the deal.[42] Substantive and procedural issues must be agreed upon in order to move forward; stakeholders must identify their interests and objectives but also be willing to compromise. When the issues are far-reaching, technical, and part of a sensitive political and security dialogue, agreement is difficult. Those trying to solve environmental problems or related disputes must confront the reality of vested economic and regional interest in addition to the practical need for getting on with the job at hand. What "can be done" must be distilled from what "should be done" under ideal circumstances. In nuclear affairs there is little trust between advocates and opponents, making progress even more difficult. Gray illustrated the sensitivity of such relationships in an example concerning a controlled release of radioactivity after the Three Mile Island nuclear power plant accident. Nuclear industry stakeholders questioned whether anti-nuclear personnel would listen to reason and whether they should be allowed to participate in the deliberations at all. They wanted up-front assurances that anti-nuclear people would not stage protests during the negotiations, while the anti-nuclear group was concerned about being assigned only token membership.[43]

Multilateral Initiatives

Moving forward with direction setting requires accurate information about the problem, often through the use of technical panels.[44] Several important studies were done on Arctic nuclear waste issues, including the European Commission's *Inventory of radioactive waste and spent fuel at the Kola Peninsula region of north-west Russia (EUR 16916)*, NATO's *Phase I* and *Phase II CCMS Reports* on cross-border contamination, the AMAP, IASAP, and ANWAP surveys of radioactivity in the Arctic, and the Congressional Office of Technology Assessment (OTA) report *Nuclear Wastes in the Arctic*. These documents helped to clarify concerns about dumped Russian marine reactors and to refocus efforts on the spent fuel problem.

Despite the sometimes dire warnings of Bellona and others about a "Chernobyl in slow motion" from the submarine spent fuel in Russia's Northwest, foreign stakeholders were not prepared to move rapidly toward significant funding and technical assistance to help resolve the problem.[45] The submarine spent fuel problem was not a crisis, budgets for foreign aid were limited, taxation and liability concerns had not gone away and working with Russia was still not easy. There remained as well apprehension in some government circles about assisting with what was essentially a Russian defense project. All of this delayed the creation of a comprehensive program and discouraging significant funding. As a consequence, much of the early activity was directed at smaller projects that were easier to agree upon, had relatively early end-dates, and could be implemented by smaller groups of stakeholders. These efforts were essential to the overall goal and hence not unimportant, but were somewhat removed from the overall plan that eventually would be needed. Public goods theory, as developed by economist Mancur Olson, helps to explain this phenomena: cooperation toward a common goal, such as many environmental projects, works better when the number of stakeholders is small and when the objectives are clear, thereby minimizing free riding and the need to build and continually maintain consensus.[46]

The Murmansk Trilateral Initiative of September 1994 involved only Norway, Russia, and the United States. Its goal was to expand the liquid waste treatment capacity of the MSC (Murmansk Shipping Company — the icebreaker organization) radioactive liquid waste treatment plant in Murmansk, making it large enough to purify liquid Radwaste from submarines in addition to icebreakers. In the Pacific Fleet, a similar plan took shape involving firms from the United States, Europe, and Japan but with leadership resting with US, Japanese, and Russian organizations to construct a floating liquid waste purification facility for Bolshoi Kamen. The

Arctic Military Environmental Cooperation (AMEC) program was begun in 1996 as a limited venture as well, involving officials from the defense ministries/departments of Norway, Russia, and the United States — although other institutional actors within each country became involved along the way. The AMEC projects were relatively limited in scope, but achievable and potentially valuable contributions toward remediation of the spent fuel and other environmental problems in Russia.

The *Lepse* project is often viewed as a microcosm for the much larger issue of Russian decommissioned submarines and their spent fuel. It too involves a small number of international actors (Russia, Norway, the European Commission, France, and [to a lesser degree] the United States) with the difficult and dangerous objective of removing damaged and highly contaminated spent fuel from the ship. The project will utilize robotic equipment to cut out the fuel assemblies and then place them in interim storage — probably modified RBMK metal-concrete containers. Plans must then be put in place to move the fuel to Mayak for storage and reprocessing or to a permanent storage location. Despite the complexity of the task, the *Lepse* project will be easier to organize and complete than the submarine spent fuel problem. It is concentrated in one location and has a coherent group of Russian and international actors, unlike the decommissioned submarines and spent fuel storage sites scattered throughout the Kola and Archangel regions. *Lepse* is also a serious and immediate Radwaste hazard: the ship could sink or suffer a collision and possibly release substantial radioactivity to a region of nearly half a million people. Collaboration is well developed and the Western companies involved are ready to go, but taxation and liability concerns must still be resolved.

IGOs

Intergovernmental organizations (IGOs) can help cooperation go beyond limited ventures and help solve more difficult international problems by providing a stable setting for negotiation. With their institutional structures, IGOs can be more long-lived and influential than bilateral or multilateral agreements which often expire upon project completion, and can therefore build on their institutional memory and record of success. The secretariats of IGOs sometimes acquire effective autonomy from their membership if they perform well and provide issue clarification and policy leadership. IGOs can also establish political cover for individual country leaders who can argue that, while a particular project was controversial or unpopular in their own country, the greater need for international solidarity required their submission to the joint action. This political ploy is common among the leadership of European Union countries who often point to the European Commission or the European Union itself as the unpopular culprit for their actions. The authority and influence of IGOs range from strong military alliances like NATO and powerful economic and political groups like the European Union, to weak talking shops like the Arctic Council.

Of some importance in the direction setting phase have been the Barents Euro-Arctic Council and the Barents Regional Council. Established in January 1993 in response to a Norwegian initiative, these IGOs are political and economic instruments to help normalize relations across the remote and hostile Russian frontier through a variety of initiatives, primarily with projects to channel and coordinate aid to Russia. Although in part altruistic, Western interests predominate because the implemented mechanisms help to ensure better knowledge and control over Russian developments, such as the balance between resource exploitation and environmental protection.[47] The Barents Euro-Arctic Council approved an Environmental Action Programme on 15 June 1994 that included objectives to help prevent radioactive and oil pollution and to prepare for oil pollution accidents. The Council seems less a talking shop than the Arctic Council and a relatively effective means of engagement with Northwest Russia. On the other hand, it has a low degree of institutionalization and depends heavily on the support of its major participants.

Of more immediate impact on the submarine spent fuel issue is the International Atomic Energy Agency Contact Experts Group for International Radwaste Projects (IAEA CEG), composed of twelve member countries and organizations and two observers. The focus of the group is on information exchange and practical measures to reduce Radwaste hazards in Russia, concentrating particularly on the submarine spent fuel problem of Russia's Northwest. The organization's meetings vary in attendance, but always include diplomats, technical experts, representatives from Russian activities, and Western companies hoping to profit from Radwaste contracts. The organization helps sort out what various stakeholders can and want to do; using Gray's terminology, the IAEA-CEG performs a norm-setting function at the domain level and "captures the imprecise, emergent, exploratory, developmental character of these interorganizational arrangements."[48] The IAEA CEG played a role in gaining general international acceptance of the 1996 MINATOM/Russian Navy priority list on Radwaste projects in Northwest Russia and has helped to prevent redundant projects. Like the Arctic Council and Barents Cooperation, however, the IAEA CEG has no decision-making authority and is institutionally weak. While its coordination and information functions have been important, there are incentives and proposals to enhance the process and institutions of the organization. Using Gray's words again, stakeholders sometimes want to manage their interactions in an increasingly systematic manner as a result of negotiation.

Regimes

IGOs are sometimes regimes, a term applied to many of the cooperative international arrangements developed in the West since World War II. Regimes are often defined as sets of implicit or explicit principles, norms, rules, and decision-making procedures around which actors' expectations converge in a given area of international relations.[49] They can be intervening variables between the conflicting interests of states and the cooperative agreements and activities that often follow. While often conflated into one category, distinctions should be made between IGOs with regime characteristics and regimes that make rules and set standards for participants to follow.

The international organizations working with the Russian submarine spent fuel issue, such as the Arctic and Barents Councils and particularly the IAEA CEG, can be classified as international regimes. With enhanced functions and organization, the IAEA CEG could become what is called a "pivot regime" around which the other activities of the Russian submarine spent fuel problem revolve. Regimes are venues for collaboration, giving Westerners and Russians alike the opportunity to decide on priorities and on which government agencies, corporations, and personalities are likely to make and keep commitments. Personal interactions create a basis for increased trust among the parties and allow for subsequent negotiations to proceed more smoothly. Gatherings and discussions can also get rid of false hopes; there is certainly no pie in the sky solution to the Russian submarine spent fuel problem, for example, and this is now well understood. The agenda, decisions, and reports of IGO meetings are good evidence of regime-like activity, although considerable worth also lies at the margins of the meetings. Outside open chambers, during coffee and (with Europeans) cigarette breaks, interested parties can establish new relationships and informally develop plans to collaborate.

Multilateral initiatives and IGO regimes have helped with the direction setting function of the Russian submarine spent fuel problem. Generally accepted ground rules and priorities for collaboration have been established and help form a basis for further common action. Subgroups have been organized and technical studies frequently authorized (too frequently say the Russians) and alternative options explored with the hope of eventually moving forward. The membership and goals of IGOs like Barents Cooperation and the IAEA CEG and those of the really important organizations of Europe, such as NATO, the European Union, and the IAEA itself, have substantial overlap. Such nesting of international regimes contributes to cooperation by allowing the disparate players to choose the most effective forum for their agenda and to ensure that key issues are well known by all interested parties.[50] Members of regimes share a common understanding of the problem that can then be communicated to policy-makers and funding sources in their own countries and with international lending institutions. All of that said, the Russian submarine spent fuel issue lacks authoritative international regimes that can effectively allocate resources; the positive outcomes thus far have resulted from a complex negotiating and inter-organizational process that remains idiosyncratic and often unreliable.

Rule-making Regimes

Two rule-making regimes directly affect the submarine spent fuel issue. Dumping radioactive material in the oceans is regulated by international negotiations and agreements under the London Convention. First approved in 1972, this pact of 80 nations (including the United States and Soviet Union) partially limited ocean disposal of nuclear waste by prohibiting the dumping of high-level radioactive waste such as reactor spent fuel. A decade later, several members of the Convention approved moratoriums on the ocean dumping of low- and intermediate-level radioactive waste as well. The Soviet Union abstained from these additions and the United States voted against them. In 1993, thirty-seven countries including the United States voted on a permanent ban of at-sea dumping of nuclear waste. Belgium, France, China, the United Kingdom and Russia abstained from this decision.[51] Despite its failure to sign, Russia has adhered to the 1993 ban of dumping nuclear waste and has therefore helped to keep additional anthropogenic radioactive contamination out of the Arctic and Russian Pacific Ocean areas. As an unintended consequence, however, adherence to anti-dumping agreements has been one of the factors tending to inhibit Russian submarine defueling operations because of the lack of adequate Radwaste storage and processing facilities.

In September 1997 a "Joint Convention on Safe Handling of Spent Fuel and Safe Handling of Radioactive Wastes" was opened for signature, with the objective of encouraging the safe management of Radwaste. Russia signed the Convention at IAEA Headquarters on 27 January 1999 as further indication of its intent to conform with international norms on these issues.[52] Russia's compliance with international Radwaste dumping prohibitions is virtually a precondition for international aid to assist with its submarine spent fuel problems. Its failure to sign the convention's 1993 amendment to ban all ocean Radwaste dumping remains a matter of concern to many in the international community, despite the country's voluntary adherence to the agreements guidelines.[53]

International agreements on nuclear liability have created a rule-making regime that also affects the Russian submarine spent fuel issue. The regime consisted of the "Paris Convention on Third Party Liability in the Field of Nuclear Energy of 1960" (later strengthened by the Brussels Supplemental Convention of 1963) and the "Vienna Convention on Civil Liability for Nuclear Damage of 1963," linked together by a Joint Protocol adopted in 1988. The agreements made operators responsible for liability and set limits on the amount of possible claims; they also limited the length of liability and required operators to have appropriate insurance. Courts within the country of the incident retained jurisdiction over liability cases and were required to ensure that non-discrimination of victims on the grounds of nationality, domicile or residence was maintained.[54] The IAEA and the Nuclear Energy Agency (NEA) of the Organization for Economic Cooperation and Development (OECD) are working to strengthen the international liability rules, particularly concerning compensation amounts.[55] In September 1997 at IAEA headquarters in Vienna, delegates adopted a protocol to amend the 1963 Vienna Convention, setting the possible limit of the operator's liability to not less than 300 million Special Drawing Rights (approximately 400 million dollars).

Neither the United States nor Russia is a participant in the formal liability regime, however, although the United States has domestic arrangements that parallel international agreements. Companies that might assist Russia with nuclear projects are fearful of lawsuits by third parties should there be a nuclear accident and are consequently hesitant to become actively involved. According to the IAEA Director General, Russia requires improved nuclear liability legislation because its current law, passed in 1995, does not clearly channel liability to facility operators as the Vienna Convention requires. The Russian government signed the convention in 1996, but the *Duma* has yet to ratify it. Even when ratified, Russia's association with the regime will not be fully established because of its poorly developed insurance industry. A functioning liability program is closely tied to private insurance coverage and to nuclear operators with deep pockets.[56] A step in the right direction was taken in late 1997 when 20 Russian insurance firms and MINATOM established a nuclear risk insurance pool that would cover up to $50 million in damages in the event of a radiological accident, with damages above that provided by Western companies and the Russian government.[57] Discussions have also begun on the possibility of Western insurance firms taking over the burden of third party liability.

Western contractors currently doing nuclear work in Russia often work under specific indemnity statements issued by the Russian government, but more ambitious projects would probably require a more fully developed liability framework.[58] Failure to solve the liability question would be a show-stopper for the implementation phase of collaboration.

Implementation

The third and final stage of collaboration is implementation. According to Gray, implementation is more than just getting the job done and includes characteristics such as dealing with constituencies, building external support, structuring, and monitoring agreements to ensure compliance.[59] Gray notes that even carefully constructed agreements to collaborate can fall apart unless deliberate attention is given to following through with the task at hand. Implementation must also confront what Gray calls the "two-table" problem where stakeholders simultaneously look to the objectives of their international negotiations and to their domestic constituency, ever mindful of the need to balance external commitments with support from back home. This is again similar to the notions of two-level games and double-edged diplomacy developed by Robert Putnam.[60] Bargaining is particularly difficult for Russian negotiators who are operating under conditions of severe economic stress and some organizational confusion. Western stakeholders must always balance the extent to which they can and should pressure Russia to allocate scarce resources for what they consider priority projects with how much environmental risk they are willing to accept without committing substantial resources of its own.

Sometimes good intentions and positive initiatives can have unintended consequences. Gray emphasizes the importance of process in planning and conducting successful collaborations; good-faith efforts at collaboration can be derailed because insufficient attention is given to designing and managing a constructive effort.[61] A case in point could be a spent fuel storage initiative made by the United States in early 1998. The ranking State Department official for Russian affairs, Strobe Talbott, announced at a meeting of the Barents Euro-Arctic Council that the United States would contribute $500 thousand toward the construction of a prototype containment vessel for marine nuclear spent fuel.[62] He was apparently referring to the 80-ton containers designed for use with Russian RBMK spent fuel but serviceable for marine spent fuel as well after appropriate modification. These very large containers are less portable than the smaller AMEC containers will be, which could mean that the spent fuel at Andreeva Bay will stay near Norway — an important stakeholder — longer than anticipated. Norway might prefer to concentrate efforts on the more portable AMEC containers and also to move toward fixed interim storage facilities. A positive initiative by Ambassador Talbott that may have been made outside the established process had the potential to disrupt collaboration already in train, at least for the short term and in a minor way.

Collaboration has occurred through multinational agreements, IGOs, and regimes and has improved communications and established priorities for further action on the Russian submarine spent fuel problem. A number of projects are in progress to chip away at the problem, like the SSBN dismantlements established by the CTR program and the liquid Radwaste projects nearing completion in Murmansk and Bolshoi Kamen. The process thus far, however, has not created an integrated plan with firm deadlines and commitments nor established a regime with sufficient authority to allocate resources to solve the problem. Other international actors may be required.

Multinational Industrial Alliances

Where IGOs and regimes have come up short, multinational industrial alliances may succeed. In November 1995, Kvaerner Moss Technology of Norway announced that it had reached agreement with Russia's Energia to defuel and dismantle all Russian nuclear submarines by the year 2010 and to take care of the Radwaste generated in the process. As discussed in Chapter 6, Norway spent nearly a million dollars on the plan but saw it fall apart when Russian agencies could not agree on its implementation.[63] Since then Kvaerner has become part of the so-called Industrial Group (IG), along with BNFL of the United Kingdom, SGN of France, and SKB of Sweden, that is working with Russian activities on portions of the defueling chain. Projects include interim fuel storage studies and environmental assessments at Mayak. Other groupings are developing as well, with Lockheed Martin of the United States allied with COGEMA of France looking for possible business opportunities in Russian Radwaste. Individual firms are also staking out particular parts of the Russian problem, developing expertise and contacts on the issue, and then positioning themselves as the obvious choice should a contract become possible. The initiative by the British firm NNC to help dispose of Russia's liquid metal reactors is a case in point.

The grand and complicated task of defueling, transporting, and storing or reprocessing large quantities of Russian submarine spent fuel may well require the resources and expertise of several Western and Russian companies in alliance for proper implementation. Without drawing too fine a neo-liberal economic point on the issue, alliances of well-funded multinational corporations may be the appropriate entities for the task. There is a "pull" effect in that these corporations may be the only organizations on earth that can actually get the job done. Nuclear industries in the West are large, experienced, and heavily capitalized; they also have close links with their national governments through frequent technical and regulatory consultations and financial transactions. Familiarity between industry and officialdom creates some confidence in the ability of Western nuclear companies, perhaps in alliance with Russian actors, to follow through on complex issues. There is also a "push" effect in that multinational corporations may have the political clout that NGOs and even IGOs and individual government agencies do not. According to Thomas Jandl of Bellona USA: "Industry will be better [than NGOs] in convincing a congressional representative that cleanup funding for nuclear storage sites in Russia is not a waste of money. American technology exports are creating jobs at home, while at the same time making the world a safer place to live — both in terms of disarmament and the environment"[64] The Kvaerner/Energia proposal and the Industrial Group activity have generated much more interest than any NGO or IGO plan. There is at least some hope that Russia and its various industrial and governmental partners may finally put together the elusive PERT chart — with funding and technology firmly committed to getting the submarine defueling chain really moving. To paraphrase Oran Young, what is really needed is a "salient solution" — something simple that makes sense.[65]

Conclusion

Barbara Gray's thesis of three phases of collaboration — problem setting, direction setting, and implementation — helps to clarify the efforts being made by international actors to alleviate Russia's submarine spent fuel issue. This chapter has taken her paradigm a step further to suggest that a relationship exists between problem setting and NGOs, direction setting and IGOs/regimes, and implementation and multinational industrial alliances. Comparison with other large-scale environmental projects will be required to determine if this observation is more than an interesting development unique to nuclear issues in Russia, but the model might be useful in other areas of environmental concern and could help participants to focus more closely on appropriate actors at different phases of collaboration. The involvement of NGOs, IGOs, and the other arrangements found in the Russian submarine spent fuel problem approaches Leon Gordenker and Thomas G. Weiss' modest but useful definition of global governance: a more ordered and reliable response to problems that goes beyond the individual and even collective capacities of states, achieving enhanced transparency, accountability and participation.[66]

Chapter 8

The Elusive PERT Chart

*There will not be any Chernobyl here [with Northern Fleet submarines].
The situation is quite complicated. We just need to stabilize it and to
decide what are our priorities.*[1]

— Viktor Gubanov
MINATOM Department of Emergency Situations

Viktor Gubanov has it about right. The problems associated with
Russian decommissioned submarines can be solved with available technology and talent, albeit at significant cost and effort. Several forums are
available to coordinate the effort and a number of collaborations are
already in progress, together representing something of a success story for
international cooperation on the environment. Progress has been difficult,
however, and there are relatively few projects that directly address the
defueling of Russian nuclear submarines and the safe management of their
spent fuel, with the CTR-funded ballistic missile submarine dismantlement program a significant exception.

Nor will the way ahead be easy. On the one hand, no known incidents
involving extensive radioactive contamination have occurred in Northwest Russia and the initial great concern about environmental damage
from the ocean dumping of Russian marine reactors has diminished. Russian sources note that the "radio-ecological situation" is normal at the
bases and repair facilities used by their nuclear powered ships and that
contamination levels do not exceed background, except for isolate cases
of "trace radioactivity."[2] Without a crisis, public and Western legislative
enthusiasm for additional financial commitments to Russia is difficult to
arouse — except perhaps in the Nordic countries. On the other hand, Russian stakeholders are getting frustrated by the lack of progress from the
international initiatives and negotiations already underway. These have
moved forward only after prolonged negotiations to identify funding
sources and to overcome technical questions and divergent organizational

expectations and political cultures. Several years of discussions and proposals have failed to produce any meaningful reduction in the amount of submarine spent fuel in the Northwest Russia or in its potential hazards, with the townspeople of Murmansk complaining that "there is a lot of talk, but very little action."[3] Indeed Western firms have profited from their eternal studies, but have produced few tangible benefits for Russia to date.[4]

This chapter summarizes the progress of the initiatives begun thus far and highlights the difficulties encountered. It concludes with an assessment of US engagement and considers what action should be encouraged so that large scale Russian submarine defueling operations and better spent fuel management can begin.

Some Progress

The Murmansk Trilateral Initiative to upgrade the Atomflot liquid waste purification plant is nearing completion after significant delays. The technical development phase was completed in 1995, but equipment procurement and construction have proceeded haltingly ever since. It now seems likely that the facility will be completed by late 1999 with a six-month test and run-in period to follow, about one to two years later than originally planned. Technical, production, and funding delays have occurred, with each side critical of the other's performance. Keeping the facility's purification capability available for the icebreaker fleet during the modification has hampered progress. Officials have commented on the makeshift character of the modifications made thus far, noting that as a minimum the project has been a learning experience.

On the Pacific coast, the liquid waste purification project for Bolshoi Kamen has been even more of an ordeal. Most notorious were the demands of Russian officials at the Komsomolsk construction yard for additional money to complete and release the facility, effectively holding it hostage for months hundreds of miles away from its final destination. A more recent delay concerned control system problems and the plant's inability to make effluent of sufficient purity. Although Russian officials blame the US lead contractor Babcock & Wilcox, the delay may be influenced by efforts to prolong construction as long as possible to continue payment to the Russian companies and workers involved. This is a poor business strategy if true, but reflects the desperate economic conditions and uncertain future common to many Russian enterprises.

The AMEC initiative among the Norwegian and Russian Defense

Ministries and the US Department of Defense is moving forward, if at times with hesitation. Although progress meetings are routinely held and press reports not uncommon, accurate information concerning construction of the metal-concrete containers for spent fuel assemblies and other aspects of the initiative is difficult to come by. This may be due to proprietary sensitivity of the metal-concrete container work and to concerns about taxation and liability, but paucity of funding and other Russian spent fuel container and interim storage projects may be confusing the effort as well. Norway has proposed linking AMEC to the Norway-Russia Framework Agreement of May 1998 as a way to energize the initiative. "When this happens, we will have a legal basis for signing contracts and transferring money," a Norwegian Defense Ministry representative suggested in August 1998.[5] With luck, a prototype container will be ready in late 1999 with production beginning shortly thereafter. Because AMEC involves cooperation among the defense establishments of Norway, Russia, and the United States, it may require redirection as the Russian Navy turns over its decommissioned submarine and spent fuel responsibilities to MINATOM.

The *Lepse* project is on hold because of taxation and liability concerns. Defueling procedures and equipment are about ready to go with the next step to test the SGN robotic system in Murmansk. Once testing is completed and the metal-concrete containers provided (probably of the modified RBMK design), the system can be put into service and fuel assembly removal can begin. Removing damaged spent fuel from the *Lepse* will be an expensive, complicated, and potentially hazardous procedure. While some preparatory work may take place in the near future, Western participants are not likely to begin fuel removal until binding agreements on liability are in place. The Framework Agreement between Norway and Russia, which included taxation and liability settlements, again suggests that an arrangement on *Lepse* can be reached in the near future. There is some peril, however, that momentum could be lost as stakeholders look to other priorities. Failure of the *Lepse* project would be a substantial setback to the cooperative edifice constructed thus far, not to mention the continued hazard to the Murmansk region posed by the ship's hazardous cargo and dilapidated condition.

With the Norwegian Framework Agreement finalized in May 1998, several Norway-funded projects are expected to move forward quickly. This should include construction of four railway cars for transporting submarine spent fuel and a new or modified defueling vessel. Under CTR, the United States will fund an additional four railway cars and possibly contribute to the defueling ship as well. The conclusion of the Industrial Group

study on interim storage of spent fuel assemblies could lead to firm decisions on construction of a high-quality storage facility on the Kola Peninsula or at Mayak, or perhaps both. Conflicts between MINATOM and
Mayak on the one hand and Western governments and companies on the
other over the type and location of the facility are among the factors holding up project approval. Meanwhile, construction and deployment of
modified RBMK and AMEC metal-concrete containers may progress to
become increasingly attractive alternatives to the expensive and controversial fixed facilities. At Mayak itself, the RT-1 reprocessing plant remains
shutdown. Construction of new vitrification facilities to restore its operating license is a vital requirement, but remains at a virtual standstill for
lack of funding.

US Restraint

The United States is a key player in efforts to resolve the Russian submarine spent fuel problem. It is a member of the Arctic Council, the IAEA
CEG, the Murmansk Trilateral Initiative, the AMEC program, the *Lepse*
Advisory Committee, an observer in Barents Cooperation, and the source
of CTR funds and equipment for defueling and dismantling Russian ballistic missile submarines. In late 1996, Secretary of Defense William J.
Perry made the following observations after a visit to a Northwest Russia
shipyard:

> It's a win for America — the submarine we saw being dismantled will
> never again threaten American cities. It's a win for the Russians — the
> workers doing the dismantlement were previously unemployed
> because of the decrease in orders for nuclear submarines. And it's a
> win for the environment — the submarine's nuclear fuel will be dis-
> posed of safely; and the sub's components are being recycled into
> materials that can be used to produce commercial products.[6]

United States engagement, however, suffers in comparison to commitments by Norway and even the European Commission. Specific US
financial obligations, not including the CTR program, are perhaps $2–3
million dollars; CTR contributions to SSBN-unique activities may add
another $30 million.[7] Norway, on the other hand, has committed at least $50
million and is likely to contribute much more. The European Commission
is a major player, although actual outlays have been modest thus far. It has
made commitments to help fund metal-concrete spent fuel containers, a

new interim storage facility for spent fuel, and the *Lepse* project, all of which are certain to run into many millions of dollars. In 1995 Senators Nunn and Lugar called for $20–30 billion for a "Decade of Stabilization" to help Russia bring its nuclear programs up to international standards. Although $1.8 billion has been committed by the United States for CTR programs, relatively little US funding has been specifically allocated for submarine spent fuel disposal.[8] Why is this the case?

Distance is one reason. For an American living in Colorado, the hazards posed by Russian submarine spent fuel are very small indeed. A severe submarine reactor accident in Northwest Russia or the Russian Pacific would affect the immediate vicinity and might contaminate parts of the Arctic Ocean and its fisheries, perhaps Alaska as well, but should not affect the continental United States in any significant way. Chernobyl, a near-worst case nuclear accident of a very large civilian reactor, caused few problems in the United States but significantly affected Central and Eastern Europe and Scandinavia. Norway, by contrast, has a common border with Russia and has territory only 30 miles away from the spent fuel storage facilities at Andreeva Bay. It is no surprise that Norwegian officials and citizens are concerned and engaged while US representatives are more detached and relaxed.

There are also legitimate security issues to consider before significant aid should be given to Russia on this project. J. Michael Waller of the American Foreign Policy Council, in testimony before the US Congress, noted that when Secretary of Defense William Perry lauded the US–funded dismantlement efforts at Severodvinsk (above quote), he failed to mention anything about the new attack and ballistic missile submarines under construction in the same shipyard.[9] Naval analyst Norman Polmar points out that the Russian submarine fleet is still making advances. When completed, the new *Severodvinsk* class of Russian attack submarine may be quieter than the *Seawolf* class, the US Navy's best. Because silence is everything in undersea warfare, the Russian Navy could enjoy an advantage over US submarines that it has never had before.[10] Since 1990, the Russian Navy has spent $4.8 billion to build modern quiet submarines.[11] The money could have been used to dismantle many if not all of its older submarines. United States assistance in upgrading and building facilities to defuel decommissioned submarines might also be used to refuel operational ships at a later date. As a bottom line, Russia has devoted significant amounts of its scarce capital to military programs despite its decade-long economic woes. According to the International Institute of Strategic Studies (IISS), the country spent $64 billion on defense in 1997 or 6 percent of GNP — the world's highest after the United States.[12]

United States officials have problems with other security related actions by Russia.[13] The 1994-95 war in Chechnya had few heroes but saw large numbers of civilian casualties as a result of Russian bombardments. In the Balkans, Russia's general support for Serbia has sometimes put it at odds with US initiatives. The Russian position on Kosovo, wrote political scientists James Goldgeier and Michael McFaul, only reaffirms the belief of many, especially in the (US) Republican party, that Russia itself is "a pariah state" whose influence in internationals affairs must be contained.[14] Russian aid to Iran's nuclear and missile programs may be the most contentious issue of all. US displeasure initially turned on Russian plans to supply gas centrifuge uranium enrichment technology and heavy-water moderated reactors to Iran — equipment that could lead directly to the production of weapons useable material. United States concern has carried over to Russian efforts to complete the Bushehr nuclear power plants. Russia defends its Iranian programs by pointing out that Bushehr can not strengthen Iran's nuclear weapons potential and that US plans to build a reactor in North Korea are equivalent activities.[15] These arguments do not play well in Washington. The "Foreign Operations Appropriation Act" was signed into law in 1997 and authorizes withholding up to 50 percent of US aid to Russia unless the President certifies Russia's conformance with a variety of export controls.[16] In early 1999 the US administration threatened to cut back or eliminate Russian launches of American-made satellites and to impose economic penalties against Russian high technology institutes because of the country's export of sensitive technology.[17]

United States assistance to Russia on nuclear issues may also be impeded by concerns from the American uranium enrichment and nuclear fuel supply industry. The Russian and US industries are competitors as providers of nuclear services to the rest of the world. The US nuclear industry has a significant proportion of the world market for commercial reactor nuclear fuel and watches carefully the production operations of MINATOM, particularly its plan to use fissile material from disassembled weapons as part of commercially available nuclear fuel. The complicated and controversial arrangements between Tenex, a MINATOM subsidiary, and US–based Pleiades Group, Ltd., to organize various fuel transactions have caused concern in the US Congress. Senator Pete Domenici complained that some of the arrangements "may provide an opportunity to divert payment for the uranium, or the uranium itself, from the proper recipients in the Russian Federation."[18]

Reticence among defense and energy officials in the United States and other Western countries could also stem from concern that proposed solutions to Russia's nuclear problems may lead to encroachment of their own

nuclear activities. The NATO/CCMS *Phase II Report*, for example, recommended that before commencement of defense-related activity that
involves the use of radioactive materials, the full life-cycle implications,
including waste management and disposal, should be considered.[19] Western security managers would likely oppose restrictions that might hamper
their ability to deploy high quality military equipment in an expeditious
manner. By a similar logic, should a significant radiological accident occur
in Russia on a project that had Western involvement, the reputation of the
nuclear firms and government agencies involved could suffer and perhaps
lead to restrictions on their own domestic nuclear activities. Environmental
NGOs in the West, like Greenpeace and Bellona, would welcome greater
controls on Western nuclear operations and maintenance and probably the
elimination of nuclear reactors and nuclear weapons altogether — both at
sea and on land.

Political scientists Nazli Choucri and Robert C. North also point out
that the United States is only a "cautious champion" of environmental
causes, while at the same time a major perpetrator of resource depletion
and degradation. Of course the United States has a much better record
than the former Soviet Union, which was "notably destructive as a stew-
ard of its vast natural domain."[20] United States support for large-scale
technology cooperation has also been dwindling. Citing the canceled
Superconducting Super Collider (SSC), the struggling International Ther-
monuclear Experimental Reactor (ITER), and the Department of Energy's
contribution to the UN Conference on Environment and Development
held in Rio in 1992, former US Secretary of Energy James D. Watkins (a
retired nuclear submarine admiral and Chief of Naval Operations) wrote
that "…the United States is fast gaining a reputation among other nations
as an unreliable S&T [science and technology] partner when launching
major new research initiatives of potential benefit to the United States and
the world."[21]

In addition, the US system of government can make international
cooperation and foreign aid very cumbersome and difficult. Former
National Security Advisor Anthony Lake pointed out that: "We have to
cooperate more internationally if we are going to retain our ability to act
nationally and for the sake of democracy. The problem is that third para-
dox, and that is that democratic politics may be the greatest barrier to
democracies being able to make this tradeoff."[22] In other words, a free people with influence on their government's policy can also be shortsighted.
Those managing today's US international cooperative efforts feel the hot
breath of a Congress unsympathetic to foreign assistance programs that
lack obvious evidence of self-interest. If University of Chicago scholar

Stephen M. Walt (no bleeding-heart) has read the post–Cold War period accurately, US restraint in the Russian submarine spent fuel problem has been typical of its other activities:

> As for the United States, the past decade has shown how much it [the United States] likes being "number one" and how determined it is to remain in a predominant position. The United States has taken advantage of its current superiority to impose its preferences wherever possible, even at the risk of irritating many of its long-standing allies. It has forced a series of one-sided arms control agreements on Russia, dominated the problematic peace effort in Bosnia, taken steps to expand NATO into Russia's backyard, and become increasingly concerned about the rising power of China. It has called repeatedly for greater reliance on multilateralism and a larger role for international institutions, but has treated agencies such as the United Nations and the World Trade Organization with disdain whenever their actions did not conform to US interests. It refused to join the rest of the world in outlawing the production of landmines and was politely uncooperative at the Kyoto environmental summit. Although US leaders are adept at cloaking their actions in the lofty rhetoric of "world order," naked self-interest lies behind most of them. Thus the end of the Cold War did not bring the end of power politics and realism is likely to remain the single most useful instrument in our intellectual toolbox.[23]

This seems an overly harsh assessment, at least as far as US dealings with Russia on nuclear issues are concerned. The CTR program is of enormous importance to Russia and other countries of the former Soviet Union, not to mention to the security interest of the United States and the rest of the world. The United States also continues to provide a significant percentage of the IAEA budget and to push for acceptance of IAEA safety and security initiatives throughout Central and Eastern Europe and the former Soviet Union. But aid for the environment is another story; while committed to cleaning up its own Radwaste and other environmental problems, the United States as a government and nation seems generally unsympathetic to Russia's needs.

Why Get Involved?

The United States can and should do more. A case for greater engagement and financial commitment can certainly be made based on interest. To work on Russian defueling and Radwaste projects could provide experience and technologies useful to America's own nuclear industry and Radwaste cleanup programs. US corporations could also profit from the engagement, as Western European companies certainly will; money contributed by Western governments generally finds its way back to the coffers of national champion firms, such as Kvaerner for Norway, SKB for Sweden, SGN for France, and BNFL for the United Kingdom. Moreover, a serious accident in Russia's nuclear programs could affect American attitudes toward their own domestic use of nuclear energy, perhaps leading to additional restrictions on civilian and military nuclear activity. Supporting further Russian defense conversion, which some of the effort would involve, may also be in US interest. According to Mark P. Poncy, Jr., the defense industry is where Russia's most talented work force are positioned so that investing in defense conversion enterprises could create business opportunities for US firms and help promote Russia's transition to a free market economy.[24] Its defense budget is probably too large for its current economy and political status, but a portion of it should be considered social welfare for its underemployed military and defense establishment.

Hans Morgenthau wrote that a country's "diplomacy must look at the political scene from the point of view of other nations."[25] Russia is a major power with diverse interests that will occasionally and inevitably clash with those of the United States, but US officials must also understand Russian attitudes and concerns. It is a very large country with both strong and unstable neighbors; it has a long border with China, a crucial nexus with Japan, Korea, and China in Asia's northwest, and frequent violence to its south. Russia requires at least some effective military power. The alternative to building new nuclear submarines and properly maintaining its more modern ones is block obsolescence of older classes and virtually no long-ranged naval power of significance within a decade or so. This might be good for US security, but consideration should also be given to Russia's contribution to order in its perimeter regions and to the possible role of Russian nuclear weapons in global stability.[26] Construction of the *Severodvinsk* and the *Yuri Dolgorykey*, in any event, is proceeding extremely slowly — if at all. With the shift of responsibility for decommissioned submarines from the Russian Navy to MINATOM, Western funds for defueling operations should have a more difficult time finding their way to projects that might increase the operational capability of the Russian Navy.

Russia's technology exports are more problematic. The proliferation of weapons of mass destruction and the technology to produce them is likely to be one of the foremost security issues of the 21st century. United States policy-makers should do all in their power to strengthen Russia's engagement with the various regimes established to reduce weapons proliferation, but must also consider Russia's need for export income before firming up opposition to export initiatives. With oil, gas, and other natural resources, and perhaps steel, common chemicals, and other bulk items, Russia has few exportable products aside from its military and nuclear technology.[27]

Another reason for US involvement in the Russian spent fuel issue is the balance of influence in post–Cold War Europe. On 1 January 1999, several European Union countries took an immense step forward in the process of integration by giving up their domestic currencies and adopting the *Euro*; other members of the European Union will probably join in the years ahead. The European Monetary Union (EMU) could become a potent rival to US financial hegemony, with the *Euro* challenging the dollar as the world's reserve currency and shifting relative economic power toward Europe. Other changes to solidify the political integrity of Europe are likely to follow, including a more distinct European security and defense identity (ESDI) that could eventually predominate within NATO or supplant it altogether. The extent of the European Commission involvement in projects related to Russian submarine nuclear issues, a military concern previously out-of-bounds for the civilian agency, is noteworthy and perhaps indicative of a larger defense role for Europe in the future. Note that much of Europe's nuclear assistance to Russia falls under DG 1A, the same Commission agency that participates in the European Union's common foreign and security policy activities. France and the United Kingdom, previous stalwarts of national sovereignty, seem less concerned about the usurpation of their security and defense prerogatives by European Union bodies than they were only a few years ago. US/European Union confrontations are most likely to be about economic policy as in the past, but could extend to foreign relations and security concerns in the future.

Russia's future is being decided right now. Will it identify itself increasingly with the developing regions of the world that are sometimes hostile to US interests and initiatives, like China, India, and some countries in the Middle East, or will it chose the West? If it chooses the West, will it be part of an Atlantic arrangement, with equal influence from Western Europe and the United States, or will it be firmly linked with the European Union through interlocking economic and security arrangements, with the United States on the outside looking in? Michael Emerson, a former EU Ambassador in Moscow, recommended using the current economic crisis in Russia to reinforce a wider European order — with the European Union as the core.[28] The *Euro* could conceivably supplant the dollar in Russia as the alternative hard currency of choice. The Russian decommissioned submarine issue is a very small part of any competition for influence, but one where the United States has a definite comparative advantage if it chooses to use it. Cooperation with individual European countries involved in the Russian spent fuel problem can also help the US position. Finland, Norway, and Sweden are actively engaged in the Russian spent fuel problem – often in collaboration with the European Commission. The United States should vigorously engage with these countries on the spent fuel issue to build on its past productive association with them.

A case can also be made for cooperation and assistance for their own sake. Altruism can be viewed as "interest over the long term;" to help a proud and prickly country through a difficult patch could produce rewards in trust and friendship that may eventually prove fruitful. Cooperation in one area can lead to cooperation in others; if Russia, the United States, and the rest of the West can successfully manage a project as complicated and sensitive as submarine spent fuel, other collaborative ventures can surely follow. Echoing Barbara Gray's work, Thomas Princen and Matthias Finger note that success may be measured "less by products – treaties or public works projects – than by processes, especially those that lead to durable institutions that respond to and promote locally desirable solutions to resource problems."[29] Policy makers must balance the environment, economics, and security through a felicitous calculus for which no formulas exist. University of Virginia scholar Michael Joseph Smith wrote that the boundaries between "us" and "them" will always be "a messy product of considerations of power and interest, historical contingency, and human choice."[30] Greater engagement by the United States in Russia would be a positive step by some calculations. Both Russia and the international community seem willing to have the United States play a leading role in Russia's submarine spent fuel problem. The selection of an American official as president of the IAEA CEG in 1998 could be interpreted as encouragement for greater US engagement and leadership. Without substantial financial commitment, however, the United States will have little voice in future deliberations and will not share in the satisfaction of important results.

The Way Ahead

The scope of the Russian submarine spent fuel problem and the difficulties of international cooperation to address it are by now well known to the major participants. It is time to move forward:

1. Projects in train must be completed. The IAEA CEG's four "highest immediate priority" items are a good place to start: completing the Murmansk purification facility, decommissioning the *Lepse*, constructing an interim storage facility at Mayak, and manufacturing metal-concrete spent fuel storage containers. To this could be added completing the Bolshoi Kamen purification barge, building new spent fuel railway cars and a defueling ship, and improving the general condition of shipyards, railways, and other facilities so that further bottlenecks to the defueling chain do not emerge at a later time. Getting a few projects completed would improve the morale of the stakeholders and show that large-scale cooperation is indeed possible.

2. Publishing an overall plan is essential. The collaboration thus far has helped to establish a degree of trust among the parties and to clarify the parameters of the problem, but has not led to an agreement on the specifics of what to do and when to do it.[31] A master PERT chart or other comprehensive plan that links problems with solutions, ships with dates, and that has widespread acceptance and financial support is a crucial step toward project completion. Such a document has been elusive because of differing priorities among the various stakeholders and because of inadequate financial commitments, not to mention Russian preferences that sometimes upset foreign partners. Each controversy should be placed on the table and worked through; it is essential to get beyond Russian complaints about too much talk and too little action by the West and Western concerns about Russian motives and competence.[32]

3. Removing Russian organizational impediments is essential. Russia needs to be less quarrelsome in its foreign and internal policies, and more openly consistent and trustworthy in its business relationships. Some of this may be forthcoming. A new civil code and federal commission on securities could better organize the country's legal affairs; initiatives to reform the tax system are also underway.[33] Russia's allegiance and compliance with international agreements on radioactive waste disposal and liability may become more codified in the near future and further assure Western countries of its good intentions.[34] Hopes persist that the various anti-corruption initiatives of the current government will be successful and that the bottom of Russia's terrible economic decline might be reached at some point in the near future. Greater prosperity could lead to more Russian commitment to environmental issues, including funds for proper disposal of submarine spent fuel.

Shifting control of decommissioned submarines and spent fuel storage facilities from Russian Navy to MINATOM should have a positive effect once the transition is complete. MINATOM is in a much better financial condition than the Russian Navy and may be a more receptive international partner, despite past conflicts with Western agencies. A number of issues will undoubtedly need to be resolved before the benefits of the change are apparent, such as who will man the decommissioned submarines and how the workers will be paid. Draftees and other members of the Russian Navy at least have to show up for work and can not go on strike as easily as civilian government employees or private contractors.

4. Securing more funding is essential. Russia's ability to contribute is very low, and even less so since the August 1998 financial crisis. In 1997, for each ruble that Russia spent on the submarine spent fuel problem, it received seven rubles of international support. National and international institutions must be tapped to a higher degree in order to cope with the task. Organizations like the World Bank, the European Bank for Reconstruction and Development, and the European Investment Bank, are already committed to safety programs for civilian nuclear power plants in the former Soviet Union and should consider funding Russian decommissioned submarine spent fuel problems as well.[35] The IAEA CEG has made the financial need known to a number of institutions, but perhaps more influential levels of the IAEA or national governments should intervene.

The Russian submarine spent fuel problem is a good place to spend some money. It may be a better investment than the International Space Station (ISS) for example, a $40 billion effort with major participation by both Russia and the United States. The benefits from helping with Russian decommissioned submarines would be more immediate while the challenge would still be great. NASA recently proposed paying Russia $600 million for a four year period beginning in late 1998 to preserve a Russian role in the ISS.[36] The marginal utility of even half that amount invested in well-designed and well-managed spent fuel projects would be enormous and might get wholesale defueling and storage operations moving forward.[37] With fairly robust economies, the West can afford both space projects and substantial contributions to Russia's environmental problems — truly exciting efforts at cooperation with a former adversary that could build new and lasting relationships.

In his 1999 State of the Union address, President Clinton called for a $4.2 billion increase in US assistance programs aimed at reducing the threat of nuclear proliferation from Russia, apparently to complement and expand the Nunn-Lugar program.[38] Some of this funding will hopefully find its way to the Russian decommissioned submarine problem. Agency managers in the West must do a better job of convincing their leadership and legislatures of the value of assisting Russia on this issue; engineers are engineers and given adequate financing almost any problem can be solved.

5. Strengthening institutions might improve progress, perhaps through the creation of an oversight board to help create and sanction a general plan. Enhanced and regularized IAEA CEG procedures are possible improvements in the short term. Regardless of the changes made, bargaining with Russia will remain tricky. Western Europe and the United States have generally prospered despite the economic and political problems experienced elsewhere in the world, while Russia's economy continues to lag. Western anxiety over nuclear issues, however, gives Russia negotiating leverage even in the asymmetrical relationship — both in petitioning for funds and in determining priorities. Hence, disagreements and miscalculations are unlikely to go away anytime soon.

6. Consider a middle ground on Radwaste technology and practices. Imposing Western ideas on Russia is probably not the most cost- or time-effective way to remedy the submarine spent fuel problem. Carefully moving to circumstances where Russian equipment and procedures that are "good enough" should be considered: there are times when getting a project done reasonably well in a short period of time takes precedence over completing it perfectly but much later.[39]

Conclusion

Ever more Russian submarines are being taken out of service, creating greater needs for defueling and proper spent fuel and other Radwaste management. A Swedish industrial representative recently toured spent fuel storage sites in and around Murmansk and commented that they were: "...quite terrible to see. It's the way a garbage dump might have looked in Sweden 20 or 30 years ago, and there's more piling up, with no modern management."[40] In a July 1998 interview, Russia's Atomflot Chief Engineer Stanislav Pichugin said: "About 85 per cent of the storage space [for spent fuel] has already been occupied. Therefore, in about three years we may be completely full, and our company and the nuclear fleet [Russian icebreakers] may have to stop operating."[41] With the large amount of spent fuel and other Radwaste in Northwest Russia, there is a finite risk of a significant radiological accident in the years ahead — causing at least localized and perhaps widespread radioactive contamination. The Russian economic crisis could also undermine the structure of the country's armed forces and industrial enterprises further than it already has, creating disorder and threatening the security and safety of spent fuel and other nuclear facilities. More attention would then be received, but with much more expense and effort required for remediation. Russian parliamentarian Alexei Arbatov noted that it remains to be seen whether the world will survive the collapse of a nuclear superpower.[42]

The 1998 London seminar on Radwaste agreed that the international community has a duty to help Russia cope with its Soviet-era nuclear problems.[43] Despite the obstacles, occasional losses of momentum, and real fears for the future, some progress is being made toward resolving the Russian submarine spent fuel problem. Christopher Watson, a nuclear expert at AEA Technology and participant in IAEA CEG meetings, gave the following assessment and recommendation:

> There is a lot to be said for spending money now [on the Russian submarine spent fuel problem]. In five years time, I would hope we will have got most of the 20,000 fuel elements still in submarines, in casks. I would also hope we will have got submarine decommissioning activity up to full speed and resolved the issue of the repository at Novaya Zemlya. A start should also have been made on constructing storage facility for solid and liquid wastes and I would like to think we will have started to deal with the contamination at Andreeva Bay and developed a strategy to deal with damaged submarines.[44]

The contacts developed between Russia and the West on this issue are continuing with no major participant giving any indication of preparing to jump ship, despite heightened differences in other area of international politics. Russia will most likely move forward on this and other environmental issues through a mixture of incentives, both formal and informal, and positive and negative.[45] We should not give up on Russia's future and its ability to become a prosperous democratic country. Of fears that the Napoleonic Wars would ruin England, Adam Smith said: "Sir, there is a great deal of ruin in a nation."[46]

Russian High Priority Projects
(In priority order, updated by June 1997)

No.   Project Name

1. Fabrication and commissioning of special train cars of TK-VG-18 type for transportation of containers with spent fuel from decommissioned nuclear submarines.

2. Construction and commissioning of a storage for spent fuel arriving to the "Mayak" enterprise for reprocessing.

3. Design and construction of facilities for interim storage of spent fuel from decommissioned nuclear submarines in Murmansk region.

4. Design, construction and commissioning of a vessel for transportation of spent fuel from decommissioned submarines in the Northern region.

5. Design, construction and commissioning of temporary storage for liquid r/a wastes at the "Zvezdochka" plant for utilization of nuclear submarines in Severodvinsk.

6. Fabrication and commissioning of mobile facility(s) for concentration of liquid r/a wastes from the Northern Navy.

7. Design, construction and commissioning of a temporary storage of solid r/a wastes at the "Nerpa" plant for utilization of nuclear submarines (Murmansk region).

8. Creation of a prototype r/a waste disposal facility at the Bashmachni Peninsula at the Novaja Zemlja Archipelago.

9. Development of a feasibility study and design on the remediation of the floating technical base-spent fuel storage "Lepse."

10. Construction of two floating facilities for unloading spent fuel from decommissioned submarines.

11. Construction of industrial liquid r/a waste treatment facilities in the Northern region.

12. Reconstruction of solid r/a waste storages at the special combine "Radon" in Murmansk.

13. Creation of a complex of facilities for treatment of solid r/a wastes from nuclear fleet in Murmansk.

14. Creation of the North-West radwaste management centre on the basis of the Leningrad Specialized Enterprise "Radon."

15. Establishment of a Training-Methodological Centre on radioactive waste management.

16. Development of a conception and structure of a normative system regulating safety in r/a waste and spent fuel management.

17. Development of a sophisticated computer based system for evaluation of radiation legacy of the former USSR (RADLEG).

18. Development of a unified data base on radiological situation in the Murmansk region.

19. Development of programme and implementation of radiological monitoring of the flood-lands of the Enisei River in the region of influence of the Mining & Chemical enterprise.

20. Radiation characteristics of unloaded spent fuel in the reactor cores of decommissioned submarines.

Declaration on the Establishment of the Arctic Council, September 19, 1996

THE REPRESENTATIVES of the Governments of Canada, Denmark, Finland, Iceland, Norway, the Russian Federation, Sweden and the United States of America (hereinafter referred to as the Arctic States) meeting in Ottawa;

AFFIRMING our commitment to the well-being of the inhabitants of the Arctic, including recognition of the special relationship and unique contributions to the Arctic of indigenous people and their communities;

AFFIRMING our commitment to sustainable development in the Arctic region, including economic and social development, improved health conditions and cultural well-being;

AFFIRMING concurrently our commitment to the protection of the Arctic environment, including the health of Arctic ecosystems, maintenance of biodiversity in the Arctic region and conservation and sustainable use of natural resources;

RECOGNIZING the contributions of the Arctic Environmental Protection Strategy to these commitments;

RECOGNIZING the traditional knowledge of the indigenous people of the Arctic and their communities and taking note of its importance and that of Arctic science and research to the collective understanding of the circumpolar Arctic;

DESIRING further to provide a means for promoting cooperative activities to address Arctic issues requiring circumpolar cooperation, and to ensure full consultation with and the full involvement of indigenous people and their communities and other inhabitants of the Arctic in such activities;

RECOGNIZING the valuable contribution and support of the Inuit Circumpolar Conference, Saami Council, and the Association of the Indigenous Minorities of the North, Siberia, and the Far East of the Russian Federation in the development of the Arctic Council;

DESIRING to provide for regular intergovernmental consideration of and consultation of Arctic issues.

HEREBY DECLARE:

1. The Arctic Council is established as a high level forum to:

    (a) provide a means for promoting cooperation, coordination and interaction among the Arctic States, with the involvement of the Arctic indigenous communities and other Arctic inhabitants on common Arctic issues,[1] in particular issues of sustainable development and environmental protection in the Arctic.

    (b) oversee and coordinate the programs established under the AEPS on the Arctic Monitoring and Assessment Program (AMAP); Conservation of Arctic Flora and Fauna (CAFF); Protection of the Arctic Marine Environment (PAME); and Emergency Prevention, Preparedness and Response (EPPR).

    (c) adopt terms of reference for, and oversee and coordinate a sustainable development program.

    (d) disseminate information, encourage education and promote interest in Arctic-related issues.

2. Members of the Arctic Council are: Canada, Denmark, Finland, Iceland, Norway, the Russian Federation, Sweden and the United States of America (the Arctic States).

    The Inuit Circumpolar Conference, the Saami Council and the Association of Indigenous Minorities of the North, Siberia and the Far East of the Russian Federation are Permanent Participants in the Arctic Council. Permanent participation equally is open to other Arctic organizations of indigenous peoples[2] with majority Arctic indigenous constituency, representing:

    (a) a single indigenous people resident in more than one Arctic State; or

    (b) more than one Arctic indigenous people resident in a single Arctic State.

The determination that such an organization has met this criterion is to be made by decision of the Council. The number of Permanent Participants should at any time be less than the number of members.

The category of Permanent Participation is created to provide for active participation and full consultation with the Arctic indigenous representatives within the Arctic Council.

3. Observer status in the Arctic Council is open to:

    (a) non-Arctic states;

    (b) inter-governmental and inter-parliamentary organizations, global and regional; and

    (c) non-governmental organizations that the Council determines can contribute to its work.

4. The Council should normally meet on a biennial basis, with meetings of senior officials taking place more frequently, to provide for liaison and coordination. Each Arctic State should designate a focal point on matters related to the Arctic Council.

5. Responsibility for hosting meetings of the Arctic Council, including provision of secretariat support functions, should rotate sequentially among the Arctic States.

6. The Arctic Council, as its first order of business, should adopt rules of procedure for its meetings and those of its working groups.

7. Decisions of the Arctic Council are to be by consensus of the Members.

8. The Indigenous Peoples' Secretariat established under AEPS is to continue under the framework of the Arctic Council.

9. The Arctic Council should regularly review the priorities and financing of its programs and associated structures.

THEREFORE, we the undersigned representatives of our respective Governments, recognizing the Arctic Council's political significance and intending to promote its results, have signed this Declaration.

SIGNED by the representatives of the Arctic States in Ottawa, this 19th day of September 1996.

FOR THE GOVERNMENT
OF CANADA

FOR THE GOVERNMENT
OF DENMARK

FOR THE GOVERNMENT
OF FINLAND

FOR THE GOVERNMENT
OF ICELAND

FOR THE GOVERNMENT
OF NORWAY

FOR THE GOVERNMENT OF
THE RUSSIAN FEDERATION

FOR THE GOVERNMENT
OF SWEDEN

FOR THE GOVERNMENT OF
THE UNITED STATES OF
AMERICA

Notes

1. The Arctic Council should not deal with matters related to military security.

2. The use of the term "peoples" in this Declaration shall not be construed as having any implications as regard the rights which may attach to the term under international law.

Royal Norwegian Ministry of Foreign Affairs Nuclear Safety and the Environment Plan of Action, February 1997, Priority area 2

Management, Storage and Disposal of Radioactive Waste and Spent Nuclear Fuel (topic headings only)

201 — NATO/NACC/CCMS pilot study on cross-border environmental problems emanating from defense-related installations and activities.

202 — Effluent treatment facility for liquid radioactive waste in Murmansk.

203 — International Advisory Committee for the storage vessel for radioactive waste, the *Lepse*.

204 — Transfer of expertise concerning plans for an underground disposal facility in north-western Russia.

205 — AMEC — Norwegian, Russian, American Arctic military environmental cooperation.

206 — International seminar under the auspices of IAEA on management of radioactive waste and spent nuclear fuel in Russia.

208 — International action programme and fund.

209 — Study of the Russian programme for dismantling of decommissioned nuclear submarines in the Northern Fleet.

211 — Specialized vessel for transport of spent nuclear fuel.

212 — Specialized railway rolling stock of the type TK-VG-18 for transport of spent nuclear fuel.

213 — Upgrading of storage tanks for liquid radioactive waste at the "Zvez-dochka" shipyard in Severodvinsk.

214 — Mobile facilities for treatment of liquid radioactive waste.

215 — Storage facility for solid radioactive waste on Kola.

216 — Emptying and discontinuing of the hazardous storage facility for spent nuclear fuel in Andreev Bay.

217 — Possible participation in the completion of environmentally safe interim storage for spent nuclear fuel at Mayak.

218 — Support for expert participation and the secretariat of the "Contact Expert Group for International Radwaste Projects," IAEA.

219 — Methods of assessing the safety of facilities for radioactive waste.

220 — Criticality assessments for nuclear fuel from Russian ships' reactors.

Norway-Russia Framework Agreement on Cooperation Related to Dismantling Nuclear Submarines and Enhancing Nuclear Safety, 26 May 1998

Article 9

1. With the exception of claims for damage or injury against individuals arising from their premeditated actions, the Russian Party shall bring no claims or legal proceedings against the Norwegian Party and its personnel or contractors, subcontractors, consultants, suppliers or equipment or services at any tier and their personnel, for indirect, direct or consequential damage to property owned by the Russian Federation. This paragraph shall not apply to legal actions brought by the Russian Party to enforce the provisions of contracts to which it or a Russian national is a party.

2. With the exception of claims for damage or injury against individuals arising from their premeditated actions, the Russian Party shall provide for the adequate legal defense of, indemnify, and shall bring no claims or legal proceedings against, the Norwegian Party and its personnel, contractors, subcontractors, consultants, suppliers of equipment or services at any tier and their personnel in connection with third-party claims in any court or forum arising from activities undertaken pursuant to this Agreement for injury, loss or damage occurring within or outside the territory of the Russian Federation that results from a nuclear incident occurring within the territory of the Russian Federation.

3. Without prejudice to paragraphs 1 and 2 of this article nothing in this article shall be interpreted to prevent legal proceedings or claims against nationals of the Russian Federation or permanent residents of the territory of the Russian Federation.

4. The provisions of this article shall not prevent indemnification by the Parties for damage in accordance with their national laws.

5. Nothing in this article shall be construed as acknowledging the jurisdiction of any court or forum outside of the Russian Federation over third-party claims, for which paragraph 2 of this article applies, except as provided for in paragraph 9 of this article and in any other case where the Russian Federation has pledged itself to acknowledge and execute a legal decision on the basis of provisions of international agreements.

6. Nothing in this article shall be construed as waiving the immunity of the Kingdom of Norway or the Russian Federation with respect to potential third-party claims that may be brought against either of the Parties.

7. The provisions of this article shall — if so requested by the contractor — be incorporated into the project agreements or contracts by the issue, by or on behalf of the Russian Party, of an indemnity confirmation letter to the contractor.

8. In case a nuclear incident has occurred which may lead to the fulfillment of the obligation to compensate damage, the Parties shall hold consultations upon request by one of the Parties.

9. As regards its obligations in this article to the contractors, subcontractors, consultants, suppliers of equipment or services at any tier and their personnel, the Russian Party undertakes to have any conflict, controversy or claim arising out of or in relation to this article, if not settled amicably within three months, referred to and finally resolved by arbitration in accordance with the UNCITRAL Arbitration Rules. The national legislation of the Parties shall not be applied for the resolution of any conflict, controversy or claim.

10. Any payments related to the indemnification in paragraph 2 of this article shall be made promptly and in a convertible currency.

11. The obligations concerning liability for nuclear damage undertaken by the Russian Party in accordance with the present article shall be valid for objects which are the subject of cooperation under this Agreement, and shall remain in effect regardless of any subsequent transfer of ownership of these objects, termination of this Agreement or the expiry of its validity.

Notes

Preface

1. Cited from Peter G. Tsouras, *Warrior's Words: A Quotation Book* (London: Arms and Armour Press, 1992), 372.

1. Russian Dilemmas

1. George F. Kennan, *Russia and the West Under Lenin and Stalin* (New York: New American Library, 1960), 370.

2. Some may take exception to this structural realist explanation of Cold War stability, but the balance of nuclear terror and bipolarity were certainly important factors in this "long peace."

3. The "intensive" industrial revolution of the late-20th century increased productivity and output through the use of computers and other new technologies; the "extensive" industrial revolution that preceded it increased production by building additional factories.

4. Early resistance in the Baltic states resulted in some loss of life as did the conflict between Azerbaijan and Armenia over Nagorno-Karabakh. Since the breakup of the Soviet Union, civil and ethnic strife has taken thousands of lives in the successor states.

5. See *Gannett News Service*, 30 June 1998 and "Nuclear Complacency," *The Economist*, 17 October 1998, 20.

6. Susanne Kopte, "Nuclear Submarine Decommissioning and Related Problems," Bonn International Center for Conversion (BICC), August 1997.

7. *Gannett News Service*, 30 June 1998.

8. "Costing a bomb: defense," *The Economist*, 4 January 1997 and *Financial Times*, 28 August 1998.

9. *New York Times*, 30 November 1998.

10. *Deutsche Presse-Agentur*, 9 March 1997.

11. See David Hoffman, "Russia's New Tycoons: An emerging power group mixes capitalism with affairs of state," *Washington Post National Weekly Edition*, 20 January 1997, for more on the Russian oligarchs.

12. *New York Times*, 25 August 1998.

13. Press conference with Minister of Nuclear Energy Yevgeny Adamov, *Official Kremlin International News Broadcast*, 25 November 1998.

14. *New York Times*, 23 November 1998.

15. *Financial Times*, 27 August 1998.

16. *New York Times*, 12 October 1998.

17. Mark P. Poncy, Jr., "The need for greater US Assistance in promoting Russian defense conversion," *Law and Policy in International Business*, Vol. 28, No. 2, 1 January 1997.

18. *Financial Times*, 18 February 1999.

19. *Financial Times*, 3 September 1998.

20. *Financial Times*, 1–2 August 1998.

21. *New York Times*, 2 November 1998.

22. *New York Times*, 23 November 1998.

23. *The Economist Intelligence Unit Ltd.*, 5 February 1998.

24. *New York Times*, 2 November 1998.

25. *Associated Press*, 10 April 1997.

26. When the United States issued new $100 bank notes in the late-1990s, Russians — not Americans — were most concerned about the look of the new bills and their efficacy in future transactions.

27. See A. Anikin, V. Fedorov, and S. Boiko, "Dynamics and regulation of the ruble exchange rate in light of world experience," *Russian & East European Finance & Trade*, May/June 1997, for analysis of Russia's fiscal policy before the August 1998 crash.

28. See Sylvia Nasar, "Denied Western Funds, Russia Makes Its Choice," *New York Times*, 18 August 1998.

29. For analysis of the Asian economic problem, see Hirofumi Ushikoshi, "Causes of the Asian Currency Crisis," *NLI Research Institute Home Page, http://www.nli-research.co.jp/ENG/RESEA/ECONO/ECO9804.htm*. See also the four part series in the *New York Times*

on "Global Contagion: A Narrative," in February 1999.

30. *New York Times*, 17 February 1999.

31. *Financial Times*, 27 August 1998.

32. *Financial Times*, 28 August 1998.

33. *Financial Times*, 29 August 1998.

34. *Denver Post*, 23 August 1998.

35. *Financial Times* 28 August 1998.

36. *New York Times*, 23 October 1998.

37. *Gazette Telegraph* (Colorado Springs), 30 December 1998.

38. *New York Times*, 26 February 1999.

39. *Washington Post National Weekly Edition*, 16 November 1998.

40. *Financial Times*, 19 January 1999.

41. *Financial Times*, 28 August 1998.

42. *New York Times*, 5 February 1999.

43. *Financial Times*, 5 June 1998.

44. *Gazette Telegraph* (Colorado Springs), 30 December 1998.

45. *New York Times*, 14 December 1998.

46. *Associated Press State and Local Wire*, 25 November 1998.

47. *New York Times*, 2 December 1998.

48. *Agence France Presse*, 12 November 1998.

49. *The Independent* (London), 17 May 1996.

50. *Times Newspaper Limited* (London), 25 November 1998.

51. *The Guardian*, 11 May 1998.

52. *Moscow News*, 14 May 1998.

53. Murray Feshbach and Alfred Friendly, Jr., *Ecocide in the USSR: Health and Nature Under Siege* (New York: Basic Books, 1992), 92.

54. Feshbach and Friendly, *Ecocide*, 93

55. Jurki Käkönen, *Politics and Sustainable Growth in the Arctic* (Newcastle upon Tyne: Dartmouth Publishing Company, 1993), 30.

56. *The Herald* (Glasgow), 3 October 1997.

57. "Project information sheet, Environment 015, Task Force Report," 14–15 December 1995, 24.

58. *The Commercial Appeal* (Memphis), 29 March 1998.

59. *Moscow Times*, 5 February 1998.

60. *Gazette Telegraph* (Colorado Springs), 26 December 1998.

61. A half-life is the time it takes for a given radionuclide to be reduced to one half of its original quantity. Usually five half-lives pretty much does away with the radionuclide; unfortunately the daughter isotopes may also be radioactive and present a problem for another five half-lives, which is one of the problems with spent nuclear fuel. See NATO/CCMS/NACC Pilot Study, *Cross-Border Environmental Problems Emanating From Defence-Related Installations and Activities, Vol. 1: Radioactive Contamination, Phase I: 1993–1995*, Report No.

204, April 1995, 115–123 for specific characteristics of various radionuclides.

62. Don J. Bradley, *Behind the Nuclear Curtain: Radioactive Waste Management in the Former Soviet Union* (Columbus, Washington: Battelle Press, 1997), 503, 518.

63. See Thomas B. Cochran, Robert S. Norris, and Oleg A. Bukharin, *Making the Russian Bomb, From Stalin to Yeltsin* (Boulder: Westview Press, 1995), 157.

64. *Financial Times*, 19/20 September 1998.

65. *Nuclear Energy Safety Challenges in the Former Soviet Union: A Consensus Report of the CSIS Congressional Study Group on Nuclear Energy Safety Challenges in the Former Soviet Union*, project chairman James R. Schlesinger (Washington, D.C.: CSIS, 1995), 6.

66. Norman Polmar, "The Soviet Navy," *US Naval Institute Proceedings*, Vol. 124, No. 2, February 1998, 87–88.

67. NATO/CCMS Pilot Study, *Cross-Border Environmental Problems Emanating From Defence-Related Installations and Activities, Phase II: 1995–1998, Vol. 3: Management of Defense Related Radioactive Waste*, Report No. 226, March 1998, 22.

68. Report on the conference "Perspectives on International Cooperation in the Dismantlement of Nuclear Submarines," held in Moscow, 11 December 1998.

69. Judith Perera, "Russia: New MINATOM department to oversee Radwaste, including naval wastes," *Nuclear Waste News*, 15 October 1998.

70. PERT stands for "Program Evaluation and Review Technique." It is a logic diagram and commonly used way to help manage complex industrial projects. The PERT system was developed and used in conjunction with the US ballistic missile and submarine construction program of the 1950s and 60s.

71. See Thomas Nilsen, Igor Kudrik, and Alexandr Nikitin, *The Russian Northern Fleet: Sources of Radioactive Contamination*, Bellona Report Volume 2: 1996, published by the Bellona Foundation, Oslo, Norway, Chapter 2, for much more on Russian nuclear submarine construction.

72. As of 1 January 1995, six Northern Fleet submarines and nine from the Pacific Fleet had been defueled and dismantled, according to *Nuclear Wastes in the Arctic: An Analysis of Arctic and Other Regional Impacts from Soviet Nuclear Contamination*, OTA-ENV-623 (Washington, D.C.: US Government Printing Office, September 1995), 133.

73. *The European*, 12 October 1998.

74. Mark Hibbs, "Murmansk Shipping Company to Offer to Bring Andreeva Bay Cores to Mayak," *Nuclear Fuels*, 22 April 1996, 4.

75. Colonel A. D. Belikov, Russian Navy, "The Radiation and Ecological Situation at Northern Fleet Facilities," in *Reducing Wastes from Decommissioned Nuclear Submarines in the Russian Northwest: Political, Technical, and Economic Aspects of International Cooperation,* Proceedings from the NATO Advanced Research Workshop, "Recycling, Remediation, and Restoration Strategies for Contaminated Civilian and Military Sites in the Arctic Far North," Kirkenes, Norway, 24–28 June 1996 (Washington, D.C.: American Association for the Advancement of Science, 1997), eds. Sanoma Lee Kellogg and Elizabeth J. Kirk, 23.

76. See Chapter 3, *Phase I CCMS Report,* for more detail on contamination in the Barents, Baltic, and Black Seas.

77. *Interpress Service,* 24 April 1998.

78. *The Guardian* (London), 26 March 1997.

79. *The Independent,* 13 December 1998.

80. *The Independent* (London), 21 December 1997.

81. Norway's "Nuclear Safety and Environment Plan of Action, 1997–98, For the Implementation of Report No. 34 (1993–94) to the Storting on Nuclear Activities and Chemical Weapons in Areas Adjacent to our Northern Borders" (Plan of Action), Royal Norwegian Ministry of Foreign Affairs, February 1997, 4.

82. *BBC Summary of World Broadcasts,* 25 October 1996.

83. Timothy W. Maier, "Russian Armada Poisons the Seas," *Insight on the News,* 5 July 1999.

84. MINATOM head Yevgeny Adamov at a press conference noted that there was a danger that American intelligence activities would try to use nuclear safety and security aid as a means to penetrate Russian restricted cities. Press conference with Nuclear Energy Minister Yevgeny Adamov, *Official Kremlin International News Broadcast,* 9 December 1998.

85. *International Herald Tribune,* 17 November 1998.

86. *Sunday Telegraph* (London), 6 October 1996.

87. *Philadelphia Inquirer,* 15 January 1999.

88. *Foreign Report,* 12 November 1998.

89. Andrew Meier, "Kept Out in the Cold: A warning about the dangers of Russia's rotting nukes trapped Alexander Nikitin in a legal maze," *Time International Edition,* 16 November 1998, 32.

90. *The Scotsman,* 1 July 1997.

91. *Nuclear Waste News,* 11 December 1997.

92. *Denver Post,* 22 January 1999.

93. *Financial Times,* 21 August 1996.

94. For a report on "the gusher that wasn't," see *New York Times,* 5 September 1997.

95. Martin Walker, "Investing in Russia: Not for the Weak of Heart," *Europe,* No. 364, March 1997, 10.

96. *Financial Times,* 21 August 1996.

97. *Financial Times,* 19–20 December 1998.

98. *Phase I CCMS Report,* 22.

99. *The Herald* (Glasgow), 10 July 1997.

100. Remarks by Secretary of Defense William J. Perry to the Society of American Engineers, *DoD press release,* 25 November 1996.

101. *Phase II CCMS Report,* 13.

102. For a comprehensive overview of US nuclear weapons production and Radwaste issues, see the Department of Energy Publication, *Linking Legacies: Connecting the Cold War Nuclear Weapons Production Processes To Their Environmental Consequences,* January 1997, DOE/em-0319.

103. See *Gazette Telegraph,* 24 July 1998.

104. Joshua Handler, "The lasting legacy — Nuclear submarine disposal," *Jane's Navy International,* 1 January 1998.

105. See David Huizenga, "Spent Nuclear Fuel Management," in Kellogg and Kirk, *Reducing Wastes from Decommissioned Nuclear Submarines,* 125–126.

106. Handler, "The lasting legacy" 1 January 1998.

107. Handler, "The lasting legacy" 1 January 1998.

108. Kopte, "Submarine Decommissioning," 45.

109. For analysis of the Russian economy, see Vitaly V. Shlykov, *The Crisis in the Russian Economy,* a monograph prepared for the US Army War College Annual Strategy Conference, 30 June 1997, Strategic Studies Institute Strategic Conference Series.

110. Bellona, *Russian Northern Fleet,* 115 and 136.

111. Preface from Georgi Kostev, *Nuclear Safety Challenges in the Operation and Dismantlement of Russian Nuclear Submarines* (Moscow: Committee for Critical Technologies and Non-Proliferation, 1997), 2.

112. *Phase II CCMS Report,* 263.

113. Kopte, "Submarine Decommissioning," 30.

114. Approximately 50 million curies were released after the Chernobyl accident, according to GAO letter report, "Nuclear Safety: Concerns with Nuclear Facilities and Other Sources of Radiation in the Former Soviet Union," 11/07/95, GAO/RCED-96-4.

115. Introduction to Kostev, *Nuclear Safety Challenges,* 5.

Chapter 2

1. *RIA News Agency*, Moscow, 4 July 1998.

2. The victory of Admiral de Grasse and his French fleet over the British fleet at Virginia Capes in September 1780 prevented relief of the British army under General Cornwallis at Yorktown. This allowed George Washington and his French allies to complete the siege and force Cornwallis' surrender. The British government soon granted independence to the thirteen colonies.

3. During the Cold War, however, the Kola Peninsula was adjacent to NATO-member Norway; in Kamchatka, military ports like Petropavlovsk had to worry about US reconnaissance aircraft and other activities based in the nearby Aleutian islands.

4. See S. G. Gorshkov, *The Sea Power of the State* (Annapolis: Naval Institute Press, 1979), 66–68, for the Soviet naval leaders' version of early Slav maritime history.

5. Peter Tsouras, "Soviet Naval Tradition," in *The Soviet Navy: Strengths and Liabilities* (Boulder: Westview Press, 1986), eds. Bruce W. Watson and Susan M. Watson, 6.

6. Allen F. Chew, *An Atlas of Russian History: Eleven Centuries of Changing Borders* (New Haven: Yale University Press, 1970), 40.

7. Cited from Gorshkov, *Sea Power of the State*, xi, originally from the Russian *Marine Regulations* of 1720.

8. Eric Morris, *The Russian Navy, Myth and Reality* (New York: Stein and Day, 1977), 3.

9. Tsouras, "Soviet Naval Tradition," 7.

10. All of this followed the climatic land Battle of Poltova in 1709 when Peter the Great and his Russian army ended Sweden's role as a great power. For the sequence of events, see R. Ernest Dupuy and Trevor N. Dupuy, *The Harper Encyclopedia of Military History, Fourth Edition* (New York: Harper Collins, 1993), 675, 676.

11. Tsouras, "Soviet Naval Tradition," 8–9.

12. Morris, *The Russian Navy*, 5–6.

13. Gorshkov, *Sea Power of the State*, 80.

14. Dupuy, *Encyclopedia of Military History*, 907.

15. See Gorshkov, *Sea Power of the State*, 92–124 and 141–155 for his version of Russian/Soviet naval activity in World Wars I and II.

16. Morris, *The Russian Navy*, 21.

17. Harrison Salisbury gives us the sweep and detail of this desperate and heroic defense in *900 Days: The Siege of Leningrad* (New York: Harper and Row, 1969).

18. Morris, *The Russian Navy*, 24.

19. Tsouras, "Soviet Naval Tradition," 18.

20. Tsouras, "Soviet Naval Tradition," 20.

21. Michele Cosentina, "Back to the Future," *US Naval Institute Proceedings*, Vol. 123, No. 3, March 1997, 45.

22. Norman Polmar, *Guide to the Soviet Navy: Fourth Edition* (Annapolis: Naval Institute Press, 1986), 1.

23. Morris, *Russian Navy*, 54.

24. The names of many Russian ships and classes of ships have been changed repeatedly in the last two decades. This book relies primarily on the more familiar Soviet designations as I understand them.

25. Paul L. Pierce, "Aircraft Carriers and Large Surface Combatants," in *The Soviet Navy: Strengths and Liabilities* (Boulder, CO: Westview Press, 1986), eds. Bruce W. Watson and Susan M. Watson, 91.

26. Testimony by Secretary of the Navy John Lehman, contained in "Hearings before the Defense Policy Panel of the Committee on Armed Services," House of Representatives, One Hundredth Congress, First Session, March 11, 13, 17, 18, 20, and 23, 1987, H.A.S.C. No 100-15, p. 14. A similar quotation appears in Polmar, *Guide to the Soviet Navy*, vii.

27. Comments of Admiral Yerofeyev during a press conference for Admiral of the Fleet Vladimir Ivanovich Kuroyedov, *Official Kremlin International News Broadcast*, 27 August 1998.

28. See, for example, Morris, *The Russian Navy*, 35–39.

29. Soviet ships operating in the Mediterranean Sea must also have been concerned about the highly capable Israeli air force.

30. Bruce W. Watson and Susan M. Watson, "Looking Toward the Future," in *The Soviet Navy: Strengths and Liabilities*, 299.

31. Military historian Eric Morris found the comparison between British-German rivalry prior to World War I and US–Soviet rivalry during the Cold War "quaint," since it viewed sea power only from an "orthodox viewpoint" and did not consider the great political value of modern naval assets. Morris, *The Russian Navy*, 130.

32. Some claim that Western navies welcomed the expansion and advances of the Soviet Navy because the new and worthy adversary helped to justify an expansion of their own capabilities.

33. W. M. Thornton and Gustavo Conde, *Submarine Insignia & Submarine Services of the World* (Annapolis: Naval Institute Press, 1997), 103.

34. Robert E. McKeown and David Robinson, "Submarines," in *The Soviet Navy: Strengths and Liabilities*, 57.

35. Thornton and Conde, *Submarine Insignia*, 103

36. Gorshkov, *Sea Power of the State*, 137.
37. McKeown and Robinson, "Submarines," 57.
38. Gorshkov, *Sea Power of the State*, 190.
39. Polmar, *Guide to the Soviet Navy*, 157.
40. Note that the first use of Rudolf Diesel's compression ignition engine was at a Busch brewery in St. Louis, MO; use of diesel engines on US inventor John P. Holland's early submarines soon followed.
41. Polmar, *Guide to the Soviet Navy, 152.* Most diesel electric submarines can run their diesels while submerged at shallow depth by snorkeling. This means raising a large mast that has an intake for fresh air and an exhaust port to get rid of the diesel combustion fumes. Snorkeling still produces considerable noise, however. Note that in the late 1990s the United States has become increasingly concerned with the proliferation of high quality late-model diesel submarines, like the Russian *Kilo* class exported to China, India, and Iran. Various air-independent-propulsion (AIP) technologies, such as fuel cells, are also in development to enhance or replace diesel-electric propulsion. For more information, see David Foxwell, "Sub proliferation sends navies diving for cover: The multiple menace of diesel-electric submarines," *Jane's International Defense Review*, Vol. 30, 1 August 1997, 30–39.
42. See Richard Rhodes, *Making of the Atomic Bomb* (New York: Simon and Schuster, 1986) for more on the squash court experiment and for excellent coverage of the development of nuclear knowledge and practice.
43. See Francis Duncan, *Rickover and the Nuclear Navy* (Annapolis: Naval Institute Press, 1990) for more on Admiral Rickover, the Shippingsport power plant, and the US Navy nuclear submarine program.
44. See Patrick Tyler, *Running Critical: The Silent War, Rickover, and General Dynamics* (New York: Harper & Row, Publishers, 1986) for further accounts of Admiral Rickover and the US Navy nuclear propulsion program.
45. Duncan, *Rickover and the Nuclear Navy*, 3.
46. Anatoly V. Kuteinikov, "Malachite Subs Post Proud Tradition," *US Naval Institute Proceedings*, Vol. 124, No. 4, April 1998, 52.
47. Kuteinikov, "Malachite Subs," 53. Soviet submarine classes were designated by US and NATO officials for allied use, but the names were often adopted by the Soviets themselves.
48. Tyler, *Running Critical*, 41–45.
49. Georgi Kostev, *Nuclear Safety Challenges in the Operation and Dismantlement of Russian Nuclear Submarines* (Moscow: Com-

mittee for Critical Technologies and Non-Proliferation, 1997), 12.
50. See Polmar, *Guide to the Soviet Navy,* 110–112 for topical analysis of Soviet submarine advances and the impact of John Walker's espionage.
51. NATO/CCMS/NACC Pilot Study, *Cross-Border Environmental Problems Emanating From Defence-Related Installations and Activities, Vol. 1: Radioactive Contamination, Phase I: 1993–1995,* Report No. 204, April 1995, 281.
52. See Tyler, *Running Critical*, for a dramatized account of the *Alfa's* development and potential.
53. Kuteinikov, "Malachite Subs," 55.
54. See Norman Polmar's testimony before the US House of Representatives Military Procurement Subcommittee of the Committee on National Security concerning the US New Attack Submarine Program, 18 March 1997. See also *Jane's Fighting Ships 1998–1999* for more on Russia's latest submarine classes.
55. Cosentina, "Back to the Future," 45.
56. Polmar, *Guide to the Soviet Navy*, 109. See also Norman Polmar's, "The Soviet Navy," *US Naval Institute Proceedings*, Vol. 124, No. 2, February 1998, for additional information on Soviet submarine construction.
57. William L. Chaze and Robert Kaylor, "Deadly Game of Hide-and-Seek," *U.S. News and World Report*, 15 June 1987.
58. *Jane's Fighting Ships 1997–1998*, 594.
59. *AP Worldstream*, 11 December 1998.
60. *Jane's Intelligence Review*, 1 March 1997, and *BBC Summary of World Broadcasts*, 6 July 1998.
61. Press conference with Admiral Vladimir Ivanovich Kuroyedov, 27 August 1998.
62. See Kostev, *Nuclear Safety Challenges*, Chapter 1, "Yesterday's Neglect of Today's Fleet," for more on post–Cold War decline of the Russian fleet.
63. "State of the Russian Navy" website, *http://www.webcom.com/~amraam/rnav.html.*
64. *ITAR-TASS*, 22 December 1998.
65. *Financial Times*, 23 October 1998.
66. Press conference with Russian Navy Commander-in-Chief, Admiral Vladimir Ivanovich Kuroyedov, *Official Kremlin International News Broadcast*, 27 August 1998.
67. *BBC Summary of World Broadcasts*, 26 May 1997.
68. *Worldwide Submarine Challenges 1997*, Office of Naval Intelligence (ONI), February 1997, 9.
69. *Worldwide Submarine Challenges 1997*, 9.
70. Cosentina, "Back to the Future," 45.
71. Richard Sharpe, ed., *Jane's Fighting*

Ships, 1998–1999 (Surrey, UK: Jane's Information Group Limited), 547 and 551.

72. Paul Mann, "Nuclear Risks Mount in Besieged Russia," *Aviation Week and Space Technology*, Vol. 149, No. 10, 7 September 1998.

73. Tsouras, "Soviet Naval Tradition," 3.

Chapter 3

1. *The Commercial Appeal* (Memphis, TN), 22 November 1998.

2. Whereas earlier in the book, the submarines under discussion were referred to as "Soviet," in this chapter and for the remainder of the book I call them "Russian."

3. The United States built only one two-reactor submarine, the *USS Triton* (SSN 586), commissioned in 1959. *Triton* was a giant submarine used for radar picket duty and was the first ship to circle the globe underwater, commanded by the legendary Edward L. Beach.

4. Hafnium is often found in zircon sand along with zirconium. They have similar chemical properties but hafnium is a strong neutron absorber while zirconium has little neutron affinity. See "Mineral Commodity Summaries," January 1996, *http://minerals.er. usgs.gov/minerals/pubs/commodity/zirconium/ 730396.txt*.

5. *Inventory of radioactive waste and spent fuel at the Kola Peninsula region of north-west Russia, EUR 16916* (Luxembourg: Office for Official Publications of the European Communities, 1996), 91. The figures given are in thermal power output, a commonly used measure of reactor power. A Chernobyl-style reactor has a thermal output of 3,200 megawatts which in turn produces about 925 megawatts of generated electricity.

6. Francis Duncan, *Rickover and the Nuclear Navy* (Annapolis: Naval Institute Press, 1990), 24.

7. Knut Gussgard, "Spent Nuclear Fuel Issues on the Kola Peninsula," in *Reducing Wastes from Decommissioned Nuclear Submarines in the Russian Northwest: Political, Technical, and Economic Aspects of International Cooperation*, Proceedings from the NATO Advanced Research Workshop: "Recycling, Remediation, and Restoration Strategies for Contaminated Civilian and Military Sites in the Arctic Far North," Kirkenes, Norway, 24–28 June 1996 (Washington, D.C.: American Association for the Advancement of Science, 1997), eds. Sanoma Lee Kellogg and Elizabeth J. Kirk, 106.

8. NATO/CCMS/NACC Pilot Study, *Cross-Border Environmental Problems Ema-*

nating From Defence-Related Installations and Activities, Vol. 1: Radioactive Contamination, Phase I: 1993–1995, Report No. 204, April 1995, 188.

9. *EUR 16916*, 74.

10. *Phase I CCMS Report*, 200.

11. NATO/CCMS Pilot Study, *Cross-Border Environmental Problems Emanating From Defence-Related Installations and Activities, Phase II: 1995–1998, Vol. 3: Management of Defense Related Radioactive Waste*, Report No. 226, March 1998, 24.

12. Reactor construction and nuclear bomb-making are very different technologies. Reactors are designed such that the fission process is closely controlled and so that the uranium fuel will last for months or years; bombs are designed to use almost all of their uranium or plutonium almost instantaneously. Reactor accidents can not duplicate the nuclear bomb explosion process but, as Chernobyl demonstrated, can still cause enormous devastation.

13. For more information on Russian submarine reactor design see Viking Olver Eriksen, *Sunken Nuclear Submarines: A Threat to the Environment* (Oslo: Norwegian University Press, 1990).

14. Thomas B. Cochran, Robert S. Norris, and Oleg A. Bukharin, *Making the Russian Bomb: From Stalin to Yeltsin* (Boulder: Westview Press, 1995), 297–298.

15. *Phase I CCMS Report*, 189.

16. *Phase I CCMS Report*, 61.

17. The "curie" is a common means of expressing the radioactivity of an object, i.e., the number of radionuclides decaying (disintegrating) per unit time. Many organizations and publications now use the "becquerel," (Bq) however: 1 curie is equal to 3.7×10^{10} becquerels and 1 becquerel is equal to 1 disintegration per second. See *Phase I CCMS Report*, "Glossary," for more definitions.

18. Joshua Handler, "Russia seeks to refloat a decaying fleet," *Jane's International Defense Review*, Vol. 30, January 1997, 46.

19. The Cherenkov effect occurs when radioactive decay emits gamma rays, a form of electromagnetic radiation of very high frequency, which then slows from the speed of light in a vacuum to the slower speed of light allowed by water. The speed change is accounted for as energy emitted in the form of blue light, an impressive effect.

20. Don J. Bradley, *Radioactive Waste Management in the Former Soviet Union*, ed. David R. Payson (Columbus, Washington: Battelle Press, 1997), 363. Potassium iodide, if taken shortly before or after a nuclear accident, can block the absorption of radioactive iodine.

Data from Poland after the Chernobyl accident suggests that the drug was useful in this regard and that the benefits outweigh the risks of side effects. See *New York Times*, 26 August 1998.

21. Of the collective effective dose from the Chernobyl accident, 40 percent will be received in the former Soviet Union, 57 percent in the rest of Europe, and 3 percent in other countries of the Northern Hemisphere. *Phase I CCMS Report*, 258.

22. Very little weapons-grade plutonium is actually produced from highly enriched submarine reactors because so little U 238, the source isotope for plutonium, is present in the fuel mixture in the first place.

23. Thomas Nilsen, Igor Kudrik, and Alexandr Nikitin, *The Russian Northern Fleet: Sources of Radioactive Contamination, Bellona Report Volume 2: 1996*, published by the Bellona Foundation, Oslo, Norway, 95.

24. See *Hostile Waters* (New York: St. Martins Press, 1997) by Peter Huchthausen, Igor Kurdin, and R. Alan White, for a dramatized version of the last patrol of the K-219, an older Russian *Yankee* class SSBN that sank east of Bermuda in 1986.

25. Georgi Kostev, *Nuclear Safety Challenges in the Operation and Dismantlement of Russian Nuclear Submarines* (Moscow: Committee for Critical Technologies and Non-Proliferation, 1997), 88.

26. Judith Perera, "Russia: New MINATOM department to oversee Radwaste, including naval wastes," *Nuclear Waste News*, 15 October 1998. Data from the "Perspectives on International Cooperation in the Dismantlement of Nuclear Submarines" conference in December 1998 is slightly more current, but does not differentiate by fleet.

27. Bellona, *Russian Northern Fleet*, 130.

28. *Phase I CCMS Report*, 281

29. Susanne Kopte, "Nuclear Submarine Decommissioning and Related Problems," Bonn International Center for Conversion (BICC), August 1997, 20.

30. According to Norway's Foreign Minister Godal, "We have reason to believe that much of the fuel from nuclear submarines needs to be reprocessed for reasons of nuclear safety. This applies primarily to uranium-aluminum fuel, which corrodes relatively rapidly." *Norwegian Foreign Ministry news release*, 29 October 1996.

31. See *Phase II CCMS Report*, B-8, B-9 and various IAEA reports for more on the nuclear safety culture concept.

32. *Nuclear Wastes in the Arctic: An Analysis of Arctic and Other Regional Impacts from Soviet Nuclear Contamination*, OTA-ENV-623

(Washington, D.C.: US Government Printing Office, September 1995), 153.

33. Excerpt from *The Post and Courier* (Charleston SC) 20 July 1997 *AP* report on Mir's difficulties: "To the amazement of some and the exasperation of others, Russian space officials have appeared to take the accidents and breakdowns in stride. In fact, about the only crisis the Russians don't seem to have with the Mir is a crisis in confidence." "The Russians have more experience improvising and more confidence that they can improvise successfully," said John Pike, a space specialist at the Federation of American Scientists in Washington.

34. *Gazette Telegraph* (Colorado Springs), 27 August 1997.

35. A demonstration by nuclear workers at Desnorgorsk was resolved only after Deputy Prime Minister Nemtsov promised to back pay wages. *FE/RL Newsline*, 17 July 1997.

36. Judith Perera, "International Officials fear old subs, waste could lead to disaster in Arctic," *Nuclear Waste News*, 11 December 1997.

37. *The Guardian* (London), 18 November 1998.

38. Joshua Handler, "Russia seeks to refloat a decaying fleet," *Jane's International Defense Review*, Vol. 30, No. 1, January 1997, 43.

39. Nikolai S. Khlopkin, "Addressing Public Concerns about Radioactive Contamination Issues in the Arctic North," in *Reducing Wastes from Decommissioned Nuclear Submarines*, 29.

40. For more on submarine design, see Roy Burcher and Louis Rydill, *Ocean Technology Series 2: Concepts in Submarine Design* (Cambridge, UK: Cambridge University Press, 1994), 25, 26.

41. Bellona, *Russian Northern Fleet*, 128.

42. Bradley, *Radioactive Waste Management*, 289.

43. For a technical evaluation of sunken reactors, see M. E. Mount, N. M. Lynn, J. M. Warden, S. J. Timms, Y. V. Sivintsev, and E. I. Yefimov, *The Arctic Nuclear Waste Assessment Program [ANWAP]: Kara Sea Marine Reactors and Russian Far Eastern Seas Source Terms*, UCRL-CR-126279, Technical Information Department, Lawrence Livermore National Laboratory, University of California, Livermore, California, 27 March 1997.

44. The possibility of a "cataclysmic chain reaction" was raised in *The Scotsman*, 1 July 1997.

45. *The Palm Beach Post*, 31 May 1997.

46. See *Phase I CCMS Report*, Section 6.8 for NATO's risk analysis of moored submarines.

47. Bradley, *Radioactive Waste*, 258–260. Bradley provides very detailed information about Russian nuclear submarine Radwaste storage in Chapter 14, "Naval Waste Management and Contamination of Oceans and Seas."

48. Bradley, *Radioactive Waste*, 246.

49. Mark Hibbs, "Murmansk Shipping Company to Offer to Bring Andreeva Bay Cores to Mayak," *Nuclear Fuels*, 22 April 1996, 4.

50. See p. 102 of Bellona's *Russian Northern Fleet* for exceptionally compelling photographs of the hazardous storage conditions at Andreeva Bay.

51. Gussgard, "Spent Nuclear Fuel Issues on the Kola Peninsula," 105.

52. *Phase I CCMS Report*, 36.

53. "Nuclear Waste Storage in Andreeva Bay," *Bellona Factsheet No. 87*, 10 October 1997, http://www.bellona.no/e/fakta/fakta87.htr.

54. *Russia Today*, 30 January 1998.

55. *Phase II CCMS Report*, 29.

56. Bellona, "Current Status," June 1998, http://www.bellona.no/e/russia/status/9806.htm.

57. *Phase II CCMS Report*, 31.

58. *Inter Press Service*, 19 June 1997.

59. Joshua Handler, "The lasting legacy — Nuclear submarine disposal," *Jane's Navy International*, Vol. 30, No. 1, 1 January 1998.

60. *Nuclear Engineering International*, 30 September 1998.

61. Nolan Fell, "Russian Remediation: Cleaning Russia's Cold War Legacy," *Nuclear Engineering International*, 31 May 1999.

62. *Inter Press Service*, 22 June 1998.

63. Kostev, *Nuclear Safety Challenges*, 111.

64. Kostev, *Nuclear Safety Challenges*, 105.

65. Kostev, *Nuclear Safety Challenges*, 69–70.

66. Kopte, "Submarine Decommissioning," 30.

67. Bradley, *Radioactive Waste Management*, 290.

68. Kopte, "Submarine Decommissioning," 29.

69. Kostev, *Nuclear Safety Challenges*, 108.

70. Kostev, *Nuclear Safety Challenges*, 80.

71. Kopte, "Submarine Decommissioning," 21.

72. Yuri A. Khitrov, "Options for Storing and Processing Radioactive Wastes" in *Reducing Wastes from Decommissioned Nuclear Submarines*, 35.

73. Bradley, *Radioactive Waste Management*, 24.

74. For a technical summary of vitrification, see Charlie Scales, "Vitrification of Nuclear Waste: Borosilicate glass formulations are being used to encapsulate civil and military waste," *Glass*, 1 September 1998.

75. Col. A. D. Belikov, Russian Navy, "The Radiation and Ecological Situation at Northern Fleet Facilities," in *Reducing Wastes from Decommissioned Nuclear Submarines*, 24.

76. Conference on "Perspectives on International Cooperation in the Dismantlement of Nuclear Submarines," Moscow, 11 December 1998.

77. Belikov, "Radiation and Ecological Situation," 24.

78. *Energy Economist*, May 1996.

79. *OTA Report*, 142.

80. Bellona, *Russian Northern Fleet*, 146.

81. Handler, "Decaying fleet," 44. Also *Interpress Service news release*, 19 June 1997.

82. Minister of Atomic Energy Viktor Mikhailov press conference, *Official Kremlin International News Broadcast*, 13 January 1997.

83. *ITAR-TASS News Agency*, 3 July 1998.

84. *OTA Report*, 144–145.

85. While the *Phase I CCMS Report*, 35, states that Russia can not reprocess zirconium clad fuel assemblies, *Making the Russian Bomb*, 83–90, gives a detailed description of the process used at the Mayak RT-1 plant to do just that. Other sources confirm the view of the *CCMS Report*.

86. Bradley, *Radioactive Waste in the Soviet Union*, 104.

87. US Department of Energy publication *Linking Legacies: Connecting the Cold War Nuclear Weapons Production Processes To Their Environmental Consequences*, DOE/EM-0319, January 1997, 175.

88. For more on fissile fuel issues see David Albright, Frans Berkhout, and William Walker, *Plutonium and Highly Enriched Uranium 1996: World Inventories, Capabilities and Politics* (SIPRI, Oxford University Press, 1997).

89. *Phase II CCMS Report*, 32.

90. Norway's "Nuclear Safety and Environment Plan of Action, 1997-98, For the Implementation of Report No. 34 (1993-94) to the Storting on Nuclear Activities and Chemical Weapons in Areas Adjacent to our Northern Borders" (Plan of Action), Royal Norwegian Ministry of Foreign Affairs, February 1997, 13.

91. "Nuclear Safety: Concerns with Nuclear Facilities and Other Sources of Radiation in the Former Soviet Union," GAO/RCED-96-4, Report to Senator Bob Graham, November 1995.

92. Andrei Ivanov and Judith Perera, "Russia: Nowhere to process nuclear waste from troubled Kola base," *Inter Press Service*, 19 June 1997.

93. Nolan Fell, "Russian Remediation: Cleaning Russia's Cold War Legacy," *Nuclear Engineering International*, 31 May 1999.

94. Mark Hibbs, "Icebreakers Paid 4.5 Million for T-1 Reprocessing in 1995," *Nuclear Fuel*, Vol. 21, No. 10, 6 May 1996, 10.

95. *BBC*, 17 May 1996.

96. *Phase I CCMS Report*, 60.

97. Susanne Kopte, "Submarine Decommissioning," 13.

98. Bellona, *Russian Northern Fleet*, 34.

99. Bradley, *Radioactive Waste Management*, 255.

100. Bellona, *Russian Northern Fleet*, 108.

101. Kopte, "Submarine Decommissioning," 18.

102. *Phase I CCMS Report*, 283.

103. Norwegian Foreign Minister Godal, *ODIN*, 29 October 1996.

Chapter 4

1. *Washington Post*, 20 March 1998.

2. See "The Task Force on Further Development of the Environment Action Programme: Report to the Barents Council," Rovaniemi, Finland, 14–15 December 1995, 7.

3. Viktor Haynes and Marko Bojcum, *The Chernobyl Disaster* (London: Hogarth Press, 1988), 4.

4. Don J. Bradley, *Radioactive Waste Management in the Former Soviet Union*, ed. David R. Payson (Columbus, Washington: Battelle Press, 1997), 61.

5. NATO/CCMS/NACC Pilot Study, *Cross-Border Environmental Problems Emanating From Defence-Related Installations and Activities, Vol. 1: Radioactive Contamination, Phase I: 1993–1995*, Report No. 204, April 1995, 187.

6. *Nuclear Energy Safety Challenges in the Former Soviet Union: A Consensus Report of the CSIS Congressional Study Group on Nuclear Energy Safety Challenges in the Former Soviet Union* (Washington, D.C.: The Center for Strategic and International Studies, 1995), 18.

7. *Financial Times*, 19/20 September 1998.

8. Haynes and Bojcum, *Chernobyl Disaster*, 6.

9. Haynes and Bojcum, *Chernobyl Disaster*, 8.

10. Grigori Medvedev, *The Truth About Chernobyl* (USA: Basic Books, 1991), 76; see also "The Chernobyl Disaster," excerpt from *Proceedings Magazine* of New Zealand, updated by Philip Ross, at *http://www.inhb.co.nz/proceedings /atomic/chernobyl.html*.

11. Haynes and Bojcum, *Chernobyl Disaster*, 9.

12. Haynes and Bojcum, *Chernobyl Disaster*, 16.

13. Haynes and Bojcum, *Chernobyl Disaster*, 18.

14. See "Ten Years After Chernobyl: What Do We Really Know?" based on the proceedings of the IAEA/WHO/EC International Conference, Vienna, April 1996, *http://www.iaea.or.at/worldatom/inforesource/other/chernoten/index.html*, for recent and authoritative data on the effects of the Chernobyl accident.

15. "Ten Years After Chernobyl," Facts.

16. Press conference with Russian Minister of Atomic Energy Viktor Mikhailov, 13 January 1997, *Official Kremlin International News Broadcast*.

17. Press conference with Federal Committee for Nuclear and Radiation Safety (GAN) Chair Yuri Vishnevsky, 13 July 1998, *Official Kremlin International News Broadcast*.

18. Bradley, *Radioactive Waste Management*, 348.

19. European Commission website, G-24 NUSAC description, *http://europa.eu.int/comm/dg11/g24nusac.htm*, 26.

20. RBMK is a Russian acronym for "high-power pressure-tube reactor;" VVER for "water-cooled, water-moderated reactor." Cited from *Nuclear Energy Safety Challenges, CSIS Report*, 1 (fn).

21. *Nuclear Energy Safety Challenges, CSIS Report*, 18.

22. *Nuclear Wastes in the Arctic: An Analysis of Arctic and Other Regional Impacts from Soviet Nuclear Contamination*, OTA-ENV-623 (Washington, D.C.: US Government Printing Office, September 1995), 161.

23. Andrew Steele, "New focus on an old threat to security: nuclear power," *Jane's Intelligence Review*, Vol. 9, No. 12, 1 December 1998.

24. *Financial Times*, 14 September 1997. See also *G-24 NUSAC News, Issue 10, November 1996*, for details of the Norwegian assistance program to the Kola Nuclear Power Plant.

25. Steele, "New focus."

26. Ann MacLachlan, "Russian imperative to replace old units limits decommissioning," *Nucleonics Week*, 26 March 1998.

27. Press conference with Minister of Atomic Energy Viktor Mikhailov, 13 January 1997, *Official Kremlin International News Broadcast*.

28. Judith Perera, "Russia's nuclear industry: Not dead yet," *Energy Economist*, October 1998.

29. Bellona website, "Nuclear Power Stations in Russia," *http://www.bellona.no/e/fakta/fakta46.htm*.

30. *Financial Times*, 26 November 1998.

31. Steele, "New focus."

32. Minister of Atomic Energy Viktor Mikhailov press conference, 13 January 1997, *Official Kremlin International News Broadcast*.

33. European Commission website, G-24 NUSAC description, *http://europa. eu.int/comm/dg11/g24nusac.htr*, 1.

34. *OTA Report*, 162.

35. Ann MacLachlan, "US Asks Data on 70 percent-power 'Testing' Regime at Kursk-1," *Nucleonics Week*, 9 April 1998.

36. "Center for the Promotion of Imports from Developing Countries" (the Netherlands) website, *http://www.kommanet.nl/ demo/ssgleb01.html*.

37. See the TACIS website on nuclear safety projects in Russia for detailed information on EU engagement on the issue: *http://europa. eu.int/comm/dg1a/tacis/contract_info/index_ tci.htm*.

38. *NUSAC News*, Issue 10, November 1996.

39. EU-Russia Relations, EU Memo 97/22 of 28 February 1997, "Spokesman's Service of the European Commission," *http://www. eurunion...t/extrel/russia.htm*.

40. See the report of the Panel of High-Level Advisors on Nuclear Safety in Central and Eastern Europe and in the New Independent States, "A Strategic View for the Future of the European Union's Phare and Tacis Programmes," for assessment of progress on nuclear safety issues: *http://europa.eu.int/ comm/dg1a/ nss/b1.htm*.

41. European Commission website, G-24 NUSAC description, *http://europa.eu.int/ comm/dg11/g24nusac.htr*, 38.

42. "NUSAC News," Issue 11, April 1997.

43. *European Commission press release*, 3 September 1997.

44. Ann MacLachlan, "Most Contracts are Now in Place for First Phase of Chernobyl Aid," *Nucleonics Week*, 24 September 1998.

45. *Financial Times*, 4 July 1997.

46. Bellona, "Current Status," May 1997, *http://www.bellona.no/e/russia/status/9705. htm*.

47. See Bradley, *Radioactive Waste Management*, Chapter 7, for detailed coverage of power reactor spent fuel issues.

48. Thomas B. Cochran, Robert S. Norris, and Oleg A. Bukharin, *Making the Russian Bomb: From Stalin to Yeltsin* (Boulder: Westview Press, 1995), 153.

49. Bradley, *Radioactive Waste Management*, 88–90.

50. Bradley, *Radioactive Waste Management*, 67.

51. Summary Sheet, "International Symposium on Storage of Spent Fuel from Power Reactors," Vienna, Austria, 9–13 November 1998.

52. GAO/RCED-96-4, "Concerns About the Safety of Russia's Plutonium Production Reactors and Reprocessing Plants," *http:// www.ida.net/users/pbmck/xsovnuc/mirrors/ goa/rced64/letters4.ht*.

53. Bradley, *Radioactive Waste Management*, 61.

54. Cochran, Norris, and Bukharin, *Making the Russian Bomb*, 74.

55. See Cochran, Norris, and Bukharin, *Making the Russian Bomb*, Chapter 5, for much more on the Russian nuclear fuel cycle.

56. Bellona website, "Handling of Spent Nuclear Power Plant Fuel," *http:// www.bellona. no/e/russia/status/9705.htm*.

57. Bradley, *Radioactive Waste Management*, 1.

58. Cochran, Norris, and Bukharin, *Making the Russian Bomb*, 113–114.

59. *Financial Times*, 19/20 September 1998.

60. Bradley, *Radioactive Waste Management*, 409–411.

61. Cochran, Norris, and Bukharin, *Making the Russian Bomb*, 107.

62. Press conference with Federal Committee for Nuclear and Radiation Safety Chair Yuri Vishnevsky, 13 July 1998, *Official Kremlin International News Broadcast*.

63. Bellona Current Status, July 1998: "Mayak Chemical Combine," *http:// www.bellona.no/e/russia/status/9807.htm*.

64. Cochran, Norris, and Bukharin, *Making the Russian Bomb*, 137.

65. Bellona Working Paper No. 4:95: "Seversk," *http://www.bellona.no/e/russia/sibir/ sibir2.htr*.

66. GAO/RCED-96-4, "Concerns About the Safety of Russia's Plutonium Production Reactors and Reprocessing Plants," *http:// www.ida.net/users/pbmck/xsovnuc/mirrors/ goa/rced64/letters4.ht*.

67. Mark Hibbs and Ann MacLachlan, "Ends plans to reprocess at Krasnoyarsk, will upgrade Mayak," *Nuclear Fuel*, 2 November 1998.

68. Cochran, Norris, and Bukharin, *Making the Russian Bomb*, 149.

69. Bellona Working Paper No. 4:95, "Zheleznogorsk," *http://www.bellona.no/e/ russia/sibir/sibir3.htm*.

70. *Phase I CCMS Report*, 18.

71. *New York Times*, 18 November 1998.

72. Bradley, *Radioactive Waste Management*, 174–175.

73. NATO/CCMS Pilot Study, *Cross-Border Environmental Problems Emanating from Defence-Related Installations and Activities, Phase II: 1995–1998, Vol. 3: Management of*

Defense Related Radioactive Waste, Report No. 226, March 1998, 42.

74. Mark Hibbs, "Russians Plan Use of Military Plants for Actinide Separation After 2002," *Nuclear Fuel*, 4 January 1993.

75. See the AEA website on the deep-well injection study at *http://www. aeat-env.com/groundwater/news6/Feature2.htm*.

76. Judith Perera, "Russia: Opposition Mounts Against Injection of Rad Waste into Tomsk Aquifers," *Nuclear Waste News*, 9 July 1998.

77. *Washington Post*, 17 August 1998.

78. Marco de Andreis and Francesco Calogero, *The Soviet Nuclear Weapon Legacy: Sipri Research Report No. 10* (New York: Oxford University Press, 1995), 4.

79. Researcher Alexander Zakharov was killed in 1997 by high radiation while conducting an experiment at the Russian Federal Nuclear Center at Sarov. Although apparently not related to the accident, the government owes the center 60 billion rubles — a situation that has led to strikes and demonstrations by the workers. Judith Perera, "Sarov Nuclear Research Halted in Wake of Fatal Lab Accident," *Nuclear Waste News*, 17 July 1997.

80. Andreis and Calogero, *Soviet Nuclear Weapons Legacy*, 73.

81. Press conference with United States Senator Richard Lugar, 24 November 1998.

82. Rodney W. Jones and Mark G. McDonough, *Tracking Nuclear Proliferation: A Guide in Maps and Charts, 1998* (Washington, D.C.: The Brookings Institution Press, 1998), 31–32.

83. *Financial Times*, 19/20 September 1998.

84. *Financial Times*, 2 September 1998.

85. *Gazette Telegraph*, 2 September 1998.

86. Norman Polmar, *Guide to the Soviet Navy: Fourth Edition* (Annapolis: Naval Institute Press, 1986), 373.

87. *Phase I CCMS Report*, 38.

88. *Phase I CCMS Report*, 38.

89. *BBC*, 10 July 1998.

90. *Star Tribune* (Minneapolis), 18 December 1998.

91. *Inventory of radioactive waste and spent fuel at the Kola Peninsula region of north-west Russia, EUR 16916* (Luxembourg: Office for Official Publications of the European Communities, 1996), 75.

92. *The Herald* (Glasgow), 3 October 1997.

93. "Periscope Daily Defense News Capsules," *Radio Free Europe*, 11 December 1998.

94. *Financial Times*, 14 September 1997.

95. *Wisconsin State Journal*, 29 June 1997.

96. *Phase I CCMS Report*, 283.

97. *CCMS Report No. 206, Summary Field Report*, 7. See also Norwegian Ministry of Environment report "Radioactive pollution in northern ocean areas," 31 July 1995.

98. *NNC Report*, "Evolution of the Radiological Situation Around the Nuclear Reactors with Spent Fuel which Have Been Scuttled in the Kara Sea," contained in the report on the Fourth Meeting (9–11 June 1997) of the Contact Expert Group for International Radwaste Projects (IAEA CEG), reproduced by the IAEA.

99. Susanne Kopte, "Nuclear Submarine Decommissioning and Related Problems," Bonn International Center for Conversion (BICC), August 1997, 16.

100. *Phase I CCMS Report*, 184.

101. *Phase I CCMS Report*, 193.

Chapter 5

1. Martin Malia, "Russia's Retreat from the West," *New York Times*, 3 September 1998

2. See Susanne Kopte, "Nuclear Submarine Decommissioning and Related Problems," Bonn International Center for Conversion (BICC), August 1997, for excellent coverage of Russia's difficulties in funding submarine defueling and dismantlement.

3. Press conference of Minister of Atomic Energy Viktor Mikhailov, 13 January 1997, *Official Kremlin International News Broadcast*.

4. Georgi Kostev, *Nuclear Safety Challenges in the Operation and Dismantlement of Russian Nuclear Submarines* (Moscow: Committee for Critical Technologies and Non-Proliferation, 1997), 32.

5. Thomas Nilsen, Igor Kudrik, and Alexandr Nikitin, *The Russian Northern Fleet: Sources of Radioactive Contamination, Bellona Report Volume 2: 1996*, published by the Bellona Foundation, Oslo, Norway, Chapter 8.

6. Kopte, "Submarine Decommissioning," 37.

7. Kostev, *Nuclear Safety Challenges*, 101.

8. *Nuclear Wastes in the Arctic: An Analysis of Arctic and Other Regional Impacts from Soviet Nuclear Contamination*, OTA-ENV-623 (Washington, D.C.: US Government Printing Office, September 1995), 138.

9. Elizabeth Kirk, "Scientific and Technical Cooperation in the Russian North West," paper presented at the 37th Annual Convention of the International Studies Association, 18–22 March 1997, Toronto, Canada.

10. Bellona, *Russian Northern Fleet*, 113.

11. *Environmental Risk Assessment for Two Defence-Related Problems*, CCMS Pilot Study Phase II, 1995–1998, I-27.

12. For more on the evolution of Soviet/ Russian submarine strategy, see Michele Consentino, "Back to the Future," *US Naval Institute Proceedings*, Vol. 123/3/1, 128, March 1997, 44–47.

13. Don J. Bradley, *Behind the Nuclear Curtain: Radioactive Waste Management in the Former Soviet Union* (Columbus, Washington: Battelle Press, 1997), 27.

14. Press conference of Minister of Atomic Energy Viktor Mikhailov, 13 January 1997, *Official Kremlin International News Broadcast.*

15. *OTA Report*, 218.

16. Press conference with Viktor Mikhailov, 13 January 1997.

17. *OTA Report*, 138 and Kostev, *Nuclear Safety Challenges*, 99.

18. See *Nuclear Energy Safety Challenges in the Former Soviet Union: A Consensus Report of the CSIS Congressional Study Group and Task Force*, CSIS 1995, 33–34.

19. Julian Cooper, "The future role of the Russian defence industry," in *Security Dilemmas in Russia and Eurasia* (Great Britain: Royal Institute of International Affairs, 1998), eds. Roy Allison and Christoph Bluth, 103.

20. Judith Perera, "Russia's nuclear industry: Not dead yet," *Energy Economist*, October 1998.

21. Michael Knapik, Mark Hibbs, Ann MacLachlan, "Too soon to tell if Mikhailov's departure signals new direction for HEU feed sales," *Nuclear Fuel*, 9 March 1998.

22. Ann MacLachlan, "Top official says Russia wants to take back HEU spent fuel," *Nuclear Fuel*, 2 November 1998.

23. *BBC Summary of World Broadcasts*, 8 May 1998.

24. Press conference with Russian Navy Commander-in-Chief, Admiral Vladimir Ivanovich Kuroyedov, 27 August 1998, *Official Kremlin International News Broadcast.*

25. Gamini Seneviratne, "New Russian dual-purpose cask might be ready to aid naval clean-up in 2000," *Nuclear Fuel*, 19 October 1998.

26. *BBC*, 8 May 1998.

27. Judith Perera, "Russia: New MINATOM Department to Oversee Radwaste, Including Naval Waste," *Nuclear Waste News*, 15 October 1998.

28. *Inventory of radioactive waste and spent fuel at the Kola Peninsula region of north-west Russia, EUR 16916* (Luxembourg: Office for Official Publications of the European Communities, 1996), 19. This document has an entire section on GAN licensing procedures.

29. Bradley, *Radioactive Waste Management*, 37.

30. Press conference with Federal Committee for Nuclear and Radiation Safety (GAN) Chair Yuri Vishnevsky, 13 July 1998.

31. Press conference with Yuri Vishnevsky, 13 July 1998.

32. For more on regulatory problems, see Bradley, *Radioactive Waste Management*, 34.

33. Press conference with Yuri Vishnevsky, 13 July 1998.

34. *OTA Report*, 139.

35. Robert L. Dunaway, *Environmental Assistance as National Security Policy: Helping the Former Soviet Union Find Solutions to its Environmental Problems*, INSS Occasional Paper 4, November 1995, 6.

36. *EUR 16916*, 5.

37. *OTA Report*, 216.

38. Paul Kennedy's *The Rise and Fall of the Great Powers* (New York: Vantage Books, 1987) provides some background on this issue, and a warning to the United States about excessive military spending.

39. For an insightful if dated article on Baikonur, see Sergri Leskov, "Notes from a Dying Spaceport," *Bulletin of Atomic Scientists*, October 1993.

40. Cooper, "Russian defence industry," 99.

41. Bellona Current Status, March 1998, "Naval repair yards in the north-west of Russia," *http://www.bellona.no/e/russia/status/9803.htm.*

42. Cooper, "Russian defence industry," 101.

43. *St. Petersburg Times*, 29 September– 5 October 1997.

44. Cooper, "Russian defence industry," 95.

45. Kostev, *Nuclear Safety Challenges*, 99.

46. See Gloria Duffy, "Cooperative Threat Reduction in Perspective" in *Dismantling the Cold War: U.S. and NIS Perspectives on the Nunn-Lugar Cooperative Threat Reduction Program*, eds. John M. Shields and William C. Potter (Cambridge, MA: MIT Press, 1997), 33–34.

47. *AF Worldstream*, 17 March 1997.

48. Bradley, *Radioactive Waste Management*, 29.

49. Storage and disposal of nuclear material is difficult in United States as well, as controversy over central storage sites in New Mexico and Nevada makes clear. See *Financial Times*, 25 September 1997.

50. *Star Tribune* (Minneapolis, MN), 18 December 1998.

51. *Boston Globe*, 22 November 1998.

52. Nils Bohmer and Thomas Nilsen, Bellona Working Paper No. 4:95, "Zheleznogorsk."

53. NATO/CCMS Pilot Study, *Cross-Border Environmental Problems Emanating From Defence-Related Installations and Activities,*

Phase II: 1995–1998, Vol. 3: Management of Defense Related Radioactive Waste, Report No. 226, March 1998, 34, 37, 38.

54. *EUR 16916*, 9.

55. Bradley, *Radioactive Waste Management*, 35.

56. See Bradley, *Radioactive Waste Management*, for further commentary and much more detail on Russian Radwaste and environmental plans and programs, e.g., 611.

57. Bellona, *Russian Northern Fleet*, 146.

58. Bellona, *Russian Northern Fleet*, 147.

59. NATO/CCMS/NACC Pilot Study, *Cross-Border Environmental Problems Emanating From Defence-Related Installations and Activities, Vol. 1: Radioactive Contamination, Phase I: 1993–1995*, Report No. 204, April 1995, 273.

60. *BBC*, 11 June 1998.

61. *OTA Report*, 141–142.

62. Bjorn Borgaas, "Developing the Technical Program for Handling Spent Nuclear Submarine Fuel in Northwestern Russia," in *Reducing Wastes from Decommissioned Nuclear Submarines in the Russian Northwest: Political, Technical, and Economic Aspects of International Cooperation*, Proceedings from the NATO Advanced Research Workshop: "Recycling, Remediation, and Restoration Strategies for Contaminated Civilian and Military Sites in the Arctic Far North," Kirkenes, Norway, 24–28 June 1996 (Washington, D.C.: American Association for the Advancement of Science, 1997), eds. Sanoma Lee Kellogg and Elizabeth J. Kirk, 148.

63. Norway's "Nuclear Safety and Environment Plan of Action, 1997–98, For the Implementation of Report No. 34 (1993–94) to the Storting on Nuclear Activities and Chemical Weapons in Areas Adjacent to our Northern Borders" (Plan of Action), Royal Norwegian Ministry of Foreign Affairs, February 1997, Annex 2, 9.

64. *BBC*, 25 October 1996.

65. *Energy Economist*, May 1996.

66. Lars-Otto Reiersen, "AMAP and NEFCO Activities," in *Reducing Wastes from Decommissioned Nuclear Submarines*, 50.

67. Nolan Fell, "Russian Remediation: Cleaning Russia's Cold War Legacy," *Nuclear Engineering International*, 31 May 1999.

68. Fell, "Russian Remediation," *Nuclear Engineering International*, 31 May 1999.

Chapter 6

1. *The European*, 12 October 1998. Nils Bohmer is a nuclear physicist working for the Bellona Foundation.

2. Georgi Kostev, *Nuclear Safety Challenges in the Operation and Dismantlement of Russian Nuclear Submarines* (Moscow: Committee for Critical Technologies and Non-Proliferation, 1997), 92–93.

3. NATO/CCMS/NACC Pilot Study, *Cross-Border Environmental Problems Emanating From Defence-Related Installations and Activities, Vol. 1: Radioactive Contamination, Phase I: 1993–1995*, Report No. 204, April 1995, 59. The United States lost the nuclear submarines *USS Thresher* in 1963 off the New England coast and the *USS Scorpion* in 1968 in the vicinity of the Azores Islands in the Atlantic Ocean; in addition to the *Komsomolets*, the Soviet Union lost a *November* class northwest of Spain and a *Yankee* class northeast of Bermuda.

4. See, for example, Richard Sharpe, ed., *Jane's Fighting Ships, 1989–1990* (Surrey, UK: Jane's Information Group Limited), 567, for comment on the *Mike* propulsion system.

5. Thomas Nilsen, Igor Kudrik, and Alexandr Nikitin, *The Russian Northern Fleet: Sources of Radioactive Contamination, Bellona Report Volume 2: 1996*, published by the Bellona Foundation, Oslo, Norway, 154–155.

6. Susanne Kopte, "Nuclear Submarine Decommissioning and Related Problems," Bonn International Center for Conversion (BICC), August 1997," 14.

7. *Washington Post*, 25 October 1991.

8. *Phase I CCMS Report*, 8.

9. *Norway Daily*, 30 June 1997.

10. *Phase I CCMS Report*, 283.

11. M. E. Mount, N. M. Lynn, J. M. Warden, S. J. Timms, Y. V. Sivintsev, and E. I. Yefimov, *The Arctic Nuclear Waste Assessment Program [ANWAP]: Kara Sea Marine Reactors and Russian Far Eastern Seas Source Terms*, UCRL-CR-126279, Technical Information Department, Lawrence Livermore National Laboratory, University of California, Livermore, California, 27 March 1997, 1.

12. Mount et al., *ANWAP Kara Sea Marine Reactors*, iii.

13. Electronic version of the 40th General Conference of the IAEA, "Measures to Strengthen International Co-operation in Nuclear, Radiation and Waste Safety," GC (40)/INF/5, 30 August 1996.

14. "Radioactive Waste Management: Excerpt from the IAEA Annual Report for 1994," 1, *http://www.iaea.or.at/worldatom/inforesource/annual/anr9404.html.*

15. Executive Summary of the IASAP Study produced for the Radiation and Waste Safety Division of the IAEA by K-L. Sjoeblom, updated on 01 August 1997, *http://www. iaea. org/ns/rasanet/programme/wastesafety/released waste/iasapconcs. htm*

16. "Radiological Assessment: Waste Disposal in the Arctic Seas," *IAEA Bulletin*, Vol. 39, No. 1, March 1997.

17. Norwegian Ministry of Environment report, "Radioactive pollution in northern ocean areas," updated 31 July 1995, *http://odin.dep.no/html/nofovalt/depter/md/publ/raktiv-e.html*.

18. Lars-Otto Reiersen, "AMAP and NEFCO Activities," *Reducing Wastes from Decommissioned Nuclear Submarines in the Russian Northwest: Political, Technical, and Economic Aspects of International Cooperation*, Proceedings from the NATO Advanced Research Workshop: "Recycling, Remediation, and Restoration Strategies for Contaminated Civilian and Military Sites in the Arctic Far North," Kirkenes, Norway, 24–28 June 1996 (Washington, D.C.: American Association for the Advancement of Science, 1997), eds. Sanoma Lee Kellogg and Elizabeth J. Kirk, 47.

19. "Arctic Pollution Issues: A State of the Environmental Report, Short Preface and Executive Summary," *http://www.grida.no/prog/polar/amap/soaer.htm*.

20. Mount, et. al., *ANWAP Kara Sea Marine Reactors*, iii.

21. Statement by Deputy Undersecretary of Defense Sherri W. Goodman, 6 December 1995.

22. Jurki Käkönen, *Politics and Sustainable Growth in the Arctic* (Newcastle upon Tyne: Dartmouth Publishing Company, 1993), 26.

23. *Agence France Presse*, 17 September 1996.

24. Consultative bodies related to the Barents Council are the Nordic Council, formed in 1952 as a forum for member parliamentary cooperation, and the Nordic Council of Ministers, formed in 1972 for intergovernmental cooperation. Denmark, Finland, Iceland, Norway, and Sweden are members. See *http://www.nefco.fi/nordic/htm*.

25. "The Barents Region: Cooperation and visions for the future," ODIN document, *http://odin.dep.no/ud/publ/1998/barents/uk_barents.htm*.

26. *Agence France Presse*, 20 January 1998.

27. Commission of the European Commission, *RAPID*, 16 January 1998.

28. Speech by Foreign Minister Godal, 6 November 1996. See also *Financial Times*, 4 September 1997.

29. *Agence France Presse*, 20 January 1998.

30. American Embassy Oslo cable, 24 March 1997 (on the Internet).

31. "The Barents Euro-Arctic Council Environmental Action Programme," 15 June 1994, 3.

32. NEFCO website, *http://www.nefco.fi/general.htm*.

33. "The Task Force on Further Development of the Environment Action Programme: Report to the Barents Council," Rovaniemi, 14–15 December 1995, 6.

34. Task Force Report to the Barents Council, 14–15 December 1995, 6.

35. *Europe Energy*, 20 October 1995.

36. "Report to the Third Ministerial Conference of the Barents Euro-Arctic Council Environmental Task Force," St. Petersburg, 9 October 1997, 9.

37. *Inventory of radioactive waste and spent fuel at the Kola Peninsula region of north-west Russia, EUR 16916* (Luxembourg: Office for Official Publications of the European Communities, 1996), iii.

38. *EUR 16916 EN*, 4.

39. *Phase I CCMS Report*, iii–v.

40. NATO/CCMS Pilot Study, *Cross-Border Environmental Problems Emanating From Defence-Related Installations and Activities, Phase II: 1995–1998, Vol. 3: Management of Defense Related Radioactive Waste*, Report No. 226, March 1998, 50.

41. *Nuclear Wastes in the Arctic: An Analysis of Arctic and Other Regional Impacts from Soviet Nuclear Contamination*, OTA-ENV-623 (Washington, D.C.: US Government Printing Office, September 1995), 15.

42. *The Times* (London), 20 November 1996.

43. Norway is also providing substantial humanitarian assistance to Northwest Russia, including food and clothing, to help the region through the winter of 1998-99. See *New York Times*, 20 November 1998.

44. Tore Gundersen, "Nuclear Activities in Northwestern Russia: Norwegian Policies and Programs," in *Reducing Wastes from Decommissioned Nuclear Submarines*, 8.

45. Norway's "Nuclear Safety and Environment Plan of Action, 1997–98, For the Implementation of Report No. 34 (1993–94) to the Storting on Nuclear Activities and Chemical Weapons in Areas Adjacent to our Northern Borders" (Plan of Action), Royal Norwegian Ministry of Foreign Affairs, February 1997, 4.

46. Norwegian "Plan of Action," 3.

47. Norwegian "Plan of Action," 3.

48. Norwegian "Plan of Action," 10.

49. Gundersen, "Nuclear Activities in Northwestern Russia," 8.

50. Judith Perera, "Four European Firms Team Up to Solve NW Russia's SF," *Nuclear Waste News*, 3 July 1997.

51. *Agence France Presse*, 28 February 1996.

52. Norwegian "Plan of Action," 4.

53. *Norway Daily* No. 231/96.
54. The complete name for the "Framework Agreement" is "Agreement between the Government of the Kingdom of Norway and the Government of the Russian Federation on environmental cooperation in connection with the dismantling of Russian nuclear powered submarines withdrawn from the Navy's service in the northern region, and the enhancement of nuclear and radiation safety," signed on 26 May 1998.
55. *Los Angeles Times*, 27 May 1998.
56. "Waste Commission Meets in Moscow," *Nuclear Engineering International*, 30 September 1998, 4.
57. Testimony by US Department of Defense Undersecretary for Environmental Security, Sherri Goodman, 6 December 1995.
58. Robert S. Dyer, "Norwegian-Russian-US Cooperation to Expand and Upgrade the Liquid Radioactive Waste Processing Facility in Murmansk, Russia," in *Reducing Wastes from Decommissioned Nuclear Submarines*, 166–68.
59. Dyer, "Norwegian-Russian-US Cooperation," 170.
60. Kopte, "Decommissioning Submarines," 37.
61. Norwegian Foreign Minister Godal, 29 October 1996. Norwegian financial aid is usually documented in kroner (NOK), converted here at $1.0 = NOK 6.2.
62. Kopte, "Submarine Decommissioning," 28.
63. In mid–1999, in conjunction with the Group of 7/8 meeting in Cologne, Germany, Japan proposed an expanded aid package for Russian submarine Radwaste problems worth $200 million, to include:

- Removing reactor cores from obsolete submarines and placing them in TK-18 transport casks and building a temporary cask storage facility at the Zvezda shipyard [near Vladivostok]
- Decommissioning Victor-class submarines at Zvezda
- Refitting the *Belyanka*-class tanker *Pinega* as a spent fuel container ship

From "Japan Plans to Expand Aid to Russian Submarine R&D" [Judith Perera], *Nuclear Waste News*, 10 June 1999.

64. *BBC*, 10 April 1997
65. *ITAR-TASS News Agency*, 11 March 1998.
66. *Washington Post*, 25 October 91.
67. Sergey Rybak, "Floating LLW Treatment Plant for Russian Navy Nears Operation," *Nucleonics Week*, 6 November 1997.

68. Rybak, "Floating LLW Treatment Plant," 6 November 1997.
69. *Kyoto News Service*, 18 August 1997.
70. *TASS*, 4 December 1998.
71. *Aberdeen Press and Journal*, 4 December 1998.
72. Henri de la Bassetière, "Plans for the Lepse Project," in *Reducing Wastes from Decommissioned Nuclear Submarines*, 136.
73. Radio Free Europe in *Periscope Daily Defense News Capsules*, 11 December 1998.
74. Radio Free Europe in *Periscope Daily Defense News Capsules*, 11 December 1998.
75. EU financial aid is usually expressed in ECU, converted here at $1.2 = ECU 1.0
76. Bassetière, "Plans for the Lepse Project," 131–142.
77. Information provided by European Commission officials.
78. *Japan Economic Newswire*, 15 May 1998.
79. *Financial Times*, 18 November 1998.
80. Andrew Steele, "New focus on an old threat to security: nuclear power," *Jane's Intelligence Review*, Vol. 9, No. 12, 1 December 1998.
81. Commission of the European Communities, *Rapid*, 26 November 1998.
82. *Ibid.*
83. Derived from *AMEC Press kit*, 2 April 1997.
84. Testimony by Sherri W. Goodman, Deputy Under Secretary, Environmental Security Department of Defense, before the Senate Armed Services Subcommittee on Readiness, 11 March 1998, *Federal Document Clearing House Congressional Testimony*.
85. Don J. Bradley, *Radioactive Waste Management in the Former Soviet Union*, ed. David R. Payson (Columbus, Washington: Battelle Press, 1997), 244.
86. *HazMat Transport News*, 1 August 1998.
87. "Murmansk Nuclear Fuel Storage Project," American Embassy, Stockholm, Sweden, *http://www.usis.usemb.se/newsflash/murmansk.html*.
88. Nigel Mote, "Multi-Purpose Casks for Managing Spent Nuclear Fuel from Power Stations: Applicable Also to Naval Fuel Management?" in *Reducing Wastes from Decommissioned Nuclear Submarines*, 153.
89. Judith Perera, "Russia: MINATOM OKs dual-use casks for storage of maritime SF," *Nuclear Waste News*, 20 August 1998.
90. "Sub container testing completed in Russia," *Nuclear News*, December 1998.
91. *Ibid.*
92. Gamini Seneviratne, "Nuclear impact on the aquatic environment," *Nuclear News*, November 1998.
93. For much more on CTR, see *Disman-*

tling the Cold War: U.S. and NIS Perspectives on the Nunn-Lugar Cooperative Threat Reduction Program (Cambridge, MA: The MIT Press, 1997), eds. John M. Shields and William C. Potter.

94. "News Conference with Senator Richard Lugar," *Federal News Service*, 24 November 1998.

95. Senator Lugar press conference, 24 November 1998.

96. Kopte, "Decommissioning Submarines," 40.

97. Senator Lugar press conference, 24 November 1998.

98. "Perspectives on International Cooperation in the Dismantlement of Nuclear Submarines" conference in Moscow, 11 December 1998.

99. Kopte, "Submarine Decommissioning," 31.

100. *ITAR-TASS News Agency*, 25 September 1997.

101. Gamini Seneviratne, "New Russian dual-purpose cask might be ready to aid naval clean-up in 2000," *Nuclear Fuel*, 19 October 1998.

102. "News briefs," *Nuclear Waste News*, 13 August 1998.

103. *AP Worldstream*, 20 January 1998

104. US Department of Energy publication *MPC&A Program: Strategic Plan*, January 1998, 2.

105. Press conference with US Secretary of Energy Federico Pena, 1 April 1998.

106. *Department of Energy MPC&A Program*, 18.

107. Wayne Barber, "NRC seeks DOE assurance of funds for international program," *Inside N.R.C.*, 12 October 1998.

108. Judith Perera, "Russia Seeks Kola Waste Disposal," *Nuclear Waste News*, 19 June 1997.

109. *New York Times*, 22 September 1997.

110. See ISTC website, for complete information, *http://www.istc.ru/*.

111. Senator Lugar press conference, 24 November 1998.

112. *New York Times*, 26 February 1999.

113. For more on Swedish initiatives, see "Co-operation between Sweden and the Russian Federation regarding spent nuclear fuel and radioactive waste." *Swedish Radiation Protection Institute Progress Report*, 22 April 1998,

114. See SKB website, *http://www.skb.se/engelska/skb/index.html*.

115. *SSI News*, Vol. 5, No. I, May 1997.

116. *Phase II CCMS*, 55–56.

117. *The Observer*, 26 April 1998.

118. *OTA Report*, 162.

119. Rodney W. Jones and Mark G. McDo-nough, *Tracking Nuclear Proliferation: A Guide in Maps and Charts, 1998* (Washington, D.C.: The Brookings Institution Press, 1998), 72.

120. *Moscow Times*, 6 June 1998.

121. *Ibid.*

122. Ariane Sains, "Kola Cleanup at Technical Impasse; Consortium Plans to use Old Navy Base," *Nuclear Fuel*, 24 August 1998.

123. Sains, "Kola Cleanup at Technical Impasse."

124. *Ibid.*

125. IAEA CEG, Fifth Meeting, 11–13 November 1997, Windemere, UK.

126. IAEA CEG, Fifth Meeting.

127. See IIASA homepage, *http://www.iiasa.ac.at/*.

128. IAEA CEG website, *http://www.iaea.org/worldatom/program/CEG/ report-reco.htr*.

129. Judith Perera, "Russia's nuclear industry: Not dead yet," *Energy Economist*, October 1998.

130. Knut Gussgard, "Spent Nuclear Fuel Issues on the Kola Peninsula," in *Reducing Wastes from Decommissioned Nuclear Submarines*, 107.

131. Bradley, *Radioactive Waste Management*, 152.

132. House Committee on Science, Subcommittee on Energy and Environment, Markup of H.R. 363 to amend Section 2118 of the Energy Policy Act of 1992 to extend the Electric and Magnetic Fields Research and Public Dissemination Program & the Department of Energy Research & NOAA, *National Narrowcast Network, L P.*, Congressional Hearing Transcripts, 9 April 1997.

133. *BBC Summary of World Broadcasts*, 8 May 1998.

134. Judith Perera, "International: U.S., Russia Plan Joint Venture to Store SF on Pacific Atoll," *Nuclear Waste News*, 3 July 1997.

135. Povl Ølgaard, "Worldwide Decommissioning of Nuclear Submarines: Plans and Problems," in *Reducing Wastes from Decommissioned Nuclear Submarines*, 44.

Chapter 7

1. Alexander L. George, *Bridging the Gap: Theory and Practice in Foreign Policy* (Washington, D.C.: United States Institute of Peace Press, 1993), 139.

2. This is of course the well known principle of the balance of power. For one of the better reviews of the topic, see Edvard Vose Gulick, *Europe's Classic Balance of Power* (New York: W. W. Norton & Company, 1955).

3. A well known exposition of realism

(structural realism actually) in the post–Cold War period is John Mearsheimer's "Back to the Future: Instability in Europe after the Cold War," *International Security*, Vol. 15, No. 1, Summer, 1990, 5–56. Rebuttal and response followed in the next two issues of the journal.

4. "Liberalism" is one of the most ambiguous terms in politics and political science. Some use the terms "idealism" or "globalism" to define the liberalism I describe. My explanation draws from the neoliberal notions expressed in works such as Robert Keohane's *After Hegemony: Cooperation and Discord in the World Political Economy* (Princeton: Princeton University Press, 1984).

5. Michael W. Doyle is credited with developing the modern version of the democratic peace hypothesis, which has been expanded and explained by numerous scholars ever since. See Michael W. Doyle, "Liberalism and World Politics," *American Political Science Review* Vol. 80, No. 4, December 1986, 1151–1169.

6. The realist-liberal debate is developed in several relatively recent and useful volumes, including David A. Baldwin, *Neorealism and Neoliberalism: The Contemporary Debate* (New York, Columbia University Press, 1993).

7. See James K. Sebenius, *Negotiating the Law of the Sea* (Cambridge, MA: Harvard University Press, 1984).

8. See in particular Andrew Moravcsik, "Negotiating the Single European Act: National Interests and Conventional Statecraft in the European Community, *International Organization*, Vol. 45, No. 1,Winter 1991, 651–688.

9. See *Double-Edged Diplomacy: International Bargaining and Domestic Politics* (Berkeley: University of California Press, 1993), eds. Peter B. Evans, Harold K. Jacobson, and Robert D. Putnam.

10. Andrew Moravcsik, "Preferences and Power in the European Community: A Liberal Intergovernmental Approach," *Journal of Common Market Studies*, Vol. 3, No. 4, December 1993, 473–524.

11. See "The Svalbard Archipelago: The Role of Surrogate Negotiators," in *Polar Politics: Creating International Environmental Regimes*, eds. Oran Young and Gail Osherenko (Ithaca: Cornell University Press, 1993), Chapter 3.

12. Anne Fikkan, Gail Osherenko, and Alexander Arikainen, "Polar Bears: The Importance of Simplicity," in *Polar Politics: Creating International Environmental Regimes* (Ithaca: Cornell University Press, 1993), eds. Oran Young and Gail Osherenko, Chapter 4.

13. See Marvin S. Soroos, "Arctic Haze: an exploration of international regime alternatives, in *Politics and Sustainable Growth in the Arctic*, eds. Jurki Käkönen (Newcastle upon Tyne: Dartmouth Publishing Company, 1993), Chapter 5.

14. See Peter M. Haas, "Stratospheric Ozone: Regime Formation in Stages," in *Polar Politics: Creating International Environmental Regimes* (Ithaca: Cornell University Press, 1993), eds. Oran Young and Gail Osherenko, Chapter 5.

15. Immanuel Wallerstein, *World-Systems Analysis: Theory and Methodology* (Beverly Hills: Sage, 1982), fully develops the core-periphery hypothesis.

16. For a vast list of polar organizations, see *http://www.spri.cam.ac.uk/lib/ organ/keyindex.htm*.

17. Young and Osherenko, *Polar Politics*, viii.

18. Barbara Gray, *Collaborating: Finding Common Ground for Multiparty Problems* (San Francisco: Jossey-Bass Publishers, 1989), 242.

19. Gray, *Collaborating*, 55.

20. Gray, *Collaborating*, 234.

21. Gray, *Collaborating*, 227–228.

22. David Mitrany, Ernst Haas, and Philippe Schmitter, among others, developed the basic ideas for functionalism, neo-functionalism, and integration theory.

23. See Charles Krupnick, "Europe's Intergovernmental NGO: The OSCE in Europe's Emerging Security Structure," in *European Security*, Vol. 7, No. 2, 42, Summer 1998. Cited from John J. Maresca, *To Helsinki: The Conference on Security and Cooperation in Europe 1973–1975* (Durham, NC: Duke UP 1987).

24. NATO/CCMS/NACC Pilot Study, *Cross-Border Environmental Problems Emanating From Defence-Related Installations and Activities, Vol. 1: Radioactive Contamination, Phase I: 1993–1995*, Report No. 204, April 1995, 8.

25. Young and Osherenko, *Polar Politics*, 15.

26. Gray, *Collaborating*, 57.

27. *Norway Daily*, 30 June 1997.

28. Bellona website, *http://www.bellona.no*.

29. Thomas Nilsen and Nils Bohmer, "Sources to Radioactive Contamination in Murmansk and Arkhangelsk Counties," Bellona Report No. 1, 1994, Oslo, 1 March 1994.

30. *Norway Daily*, 9 June 1997 notes Bellona's falling out with the Norwegian Conservative Party over the issue of gas-fired power plants.

31. Thomas Princen and Matthias Finger, *Environmental NGOs in World Politics: Linking the local and the global* (London: Rutledge, 1994), 232 and 211.

32. Mary Douglas and Aaron Wildavsky, *Risk and Culture: An Essay on the Selection of Technical and Environmental Dangers* (Berkeley: University of California Press, 1982).

33. Thomas G. Weiss and Leon Gordenker, eds., *NGOs, the UN, and Global Governance* (Boulder: Lynne Rienner, 1996), 217.

34. *New York Times*, 2 May 1997.

35. *Financial Times*, 26 May 1997.

36. See Weiss and Gordenker, *NGOs, the UN, and Global Governance*, 210 for further comments on the roles and limitations of NGOs and IGOs.

37. Don Munton, "Scientists as Scientist, Experts versus Experts, Policy versus Science: Toward a Broadened Concept of Epistemic Communities," paper presented to the Annual Meeting of the International Studies Association, Minneapolis, MN, March 1998, 1.

38. *Agence France Presse*, 17 September 1996.

39. See Andrew Cockburn and Leslie Cockburn, *One Point Safe* (New York: Anchor Books, 1997), for more on relations between US agencies and MINATOM. In a 5 February 1998 article for *The New York Review of Books*, Jack F. Matlock, Jr. pointed out a lack of "clarity of purpose" in US policy toward MINATOM and Russian nuclear problems in general after the Cold War ended.

40. Gray, *Collaborating*, 73.

41. Thomas Jandl, "Secrecy vs. the Need for Ecological Information: Challenges to Environmental Activism in Russia," *Environmental Change and Security Project*, Issue 4, Spring 1998, Woodrow Wilson Center, 48.

42. Gray, *Collaborating*, 74.

43. Gray, *Collaborating*, 67.

44. Gray, *Collaborating*, 82–83.

45. A phrase often used by Bellona representatives to describe the Radwaste problems of Northwest Russia. See, for example, *The Guardian* (London), 21 October 1998.

46. See Mancur Olson Jr., *The Logic of Collective Action* (Cambridge, MA: Harvard University Press, 1965).

47. Betzy Ellingsen Tunold, "Nuclear Activities in Northwestern Russia: Selected Projects Within the Norwegian Plan of Action," in Kellogg and Kirk, *Reducing Wastes from Decommissioned Nuclear*, 18.

48. Gray, *Collaborating*, 230.

49. Stephen D. Krasner, ed., *International Regimes* (Ithaca, New York: Cornell University Press, 1983), 2.

50. See Robert O. Keohane, *After Hegemony: Cooperation and Discord in the World Political Economy* (Princeton: Princeton University Press, 1984), 90–91, for more on nested regimes.

51. Susanne Kopte, "Nuclear Submarine Decommissioning and Related Problems," Bonn International Center for Conversion (BICC), August 1997," 14.

52. News conference with Russian Foreign Ministry Information Director Vladimir Rakhmanin, *Official Kremlin International News Broadcast*, 28 January 1999.

53. *OTA Report*, 22.

54. Drawn from the IAEA document, "Civil Liability for Nuclear Damage: International Framework," *http://www.iaea.org/worldatom/glance/legal/liability.html*.

55. IAEA Director General comments, 18 March 1996.

56. Mark Hibbs, "Russian Reactors not Complying with Insurance-for-License Rule," *Nucleonics Week*, 5 February 1998. According to Dirk Harbruecker, head of DKVG (Germany's nuclear insurance pool), Russia's RBMK reactors "are in our view not insurable."

57. Sergey Rybak, "Russian Insurers Set Up Nuclear Pool; Vienna Convention Eyed," *Nucleonics Week*, 20 November 1997.

58. Ann MacLachlan, "Seminar Shows Russians Far from Viable Nuclear Insurance," *Nucleonics Week*, 15 May 1997.

59. Gray, *Collaborating*, 86.

60. See Peter B. Evans, Harold K. Jacobson, and Robert D. Putnam, *Double-Edged Diplomacy: International Bargaining and Domestic Politics* (Berkeley: University of California Press, 1993).

61. Gray, *Collaborating*, 93.

62. Statement by Deputy Secretary of State Strobe Talbott to the Barents Euro-Arctic Council Ministerial, 20 January 1998, and other sources.

63. *Agence France Presse*, 28 February 1996.

64. Jandl, "Secrecy vs. Ecological Information," 50.

65. Young and Osherenko, *Polar Politics*, 14–15.

66. Gordenker and Weiss, *NGOs, the UN, and Global Governance*, 221.

Chapter 8

1. *Inter Press Service*, 22 June 1998.

2. Col. A. D. Belikov, Russian Navy, "The Radiation and Ecological Situation at Northern Fleet Facilities," in *Reducing Wastes from Decommissioned Nuclear Submarines in the Russian Northwest: Political, Technical, and Economic Aspects of International Cooperation*. Proceedings from the NATO Advanced Research Workshop, "Recycling, Remedia-

tion, and Restoration Strategies for Contaminated Civilian and Military Sites in the Arctic Far North," Kirkenes, Norway, 24–28 June 1996 (Washington, D.C.: American Association for the Advancement of Science, 1997), eds. Sanoma Lee Kellogg and Elizabeth J. Kirk, 22.

3. *Financial Times*, 14 September 1997.

4. Babcock & Wilcox, however, may be suffering financially because of the delays at the Bolshoi Kamen liquid waste purification facility.

5. *BBC Summary of World Broadcasts*, 3 August 1998.

6. Remarks by Secretary of Defense William J. Perry to the Society of American Engineers, *DoD Press Release*, 25 November 1996.

7. John M. Shields and William C. Potter, eds., *Dismantling the Cold War: U.S. and NIS Perspectives on the Nunn-Lugar Cooperative Threat Reduction Program* (Cambridge MA: The MIT Press), 1997, Appendix.

8. *Nuclear Energy Safety Challenges in the Former Soviet Union: A Consensus Report of the CSIS Congressional Study Group on Nuclear Energy Safety Challenges in the Former Soviet Union* (Washington, D.C.: The Center for Strategic and International Studies, 1995), 3.

9. Prepared statement by J. Michael Waller, Vice President, American Foreign Policy Council, before the House Committee on National Security Subcommittee on Military Research and Development, 13 March 1997, *Federal News Service*.

10. Statement by Norman Polmar before the Military Procurement Subcommittee of the Committee on National Security, House of Representatives, 1 March 1997, in *Federal Document Clearing House Congressional Testimony*, 18 March 1997.

11. "The New Russian Submarine Fleet," *Russia Express Update*, 1 April 1996.

12. *Financial Times*, 23 October 1998.

13. See Gloria Duffy, "Cooperative Threat Reduction in Perspective" in *Dismantling the Cold War: U.S. and NIS Perspectives on the Nunn-Lugar Cooperative Threat Reduction Program* (Cambridge, MA: MIT Press, 1997), eds. John M. Shields and William C. Potter, 31–36 for analysis and criticism of the CTR program.

14. *Financial Times*, 24–25 October 1998.

15. Press conference with Minister of Nuclear Energy Yevgeny Adamov, 25 November 1998, *Official Kremlin International News Broadcast*.

16. Rodney W. Jones and Mark G. McDonough, *Tracking Nuclear Proliferation: A Guide in Maps and Charts, 1998* (Washington, D.C.: The Brookings Institution Press, 1998), 34.

17. *New York Times*, 13 January 1999.

18. Michael Knapik, Sergey Rybak, Ann MacLachlan, and Mark Hibbs, "Mikhailov out as head of MINATON, RBMK designer Adamov named to post," *Nucleonics Week*, 5 March 1998.

19. NATO/CCMS Pilot Study, *Cross-Border Environmental Problems Emanating From Defence-Related Installations and Activities, Phase II: 1995–1998, Vol. 3: Management of Defense Related Radioactive Waste*, Report No. 226, March 1998, 49.

20. Nazli Choucri and Robert C. North, "Global Accord: Imperatives for the Twenty-First Century," *Global Accord: Environmental Challenges and International Responses* (Cambridge, MA: The MIT Press, 1993), Nazli Choucri, ed., 498.

21. James D. Watkins, "Science and Technology in Foreign Affairs," *Science*, Vol. 277, 1 August 1997.

22. "Carnegie Council on Ethics and International Relations Newsletter," June 1998, 4.

23. Stephen M. Walt, "International Relations: One World, Many Theories," in *Understanding International Relations: The Value of Alternative Lenses, Third Edition* (New York: McGraw-Hill, 1998), eds. Daniel J. Kaufman, Jay M. Parker, Grant R. Doty, and Harry L. Cohen, 111.

24. Mark P. Poncy, Jr., "The need for greater US Assistance in promoting Russian defense conversion," *Law and Policy in International Business*, Vol. 28, No. 2, 1 January 1997.

25. Hans J. Morgenthau and Kenneth W. Thompson, *Politics Among Nations: the Struggle for Power and Peace, Sixth Edition* (New York: Alfred A. Knopf, 1985).

26. See Roy Allison and Christopher Bluth, *Security Dilemmas in Russia and Eurasia* (London: Royal Institute of International Affairs, 1998) for analysis of current concerns within the former Soviet Union.

27. In February 1999, US officials complained about Russian dumping of steel on the world market and forced a 70 percent cut in Russian steel exports to the United States.

28. *Financial Times*, 16 September 1998.

29. Thomas Princen and Matthias Finger, *Environmental NGOs in World Politics: Linking the local and the global* (London: Rutledge, 1994), 32.

30. "Carnegie Council on Ethics and International Relations Newsletter," June 1998, 3.

31. Drawing from Barbara Gray, *Collaborating: Finding Common Ground for Multiparty Problems* (San Francisco: Jossey-Bass Publishers, 1989), 243.

32. See *Bellona Working Paper No. 1:98*, Nils Boehmer, January 1999, for a reasoned assess-

ment about what more needs to be done. *http://www.bellona.no/e/ russia/wp99-1/wp 990101.htm.*

33. Martin Walker, "Investing in Russia: Not for the Weak of Heart," *Europe*, No. 364, March 1997, 10.

34. *Financial Times*, 19 September 1997, tax reforms in this case are specifically aimed at the oil industry.

35. Susanne Kopte, "Nuclear Submarine Decommissioning and Related Problems," Bonn International Center for Conversion (BICC), August 1997, 41.

36. *Gazette Telegraph* (Colorado Springs), 4 October 1998.

37. Russia alone has funds enough to disassemble only three or four submarines per year; with international assistance the program could be completed much faster. Judith Pereras, "International officials fear old subs, waste could lead to disaster in Arctic," *Nuclear Waste News*, 11 December 1997.

38. *Philadelphia Inquirer*, 20 January 1999.

39. Shields and Potter, *Dismantling the Cold War*, 389–390, give recommendations for improvement in the CTR program. Some of these could be applied to the Russian submarine spent fuel problem as well.

40. Aiane Sains, "Kola Cleanup at Technical Impasse; Consortium Plans to use Old Navy Base," *Nuclear Fuel*, 24 August 1998, Vol. 23, No. 17, p. 4.

41. *BBC Summary of World Broadcasts*, 10 July 1998.

42. Cited from Christoph Bluth, "Arms control and proliferation" in *Security Dilemmas in Russia and Eurasia* (Great Britain: Royal Institute of International Affairs, 1998), eds. Roy Allison and Christoph Bluth. 320.

43. *Radio Free Europe in Periscope Daily Defense News Capsules*, 11 December 1998.

44. Nolan Fell, "Russian Remediation: Cleaning Russia's Cold War Legacy," *Nuclear Engineering International*, 31 May 1999.

45. See David G. Victor and Eugene B. Skolnikoff, "Translating intent into action: implementing environmental commitments," *Environment*, Vol. 41, No. 2, 1 March 1999, for similar arguments concerning Russian participation in a variety of environmental regimes.

46. Cited from Robert Jervis, "Cooperation Under the Security Dilemma," in *Understanding International Relations*, 62.

Selected Bibliography

Government and International Organizations

Arctic Council. Arctic Council documents are available at: http://arctic-council.usgs.gov/papers.html.

"Arctic Pollution Issues: A State of the Environment Report — Executive Summary." This and other relevant reports from the Fourth Ministerial Conference on the Arctic Environmental Protection Strategy (AEPS), Alta, Norway, 12–13 June 1997, available at: http://www.grida.no/prog/polar/aeps/.

Barber, Wayne. "NRC seeks DOE assurance of funds for international program." *Inside N.R.C.* Vol. 20, No. 21, 12 October 1998: 10.

Barents Euro-Arctic Council. Information on the Barents Council available at: http://virtual.finland.fi/finfo/english/barents.html and http://www.state.gov/ www/regions/eur/nei/000315_js_barents.html.

Barents Euro-Arctic Council. "The Barents Euro-Arctic Council Environment Action Programme." Bodø, Norway, 15 June 1994.

Bellona. Bellona Foundation reports available at: http://www.bellona.no/imaker?

European Union. *Inventory of radioactive waste and spent fuel at the Kola Peninsula region of north-west Russia.* EUR 16916. Luxembourg: Office for Official Publications of the European Communities, 1996.

European Union. Tacis and other relevant EU programs available at: http://europa.eu.int/comm/dg1a/nss/b1.htm.

G-24 Nuclear Coordination Secretariat. G-24 NUSAC information available at: http:// europa.eu.int/comm/environment/g24/g24home.htm.

International Atomic Energy Agency. IAEA reports and studies available at: http://www.iaea.org/worldatom/.

International Atomic Energy Agency. "Radiological Assessment: Waste Disposal in the Arctic Seas." *IAEA Bulletin*, Vol. 39, No. 1, March 1997, available at: http://www.iaea.org/worldatom/Periodicals/Bulletin/Bull39 1/specialreport.htm.

International Atomic Energy Agency. "Ten Years After Chernobyl: What Do We Really Know?" IAEA/WHO/EC International Conference proceedings on Chernobyl, April 1996, available at: http://www.iaea.or.at/worldatom/inforesource/other/chernoten/index.html.

International Atomic Energy Agency Contact Expert Group on International Radwaste Projects. "Evolution of the Radiological Situation Around the Nuclear Reactors with Spent Fuel which Have Been Scuttled in the Kara Sea." *NNC Report*, contained in report on the Fourth Meeting of the Contact Expert Group for International Radwaste Projects (IAEA CEG), 9–11 June 1997.

International Atomic Energy Agency Contact Expert Group for International Radwaste Projects. IAEA CEG reports available at: http://www.iaea.org/worldatom/program/CEG/report-reco.htr.

International Institute for Applied Systems Analysis. IIASA information available at: http://www.iiasa.ac.at/.

International Science and Technology Center. ISTC information available at: http://www.istc.ru/.

Mount, Mark E., N. M. Lynn, J. M. Warden, S. J. Timms, Y. V. Sivintsev, and E. I. Yefimov. *The Arctic Nuclear Waste Assessment Pro-*

gram [ANWAP]: Kara Sea Marine Reactors and Russian Far Eastern Seas Source Terms. UCRL-CR-126279. Livermore, CA: Technical Information Department, Lawrence Livermore National Laboratory, University of California, 27 March 1997.

Nordic Environmental Finance Corporation. NEFCO information available at: http://www.nefco.fi/general.htm.

North Atlantic Treaty Organization. NATO/ CCMS/NACC Pilot Study, Cross-Border Environmental Problems Emanating From Defence-Related Installations and Activities. Phase I, 1993–1995. Reports No. 204, 205, and 206. Brussels, 1995.

North Atlantic Treaty Organization. NATO/ CCMS Pilot Study: Cross-Border Environmental Problems Emanating from Defence-Related Installations and Activities. Phase II, 1995–1998. Reports No. 223, 224, 225, 226, and 227. Brussels, 1998.

Norway. Norwegian Foreign Ministry ODIN reports available at: http://odin. dep.no/odin/engelsk/index-b-n-a.html.

Norway. "Nuclear Safety and the Environment: Plan of Action, 1997–98, for the Implementation of Report No. 34 (1993–94) to the Storting on Nuclear Activities and Chemical Weapons in Areas Adjacent to our Northern Borders." Royal Norwegian Ministry of Foreign Affairs, February 1997.

Norway and Russia. "Agreement between the Government of the Kingdom of Norway and the Government of the Russian Federation on environmental cooperation in connection with the dismantling of Russian nuclear powered submarines withdrawn from the Navy's service in the northern region, and the enhancement of nuclear and radiation safety." Signed in Moscow, 26 May 1998.

"Norwegian — U.S. — Russian Initiatives for Environmental Cooperation in North-West Russia: Management, Treatment and Disposal of Nuclear Waste and Spent Nuclear Fuel." Report on seminar held at Union Station, Washington, D.C., 4 December 1997.

Scott Polar Research Institute. "Directory of Polar and Cold Region Organizations." Compiled by William Mills, updated 29 September 2000, available at: http://www.spri.cam.ac.uk/lib/organ/keyindex.htm.

Sweden. "Co-operation between Sweden and the Russian Federation regarding spent nuclear fuel and radioactive waste." Swedish Radiation Protection Institute Progress Report, 22 April 1998.

United States Department of Defense. Remarks by Secretary of Defense William J. Perry to the Society of American Engineers. DoD press release, 25 November 1996.

United States Department of Energy. Linking Legacies: Connecting the Cold War Nuclear Weapons Production Processes to Their Environmental Consequences. DOE/EM-0319, January 1997, available at: http://legacystory.apps.em.doe.gov/thestory/pdfpic.asp?doc=link.

United States Department of Energy. MPC&A Program: Strategic Plan. US Department of Energy publication, January 1998, available at: http://www.nn.doe. gov/mpca/text/t-stratplan.htm.

United States House of Representatives. Testimony by Secretary of the Navy John Lehman, contained in "Hearings before the Defense Policy Panel of the Committee on Armed Services." House of Representatives, One Hundredth Congress, First Session, March 11, 13, 17, 18, 20, and 23, 1987. H.A.S.C. No. 100-15, 14.

United States House of Representatives. Testimony by Norman Polmar before the House Committee on National Security Subcommittee on Military Procurement, 1 March 1997. Washington, D.C.: Federal Document Clearing House Congressional Testimony, 18 March 1997.

United States House of Representatives. Testimony by J. Michael Waller, Vice President, American Foreign Policy Council, before the House Committee on National Security Subcommittee on Military Research and Development. Federal News Service, 13 March 1997.

United States Navy. Worldwide Submarine Challenges 1997. Washington, D.C.: Office of Naval Intelligence (ONI), February 1997.

United States Office of Technical Assessment. Nuclear Wastes in the Arctic: An Analysis of Arctic and Other Regional Impacts from Soviet Nuclear Contamination. OTA-ENV-623. Washington, D.C.: US Government Printing Office, September 1995.

United States Senate. "Nuclear Safety: Concerns with Nuclear Facilities and Other Sources of Radiation in the Former Soviet Union." GAO/RCED-96-4, letter report to Senator Bob Graham, 7 November 1995.

United States, Norway, and Russia. "Declaration among the Department of Defense of the United States of America, the Royal Ministry of Defence of the Kingdom of Norway, and the Ministry of Defence of the Russian Federation on Arctic Military Environmental Cooperation." Signed in Bergen, Norway, 26 September 1996.

Books

Albright, David, Frans Berkhout, and William Walker. *Plutonium and Highly Enriched Uranium 1996: World Inventories, Capabilities and Politics.* New York: SIPRI, Oxford University Press, 1997.

Allison, Roy, and Christoph Bluth, eds. *Security Dilemmas in Russia and Eurasia.* Great Britain: Royal Institute of International Affairs, 1998.

Baldwin, David A. *Neorealism and Neoliberalism: The Contemporary Debate.* New York: Columbia University Press, 1993.

Bradley, Don J. *Behind the Nuclear Curtain: Radioactive Waste Management in the Former Soviet Union.* Ed. David R. Payson. Columbus WA: Battelle Press, 1997.

Burcher, Roy, and Louis Rydill. *Ocean Technology Series 2: Concepts in Submarine Design.* Cambridge: Cambridge University Press, 1994.

Chew, Allen F. *An Atlas of Russian History: Eleven Centuries of Changing Borders.* New Haven: Yale University Press, 1970.

Choucri, Nazli, ed. *Global Accord: Environmental Challenges and International Responses.* Cambridge MA: MIT Press, 1993.

Cochran, Thomas B., Robert S. Norris, and Oleg A. Bukharin. *Making the Russian Bomb, From Stalin to Yeltsin.* Boulder: Westview Press, 1995.

Cockburn, Andrew, and Leslie Cockburn. *One Point Safe.* New York: Anchor Books, 1997.

De Andreis, Marco, and Francesco Calogero. *The Soviet Nuclear Weapon Legacy: SIPRI Research Report No. 10.* New York: SIPRI, Oxford University Press, 1995.

Douglas, Mary, and Aaron Wildavsky. *Risk and Culture: An Essay on the Selection of Technical and Environmental Dangers.* Berkeley: University of California Press, 1982.

Dunaway, Robert L. *Environmental Assistance as National Security Policy: Helping the Former Soviet Union Find Solutions to its Environmental Problems.* INSS Occasional Paper 4. USAF Academy CO: USAF Institute for National Security Studies, 1995.

Duncan, Francis. *Rickover and the Nuclear Navy.* Annapolis: Naval Institute Press, 1990.

Dupuy, R. Ernest, and Trevor N. Dupuy. *The Harper Encyclopedia of Military History, Fourth Edition.* New York: Harper Collins, 1993.

Eriksen, Viking Olver. *Sunken Nuclear Submarines: A Threat to the Environment.* Oslo: Norwegian University Press, 1990.

Evans, Peter B., Harold K. Jacobson, and Robert D. Putnam, eds. *Double-Edged Diplomacy: International Bargaining and Domestic Politics.* Berkeley: University of California Press, 1993.

Feshbach, Murray, and Alfred Friendly, Jr. *Ecocide in the USSR: Health and Nature Under Siege.* New York: Basic Books, 1992.

Gorshkov, Sergei G. *The Sea Power of the State.* Annapolis: Naval Institute Press, 1979.

Gray, Barbara. *Collaborating: Finding Common Ground for Multiparty Problems.* San Francisco: Jossey-Bass Publishers, 1989.

Haynes, Viktor, and Marko Bojcum. *The Chernobyl Disaster.* London: Hogarth Press, 1988.

Huchthausen, Peter, Igor Kurdin, and R. Alan White. *Hostile Waters.* New York: St. Martins Press, 1997.

Jones, Rodney W., and Mark G. McDonough. *Tracking Nuclear Proliferation: A Guide in Maps and Charts, 1998.* Washington, D.C.: Brookings Institution Press, 1998.

Käkönen, Jurki. *Politics and Sustainable Growth in the Arctic.* Newcastle upon Tyne UK: Dartmouth Publishing Company, 1993.

Kellogg, Sanoma Lee, and Elizabeth J. Kirk, eds. *Reducing Wastes from Decommissioned Nuclear Submarines in the Russian Northwest: Political, Technical, and Economic Aspects of International Cooperation.* Proceedings from the NATO Advanced Research Workshop "Recycling, Remediation, and Restoration Strategies for Contaminated Civilian and Military Sites in the Arctic Far North," Kirkenes, Norway, 24–28 June 1996. Washington, D.C.: American Association for the Advancement of Science, 1997.

Kennedy, Paul. *The Rise and Fall of the Great Powers.* New York: Vantage Books, 1987.

Keohane, Robert. *After Hegemony: Cooperation and Discord in the World Political Economy.* Princeton: Princeton University Press, 1984.

Kostev, Georgi. *Nuclear Safety Challenges in the Operation and Dismantlement of Russian Nuclear Submarines.* Moscow: Committee for Critical Technologies and Non-Proliferation, 1997.

Krasner, Stephen D., ed. *International Regimes.* Ithaca NY: Cornell University Press, 1983.

Medvedev, Grigori. *The Truth About Chernobyl.* United States: Basic Books, 1991.

Morris, Eric. *The Russian Navy, Myth and Reality.* New York: Stein and Day, 1977.

Nilsen, Thomas, Igor Kudrik, and Alexandr Nikitin. *The Russian Northern Fleet: Sources of Radioactive Contamination, Bellona*

Report Volume 2. Oslo: Bellona Foundation, 1996.

Olson, Mancur Jr. *The Logic of Collective Action.* Cambridge MA: Harvard University Press, 1965.

Polmar, Norman. *Guide to the Soviet Navy: Fourth Edition.* Annapolis: Naval Institute Press, 1986.

Princen, Thomas, and Matthias Finger. *Environmental NGOs in World Politics: Linking the local and the global.* London: Rutledge, 1994.

Rhodes, Richard. *Making of the Atomic Bomb.* New York: Simon and Schuster, 1986.

Schlesinger, James R., Project Chairman. *Nuclear Energy Safety Challenges in the Former Soviet Union: A Consensus Report of the CSIS Congressional Study Group on Nuclear Energy Safety Challenges in the Former Soviet Union.* Washington, D.C.: Center for Strategic and International Studies (CSIS), 1995.

Sebenius, James K. *Negotiating the Law of the Sea.* Cambridge MA: Harvard University Press, 1984.

Sharpe, Richard, ed. *Jane's Fighting Ships 1989–1990.* Surrey UK: Jane's Information Group Limited.

Sharpe, Richard, ed. *Jane's Fighting Ships 1997–1998.* Surrey UK: Jane's Information Group Limited.

Sharpe, Richard, ed. *Jane's Fighting Ships 1998–1999.* Surrey UK: Jane's Information Group Limited.

Shields, John M., and William C. Potter, eds. *Dismantling the Cold War: U.S. and NIS Perspectives on the Nunn-Lugar Cooperative Threat Reduction Program.* Cambridge MA: MIT Press, 1997.

Shlykov, Vitaly V. *The Crisis in the Russian Economy.* Carlisle Barracks PA: Strategic Studies Institute, US Army War College, 1997.

Thornton, W. M., and Gustavo Conde. *Submarine Insignia & Submarine Services of the World.* Annapolis: Naval Institute Press, 1997.

Tyler, Patrick. *Running Critical: The Silent War, Rickover, and General Dynamics.* New York: Harper & Row, 1986.

Watson, Bruce W., and Susan M. Watson, eds. *The Soviet Navy: Strengths and Liabilities.* Boulder: Westview Press, 1986.

Weiss, Thomas G., and Leon Gordenker, eds. *NGOs, the UN, and Global Governance.* Boulder: Lynne Rienner, 1996.

Young, Oran, and Gail Osherenko, eds. *Polar Politics: Creating International Environmental Regimes.* Ithaca NY: Cornell University Press, 1993.

Articles and Papers

A great deal of information for this book was drawn from the *Financial Times, New York Times,* and other newspapers and from short articles in nuclear/energy industry trade journals such as *Nuclear Engineering International, Nuclear Fuel, Nuclear Waste News, Nucleonics Week,* and the *Energy Economist.* Much was accessed using Lexis-Nexis. Because of the large number of individual citations, they are not listed in this bibliography. Prominent in reporting issues relevant to this book, however, were journalists Judith Perera and Mark Hibbs.

Anikin, A., V. Fedorov, and S. Boiko. "Dynamics and regulation of the ruble exchange rate in light of world experience." *Russian & East European Finance & Trade* Vol. 33, No. 3, May/June 1997: 81–95.

Chaze, William L., and Robert Kaylor. "Deadly Game of Hide-and-Seek." *U.S. News and World Report* Vol. 102, No. 23, 15 June 1987: 36–41.

Cosentina, Michele. "Back to the Future." *US Naval Institute Proceedings* Vol. 123, No. 3, March 1997: 44–47.

Doyle, Michael W. "Liberalism and World Politics," *American Political Science Review* Vol. 80, No. 4, December 1986: 1151–1169.

Foxwell, David. "Sub Proliferation Sends Navies Diving for Cover: The Multiple Menace of Diesel-Electric Submarines." *International Defense Review,* Vol. 30, 1 August 1997, 30–39.

Handler, Joshua Handler, "Russia's Seeks to Refloat a Decaying Fleet," *Jane's International Defense Review* Vol. 30, No. 1, January 1997: 43.

Handler, Joshua. "The Lasting Legacy — Nuclear Submarine Disposal." *Jane's Navy International* Vol. 103, No. 1, January/February 1998: 12–20.

Jandl, Thomas. "Secrecy vs. the Need for Ecological Information: Challenges to Environmental Activism in Russia." *Environmental Change and Security Project Report* 4, Woodrow Wilson Center, Spring 1998, available at: http://ecsp.si. edu.

Kirk, Elizabeth. "Scientific and Technical Cooperation in the Russian North West." Paper presented at the 38th Annual Convention of the International Studies Association, 18–22 March 1997, Toronto, Canada.

Kopte, Susanne. "Nuclear Submarine Decommissioning and Related Problems." Bonn International Center for Conversion (BICC) Paper 12, August 1997, available at:

http://www.bicc.de/weapons/paper12/content.html.

Krupnick, Charles. "Europe's Intergovernmental NGO: The OSCE in Europe's Emerging Security Structure." *European Security* Vol. 7, No. 2, Summer 1998: 30–53.

Polmar, Norman. "The Soviet Navy." *US Naval Institute Proceedings* Vol. 124, No. 2, February 1998: 87–88.

Kuteinikov, Anatoly V. "Malachite Subs Post Proud Tradition." *US Naval Institute Proceedings* Vol. 124, No. 4, April 1998: 52–56.

Leskov, Sergri. "Notes from a Dying Spaceport." *Bulletin of Atomic Scientists* Vol. 49, No. 8, October 1993: 40–43.

Mann, Paul, "Nuclear Risks Mount in Besieged Russia." *Aviation Week and Space Technology* Vol. 149, No. 10, 7 September 1998: 60–64.

Mearsheimer, John. "Back to the Future: Instability in Europe after the Cold War." *International Security* Vol. 15, No. 1, Summer 1990: 5–56.

Moravcsik, Andrew. "Negotiating the Single European Act: National Interests and Conventional Statecraft in the European Community." *International Organization* Vol. 45, No. 1, Winter 1991: 651–688.

Moravcsik, Andrew. "Preferences and Power in the European Community: A Liberal Intergovernmental Approach." *Journal of Common Market Studies* Vol. 3, No. 4, December 1993: 473–524.

Munton, Don. "Scientists as Scientist, Experts versus Experts, Policy versus Science: Toward a Broadened Concept of Epistemic Communities." Paper presented at the 39th Annual Convention of the International Studies Association, 17–21 March 1998, Minneapolis, MN.

Poncy, Mark P. Jr. "The need for greater US Assistance in promoting Russian defense conversion." *Law and Policy in International Business* Vol. 28, No. 2, Winter 1997: 509–548.

Porter, John, and Khalil Ghabaee. "Modelling deep well injection of liquid radioactive waste." AEA Technology *GW News*, No. 6, 6 July 1997, available at: http:// www.aeat-env.com/groundwater/news6/Feature2.htm.

Scales, Charlie. "Vitrification of Nuclear Waste: Borosilicate glass formulations are being used to encapsulate civil and military waste." *Glass* Vol. 75, No. 9, 1 September 1998: 307.

Steele, Andrew. "New focus on an old threat to security: nuclear power." *Jane's Intelligence Review* Vol. 9, No. 12, December 1997: 552.

Victor, David G., and Eugene B. Skolnikoff. "Translating intent into action: implementing environmental commitments." *Environment* Vol. 41, No. 2, 1 March 1999: 14–20 and 39–44.

Walker, Martin. "Investing in Russia: Not for the Weak of Heart." *Europe*, No. 364, March 1997: 9–11.

Watkins, James D. "Science and Technology in Foreign Affairs." *Science* Vol. 277, No. 5326, 1 August 1997: 650–651.

Index